Education in an Industrial Society

Education
in an
Industrial Society

G. H. BANTOCK

FABER AND FABER

3 Queen Square

London

First published in 1963
by Faber and Faber Limited
Second edition 1973
Printed in Great Britain by
John Dickens & Co Ltd Northampton

ISBN 0 571 04791 2

Some think that a very moderate amount of virtue is enough, but set no limit to their desires of wealth, property, power, reputation, and the like. To whom we reply by an appeal to facts, which easily prove that mankind do not acquire or preserve virtue by the help of external goods, but external goods by the help of virtue, and that happiness, whether consisting in pleasure or virtue, or both, is more often found with those who are most highly cultivated in their mind and in their character, and have only a moderate share of external goods, than among those who possess external goods to a useless extent but are deficient in higher qualities; and this is not only matter of experience, but, if reflected upon, will easily appear to be in accordance with reason. For, whereas external goods have a limit, like any other instrument, and all things useful are of such a nature that where there is too much of them they must either do harm, or at any rate be of no use, to their possessors, every good of the soul, the greater it is, is also of greater use, if the epithet 'useful' as well as 'noble' is appropriate to such subjects. No proof is required to show that the best state of one thing in relation to another is proportioned to the degree of excellence by which the natures corresponding to those states are separated from each other: so that, if the soul is more noble than our possessions or our bodies, both absolutely and in relation to us, it must be admitted that the best state of either has a similar ratio to the other. Again, it is for the sake of the soul that goods external and goods of the body are eligible at all, and all wise men ought to choose them for the sake of the soul, and not the soul for the sake of them.

(ARISTOTLE: *Politics*)

Such prepotency as this country may hope for in the English-speaking world of the future must lie in the cultural realm, and that it should exert such a prepotency—as focus of the finer life of cultural tradition (which is a very different matter from being given over to inert traditionalism, academic gentility and museum-conservation of the forms of past life)—is very much to be desired.

(F. R. Leavis: *Education and the University*)

Acknowledgments

I am indebted to Dr. F. R. Leavis and Messrs. Chatto and Windus for permission to quote from *The Common Pursuit* and *Education and the University*; to Messrs. Routledge and Kegan Paul for permission to quote from the late Karl Mannheim's *Ideology and Utopia*; to Professor Richard Hoggart and to Mr. David Holbrook for permission to quote from articles in periodicals. I wish, too, to express my thanks to all the other authors whose works have been quoted, and their publishers.

Contents

Preface

————————◆————————

Initially, this book was a good deal longer. On the advice of my publishers, however, I have removed a number of chapters which dealt in general with the question of affective education; these I hope to add to and publish as a separate volume. What, therefore, is said about affective education here is a preliminary to the fuller treatment.

A good deal of the book is published for the first time; but parts have appeared before in the following journals: *Cambridge Journal*, *The Times Educational Supplement*, *The Listener* and *The Advancement of Science*. To the editors of these journals I am grateful for permission to reprint. I would also like to express my gratitude to Dr. F. Musgrove for having read and commented on the section on 'The Social Role of the School' and to Mr. Brian Simon in relation to 'Some Social and Ideological Roots of Modern Education'. Such errors as the reader may observe remain, of course, my own.

But most of all I would like to thank Mr. T. S. Eliot who has done so much to encourage me in my work and whose concern about this book has been a constant stimulus to improve it.

I am, as ever, grateful to my wife for her laborious work in typing the manuscript (much of it several times) and for preparing the index. I owe a great deal, too, to the many discussions I have had with her about the subject-matter of the book.

Rearsby   G.H.B.
1963

Introduction to Second Edition

—————————◆—————————

It is ten years since this book was first written; indeed parts of it date from several years before that. Since then I have seen no reason to alter its fundamental orientation, but I have, I think, gone some way to deepen my understanding of the issues involved. I have, for instance, come to appreciate more fully the cultural factors which lie at the heart of the book; and this deeper understanding has implication for the analysis of both elite and mass culture on which the book as first published offered some preliminary soundings.

Ultimately education, both formal and informal, is concerned with cultural transmission; this is the case whether what is being transmitted is a classical text or a capacity to recognize and solve certain types of practical problem. In the former case, the point is obvious; in the latter, it is only necessary to note that the ability to appreciate even the incidence of problems implies a firm grasp of concepts and categories relevant to the field involved, and that these have to be learned; they don't arrive by the light of nature, *pace* Rousseau, as I hope I have made clear in my essay on 'Discovery Methods'.[1]

The book, indeed, took its original impetus from a realization of some of the shortcomings in the cultural orientations of an advanced industrial society with its emphasis on consumption at the expense, for many, of work satisfaction, and its tendency to cultural homogenization outside the need to recruit certain

[1] In *The Black Papers on Education*, ed. B. Cox & A. E. Dyson (Davis Poynter 1971).

1

specific sorts of expertise. The questionable elements are the machine with its provision of material plenty at the cost (because of its dependence on certain limited kinds of expertise) of a certain cultural emptiness; and the related phenomenon of cultural homogenization. Hence my stress on 'the wrong sort of hierarchy and the wrong sort of equality' (p. 224). In specifically educational terms these features were manifest in some of the arguments about the comprehensive school with their peculiarly ambiguous stress on the need at once to afford a more equal opportunity for more to become unequal (and hence recruit to the meritocracy in terms of 'educated manpower') and at the same time to promote a terminal experiential equality, so that all can 'participate' in a harmonious democratic society by sharing a common meaning. Our society shows a typical incoherence in attempting to promote both these aims through the same educational 'reform'; and in the last ten years I have come to appreciate more fully the implications of both orientations.

In an essay on 'Equality and Education'[1] I have analysed the attempts to promote a common understanding implicit in Dewey's democracy of shared interests, and at the same time (I hope) revealed the confusions in his attempts at once to promote uniqueness of personality, and at the same time to foster democratic cohesiveness in terms of a common understanding: 'to have the same ideas about things which others have, to be like-minded with them, and thus to be really members of a social group, is to attach the same meanings to things and to acts which others attach' (cf. below p. 100). On the crucial matter of cultural meaning, indeed, the bankruptcy of the egalitarian is made manifest. He must either promote like-mindedness artificially through the most appalling tyranny (in the manner of *1984*, so that 'war' becomes 'peace' or whatever meaning he likes to impose at any one moment) or accept diversity springing out of the uniqueness of human experience. Once he admits the latter, then he must allow for different levels of understanding and accuracy, and the possibility that one version of 'experience' may provide a more valuable (in the sense here of more accurate, more in tune with its density) version than another.

Clearly my book is a plea for such diversity and especially

[1] To be published in a compilation of that name by Allen & Unwin, ed. Tibor Szamuely.

for diversity in humanistic as well as scientific terms. No-one can deny the complexity of science; but efforts have been and are being made to deny the richness and diversity of human experience in the arts. During the last ten years I have come to appreciate much more fully the degree of cultural homogenization which is taking place in some of the arts—though it is true that I should have read the signs earlier. Indeed, in art itself, they point back to the Dada movement of the first war years as a symptomatic reaction against the whole elite Renaissance tradition. Dada stressed the unconscious (where we can all be allowed to be equal), chance, the arbitrary act of choice, the surrender to whim, free association. By seeking to release the individual from the pain of effort under the pretence of self-realization, it bound him to the greatest of tyrants, himself, his own unregenerated nature. And indeed, the whole elitist anti-elitist movement to which I am referring (and of which Dada was an early warning) has been profoundly influenced by that reversal of the roles of nature and culture to which Rousseau even earlier gave voice. Two features of *Emile* have become part of the consciousness of our age—its anti-historical stance and its naturalism, both of which, of course, are closely inter-related. Emile was to constitute the fresh start and he was to be the child of 'natural' impulse; both traits involve a repudiation of historical culture. The same ethos speaks in the voice of Hans Arp,[1] one of the earliest Dadaists:

> Automatic poetry springs directly from the poet's bowels or other organs, which have stored up reserves of usable material. Neither the Postillon of Longjumeau nor the hexameter, neither grammar nor aesthetics, neither Buddha nor the Sixth Commandment should hold him back. The poet crows, curses, sighs, stutters, yodels, as he pleases. His poems are like Nature. Unregarded trifles, or what men call trifles, are as precious to him as the sublimest rhetoric; for, in Nature, a tiny particle is as beautiful and important as a star.[2]

The paradoxically historical results of this movement are everywhere apparent in current art theorizing and in the elite anti-

[1] To be fair to him, Arp was more friendly to an element of consciousness and rationality than some of his fellow Dadaists; it was Tzara, we are told by Hans Richter, who 'left the task of (artistic) selection to nature. He refused the conscious self any part in the process' (p. 60).

[2] Hans Richter: *Dada*, pp. 30–31.

3

elitism to which I have previously referred. In a recent B.B.C. series 'Is an elite necessary', the reply of the avant-garde was almost exclusively 'No'.

I have analysed the role of the avant-garde and of the 'counter-culture' it has evoked in a recent essay 'Current Dilemmas in the Education of the Elite'.[1] There are those who see in the counter-culture 'the saving vision our endangered civilization requires'. I have given reason there why I am highly sceptical of this, to me, naive faith in the benevolence of the counter-culture which I see as a manifestation of romantic decadence rather than as a saving vision. I see in current manifestations of the avant-garde a tie-up with certain popular modes that point to a common origin—an origin in irrationality, a repudiation of traditional culture and responsibility—and a dangerous degree of cultural homogenization as both become the prey of whim and fashion, restlessly seeking the new, the sensational, the purely visceral excitement, whether through the violence of action painting or the sensory overload of 'rock-pop'.[2]

Indeed, my fuller appreciation of the role and diversity of counter-cultural modes affords me my one element of unease about the critical orientation of this present book. There is, I hope, a distinction to be made between responsible and irresponsible criticism; yet one current cultural manifestation deserves more comment than it customarily receives; the very orientation of our culture to the critical and the sceptical, manifest as protest and revolt. It is in some ways the unhealthiest of all current expressions, for life, to preserve balance, must be celebration as well as denunciation, piety (in the sense of reverence, *pietas*) as well as protest. The world is always an evil place—but it is also an opportunity for richness and plenitude. One of the roles of artistic creativity is to enhance existence —as Leavis has endlessly pointed out.

For to evoke art and literature is to adumbrate the possibility of a finer order, a more releasing discipline; the lesson of the greatest artistic creativity is transcendence, not relaxation. Not the least of the curses that romantic progressivism has bestowed on us is the belief that achievement results from the lifting of

---

[1] Published in *Melbourne Studies in Education* 1972, ed. R. J. W. Selleck—one of the Theodore Fink seminars.

[2] A revealing analysis of pop culture will be found in George Melly's *Revolt into Style* (Penguin 1972).

restraints rather than from their conquest, that creativity springs from a spontaneous outpouring rather than from knowledge and discipline. I hope the criticism of our society in this book has been sufficiently balanced by a responsible sense of our society's achievements and a sufficiently implied realization that the way to improve is not to denigrate and besmirch but to seek a more responsible order. The danger is, to-day, that we are educating many people just sufficiently to enable them to destroy the culture they have inherited. We fill them with ideas of freedom and self-expression, of criticising and rejecting, before they have developed the understanding necessary to take a measure of the world and its possibilities. For another legacy we have inherited from the eighteenth century is the curse of perfectionism, forgetting that 'striving to better, oft we mar what's well'.

The lesson of this for our venture in secondary reorganization should be obvious: I will refer more fully to that unhappy exercise shortly. For the moment I will content myself with suggesting that, in addition to this pervasive emphasis on criticism with its resultant orientation to change, it might also be a good idea to bring up our young to thanksgiving and praise: for the artistic riches our civilization has produced in the past and which the present age (except perhaps in the field of industrial design and in *interpretation*) cannot emulate; for their schools and universities which afford them, however at times inadequately, at least the opportunity of education; for medical care which has so improved health and the expectation of life; for technological abundance which, whatever its problems—and they are not shirked in this book—has enabled us, in Western society, to make poverty a peripheral rather than a central problem. It is a trifle odd that so many should resent our thanking God at our morning assemblies for our daily bread at a moment when, for the first time in human history, He has taken to providing it with some abundance.

For a civilization to flourish it needs pride and confidence as well as an awareness of shortcomings. This is why I am not as happy as I was with the doctrine of self-realization (p. 131) I promulgated ten years ago. For one thing, I have realized the importance of the community order and its continuity; 'self-realization' needs to be oriented to something beyond itself to produce a self which doesn't degenerate into an undesirable egotism. Furthermore, this means something more than 'helping others' or 'co-operation'; the civic pride of the Renaissance state manifests itself in a creativity which has enriched the human race—for man cannot live by bread alone.

There is a passage in a Henry James' play (*The High Bid*) which expresses exactly my meaning here:

YULE: I see something else in the world than the beauty of old show-houses and the glory of old show-families. There are thousands of people in England who can show no houses *at all*, and I don't feel it utterly shameful to share their poor fate.

MRS. GRACEDEW: We share the poor fate of humanity whatever we do, and we do much to help and console when we've something precious to *show*. What on earth is more precious than what the Ages have slowly *wrought*? They've trusted us—the brave centuries—to *keep* it; to do something, in our turn, for them. It's such a virtue, in anything, to have lasted; it's such an honour, for anything, to have been *spared*. To all strugglers from the Wreck of Time hold out a pitying hand!

Education cannot build houses: its function is to sustain the strugglers from the Wreck of Time—and never more than at a time when the young are learning to spit on their heritage. The ultimate indictment of 'pop' culture lies in its 'deliberate built-in obsolescence'.[1]

Self and society, indeed, are inextricably intertwined, and no enriched self is likely to be realized by most people apart from the sustainment that an enriched social order can provide. As T. S. Eliot—himself the quite conscious product of a realized tradition—pointed out:

'. . . the schools can transmit only a part (of our culture), and they can only transmit this part effectively if the outside influences, not only of family and environment, but of work and play, of newsprint and spectacles and entertainments and sport, are in harmony with them'.

I have dealt more fully with Eliot's seminal thinking on education in *T. S. Eliot & Education*; but I have come to realize, recently, more fully from him, the inadequacy of the notion of an 'embattled minority' as any sort of answer to our cultural problems. Eliot rightly insists that in any healthy cultural order, each level of the community must make its appropriate cultural

[1] Melley: *op. cit.* p. 12.

offering at the level of consciousness appropriate to its ability. Less palatable to our age, of course, is his belief that informal education through the family is as important as, if not more important than, the formal system; hence, at the highest levels, the need for certain persisting families which will enable *the* elite to be made up of more than a collection of what he terms 'caciques, bonzes and tycoons'.

The former point—relating to the inevitable inter-connectedness of a culture—needs insisting on, especially at a time when a debased popular culture is so clearly invading the traditional reserve of high culture. I have already alluded to this phenomenon, and now I must spell out some of the implications I have more recently seen for our popular education. Formal education is primarily a matter of consciousness; the school, though it may also incidentally transmit only half appreciated or half unconscious attitudes, exists for the purpose of transmitting quite specific thought structures and skills. The aim of the academic in its widest sense is the clarification of the world— as environment and inner life—by introducing coherence and order into the numerous inchoate 'experiences' we encounter in our lives (science is concerned with the structure of material and organic life, history with the past, vestiges of which form part of our environment etc.); its tools are the teacher—and the book, which is also in part the teacher's teacher. The whole culture of the school rests largely (though not exclusively) on the printed word. Symptomatically, the first systematic learning the child encounters in the infant school is the need to learn to read.

I have alluded briefly to the role of reading in this book; but when I originally wrote it I had not found an answer to the question which had been buzzing round in my head for a number of years but which educationists in general seem to have ignored —perhaps because of its very obviousness and simplicity. What do you do to people, what demands do you make on them, when you teach them how to read? After all, in the history of mankind it is a most unusual and eccentric demand. I discovered too late for this volume, that Marshall Macluhan had probed the problem; he led me on to Father Ong, a sounder and more reliable scholar, and other considerations of literacy and pre-literacy, and the implications for consciousness and thought structure that the coming of the alphabet and the resulting manuscript culture, and finally the invention of movable type and the widespread dissemination of print, had had for cultural development. And I made some of my investigations the subject of my inaugural lecture in 1965, 'The Implications of Literacy'.[1]

It seems to me that once one is trying to probe at this level, one is touching something basic in the culture and the education whose job it is to transmit aspects of that culture. It is *not* true to say that 'the medium is the message'; but it is undoubtedly true that the nature of the message is inevitably affected in quite basic ways by the form in which it appears. Consider simply the role of memory in pre-literate and post-literate cultures; in the former recall is only possible through elaborate mnemonic devices which have been so admirably chronicled by Miss Frances Yates;[2] in the post-literate period access to books is all that is needed. Indeed, Father Ong has suggested that romantic breakaway and alienation is only possible in a civilization which has learned to store its memory in print; the avant-garde is the child of literacy. It is no accident, he thinks, that romanticism post-dates the publication of Diderot's *Encyclopédie*. The suggestion is interesting if not definitive; the implications of 'setting it down' (in writing) must have been apparent to the Jacobeans, as *Hamlet* makes clear ('My tables, meet it is I set it down'). Nevertheless literacy makes psychological and sociological demands (the development of certain sorts of inwardness[3]—and the need for a zone of social silence) which inevitably raise the question of the ability and motivation of certain sections of the community to benefit. Hence the suggestion that our current educational malaise might be better served and recuperated by developing new ranges of meanings adapted to the understanding of the folk for whom it is intended rather than through the perpetual attempt to foster new ways of transmitting the old meanings which goes to make up what constitutes 'curriculum reform' these days. My first attempt to define this new range of meanings comes in Chapter 7 of this book. Since then I have, I think, extended the range of arguments by which I have come to the conclusions there stated,

[1] Reprinted in *Education, Culture & The Emotions*.
[2] *The Art of Memory* (Penguin 1969).
[3] Notably the ability, with the help of writing and books, to construct certain sorts of linear arguments impossible in a pre-literate age. Hence, in fact, the decay of metaphor and the development of scientific rationalism.

but I have not radically altered these conclusions; rather they have been regrouped.

In brief, I have come to see the problem of building suitable curricula for different sections of the community in terms of the relative claims on them of action and consciousness. As I have dealt with this at length in an essay called 'The Reluctant Learner', which formed the second of my Fink lectures,[1] perhaps I may be simply permitted here a brief summary. The Renaissance ideal, in the new humanistic literacy which was now foisted on the developing aristocratic bureaucracy which marked the increasing state centralization of the following centuries, had thought to marry action and consciousness ('contemplation') in a splendid neo-Platonic synthesis. Symbolically the newly refurbished ideal may be symbolized by the great Duke Federigo of Urbino sitting, dressed in armour, and reading his book. But an imbalance between the claims of activity or 'busyness' and awareness or consciousness is early apparent in *Hamlet*, the inhibited Renaissance Scholar-Prince. By the nineteenth century the problem had become acute—as Nietzsche pointed out; and Lawrence repeats the charge. Indeed, Lawrence's work can, in part, be considered as an extended comment on the problem of spontaneity in an idea-inhibited civilization.

In Lawrence, spontaneity springs from the centres of affectivity rather than those of consciousness and rationality; and he associates affectivity especially with his own people (the working classes), those, as he himself defines in 'Education of the People', most recalcitrant to the watered down cognitive curriculum offered them in the elementary schools. (Need I add that Lawrence was a trained teacher of six years' experience?) The clue seemed worth following up, and I have attempted to do so by making action ('movement') rather than consciousness ('reading') the gateway to the education, in the first place, of the 'reluctant learner'. Hence the explicit emphasis (which is implicit in Chapter 7) on 'movement' education in various guises as a means to a reconstituted education for the folk. Thus the kinetic principle will lead into consciousness (which is unavoidable anyway—as Lawrence pointed out, man cannot be spontaneous as the thrush can be), not as in progressive 'activity', a refurbished way of doing the old things, but as a source for the expression of imagination and skill in a variety

[1] Also to be published in *Melbourne Studies in Education* (1972).

of modes—through dance, mime, drama, craft—various forms of 'making', indeed, imaginative and technical.

This is not mindlessness, indeed, but mind approached from a new angle. *Reading will still be essential* but its purposes will be controlled by the demands implicit in the new active principle; nor is it a sop for the recalcitrant like so much vocationalism that is creeping into the schools in desperation, but an alternative form of liberalization, a route into a different *but not inherently inferior* richness, one in line with the traditional orientations of the folk—affectively rather than cognitively biassed (I have indicated that these are not to be regarded as discrete categories in an essay on 'The Education of the Emotions'[1]). Hence I have sought the sort of consciousness by which the folk can best contribute to the revivified cultural order adumbrated in Eliot's analysis. My stand is in terms of alternative disciplines, not the abnegations of current permissiveness and the illusions of contemporary 'freedom'. It will not, of course, catch all the recalcitrants—this I regard as an impossible task—but it may net more than we are doing at present.

And indeed, could the bankruptcy of present policy at secondary level be better illustrated than from the fact that, at the very moment when we are being congratulated on being 'half way there'—to comprehensive reorganization that is—the first serious break—at journalistic level—in the post-war optimism about the efficacy of schooling is being registered in current depression about violence in schools—and in the disenchantment implicit in the incipient movement towards de-schooling. It is surely now clear that the doubts expressed in this book about the relevance of the comprehensive experiment in a situation which cried out for a much deeper cultural analysis of the malaise have been justified in the event; that at most what we are accomplishing is the replacement of one set of problems by another—and these not necessarily less serious. The attempt to mix the classes is a failure; the danger to the able has not been avoided; and the problem of the reluctant learner has, if anything, been exacerbated. The first is implicit in some of the few pieces of hard research that have been allowed;[2] and the second is becoming more and more apparent as the dismal tale

[1] Published in *Education, Culture & The Emotions*.
[2] Cf. *Comprehensive Education in Action*, ed. T. G. Monks (N.F.E.R., 1970).

implicit in continental and American experience is being repeated here. So that various forms of selection and streaming
are being reintroduced in those countries (Russia, Czechoslo-
vakia, U.S.A.) which had made various attempts at abandonment. A distinguished Australian literary critic and the doyen
of English teachers in that country, Mr. A. A. Phillips, expressed the situation tersely and dramatically when he said
that 'The new type of (secondary school) pupil is being allowed
to erode the standards of our elite education, and simultaneously
to suffer a type of education not designed for his needs'. I have
suggested elsewhere that the value of the comprehensive experiment may be, for future generations, in the more flexible awareness it has fostered of the diversity of talent with which we are
faced; but whether this outweighs the harm it has done is a
moot point.

And this takes me back to Eliot's second point—the role of
informal education and the need for persisting families to foster
the continuity of elite culture. That this is likely may be inferred
from the current realization of the crucial role of the family in
the matter of cultural deprivation: if at one end of the scale, why
not at the other? If a family can be a source of deprivation—
which the researches of Dr. Douglas and others seem to have
established—why should it not also prove a fostering ground
for great achievement—or at least in the preservation of certain
standards? I suggested earlier (p. 71) a 'diffusion of education
. . . seems to have had a deleterious effect on the highest
cultural standards'; and this paradox has given me food for
thought in the intervening years.

Part of the explanation has just, it seems to me, been suggested; the history of mankind demonstrates that a universal
system of education is not necessary for a state of high civilization; and schooling as such has often demonstrably played a
fairly subordinate role in the periods of great creativity. The
schooling of the Renaissance period in Italy, apart from that
provided by a few talented teachers like Guarino and da Feltre,
was in certain respects pretty barren:

> . . . that flowering of the Renaissance which was responsible
> for most of what is valuable in neo-Latin literature, for the
> first triumphs of classical scholarship . . ., for the revival of
> Platonism, for painters like Leonardo and Botticelli, for

11

writers like Petrarch, Boccaccio . . . was a product of *avant-garde* enthusiasm and owed little or nothing to the general education of the time.[1]

Dr. Bolgar omits perhaps one benefit—the severity of education to a degree which leads Father Ong to classify it as a puberty initiation rite. It was, that is to say, taken seriously—but it was neither comprehensive (no pun intended!) nor efficient even within its limits; the great conquests of the Renaissance depended, as Dr. Bolgar makes clear, on self education.

To-day, with a system of universal education we have still insufficiently asked the question 'what can most effectively be transmitted by formal schooling'. For we have to contend with two fundamental drawbacks, the inherent deficiencies implicit in any formal system of instruction (whether on 'progressive' or formal lines), and—closely linked with it—the cultural deficiencies of the teachers. The sheer organizational requirements implicit in the deployment of large numbers of learners would seem to imply that only certain types of transmission can be effectively generated[2]—which is why the 'certainties' of science and technology are likely to be more successfully passed on than the subtler nuances of the humanistic subjects. In the former, meaning is certain; in the latter equivocal. It is this ability to appreciate nuance and ambiguity which is most difficult to acquire by those who have been nurtured on the 'plain prose sense' of the developing scientific and technological society, and it is here where the deficiencies of our teachers show up most alarmingly. Literature has always been the worst taught subject in schools, and many of the other arts are sorely neglected. 'Pop' science plays a very minor role and no-one mistakes it for the real thing; but in the arts there has long been the feeling that the identification of excellence is a purely personal subjective decision—taste cannot be impugned.

The substitution of meritocracy for aristocracy and the resultant mobility has transferred the guardianship of high culture from the aristocratic element of society to the schools

---

[1] 'Humanist Education and its contribution to the Renaissance', by R. R. Bolgar in *The Changing Curriculum*, edited by History of Education Society, p. 14.

[2] Recent essays by Pierre Bourdieu ('Systems of Education & Systems of Thought', reprinted in *Readings in the Theory of Educational Systems*, ed. E. Hopper) and Professor Bernstein ('On the Classification & Framing of Educational Knowledge', reprinted in *Class, Order & Control*) hold out the possibility of a much fuller sociology of the school which may throw light on these problems.

and universities. In this situation science and technology have flourished while the arts have languished if not disintegrated. To suggest the schools and the universities as the guardians of the arts is to see at once the ludicrousness of the pretension; outside the specialism, philistinism and ignorance are rampant in the schools—and too often in the universities too. Even on empirical grounds Mr. H. L. Wilensky, after examining the tastes of a cross-section of 1,254 members by standards which could hardly be thought exacting, has come to the opinion that 'it may take rather close family supervision over more than a generation to cultivate a taste for high culture': of the 19 who had made 'rather heroic efforts to cultivate the best in the media' (among whom, happily, were a high percentage of university professors!) most had come from families of already high status. It is this that brings Mr. Wilensky to the conclusion quoted above.[1]

This situation has given me serious reason for pause in recommending the curriculum for our least able children—not that I doubt its suitability or educational potential, but that I doubt the capacities of the teachers to seize on the potential which is within it.[2] The real crisis in teacher education arises not out of the supposed organizational shortcomings identified by the James Committee, but from the fact that a considerable minority of teachers are seeking to convey a culture in which they don't believe to a school population of which a clear majority probably doesn't want it. My fear is that in seeking the implementation of what I am recommending I may simply be opening the floodgates to an avalanche of exploitable pop instead of the training (slow but possible) in affective discrimination I intend. It won't be Eisenstein who will figure in the film programmes but some costumed banality from Wardour Street (on the grounds that it's historical and therefore *ipso facto* educative). Indeed it could be worse still; the greater menace is probably some 'enlightened' young ignoramus proffering semi-pornography to his charges in the name of freedom, enlightenment and emancipation. I can't help feeling it would be better to bore them stiff.

[1] H. L. Wilensky: 'Mass Society & Mass Culture: interdependence or independence?' *American Sociological Review*, Vol. 29, No. 2, April 1964.
[2] There is not a great deal of empirical evidence on the culture of teachers; but *cf.* 'Measuring General Culture among Student Teachers' by W. Hopkins (*Educational Research*, Vol. 14, No. 2, Feb. 1972).

Still, perhaps the risk should be taken, for many even of the dullest children in our schools are to-day palpably under-functioning. And enrichment can take place. Experience of backward children in primary schools demonstrates the ability to awaken their senses and their emotions through story, drama, mime, pictorial image; but it has to be fed *to* them—it can't arise 'spontaneously' out of their meagre 'creative' capacities. They should *hear* stories, dramatize myths and legends they have encountered, mime characters created by others, look at pictures. To-day's educational fetish is creativity for all. No greater error exists in current education than the belief that 'creativity' can come out of a vacuum. The great masters have ever followed the tradition, defined by Professor Gombrich in the terms 'making comes before matching'—which is another way of saying that art (creativity) is the product of art rather than of nature.

One hope it might be possible to admit—and that is that my revised syllabus might be more attractive to teach than the present watered-down high cultural curriculum. Heaven knows we are breaking into areas of taste and discrimination, of emotional rather than intellectual refinement which arouse the gravest apprehensions, as I have indicated. It's true that we teach literature in the schools—but then there is a certain tradi-tion of discrimination (though even this seems to be breaking down when one considers what is being offered to children and students in schools these days in the name of good literature). But where are the canons of taste in the world of the film or T.V?

I think we've got to take the risks. We must hammer home that what is being offered is an alternative form of hard work, not a soft option. But film and T.V. are part of the young teacher's world, and for some more immediately appealing forms of communication than print. To say this in no way in-volves a criticism of print culture, which remains a magnificent one and one which must be kept up. But our community is large and it offers opportunity for diversity. One thing pro-gressivism has taught us, to its credit, and that is to respect individual difference; if some choose to find themselves through iconography rather than words they should be allowed to do so; and the same is true of those who wish to project themselves through movement and drama. Here too are ways of coming to understand our common world; and it is after all, such under-standing that it is the business of education to foster.

CHAPTER ONE

Introduction

'So complete', said John Stuart Mill in his *Autobiography*, 'was my father's reliance on the influence of reason over the minds of mankind whenever it is allowed to reach them, that he felt as if all would be gained, if the whole population were taught to read, if all sorts of opinions were allowed to be expressed to them by word and in writing, and if by means of the suffrage they could nominate a legislature to give effect to the opinions they adopted.' It hasn't happened quite like that. James Mill's view of human nature omitted aspects which have taken their subtle revenge on his hopes and expectations. Universal schooling has been with us these eighty years, but universal rational man has eluded us. And because so much of our education has been geared in theory to his production, a good deal of it has proved a failure.

Rational man, despite his affiliations to enlightened *self-*interest, has always had his minimum social responsibilities. In this century, as disappointment with the liberal 'harmony' has grown, these have tended to be increasingly stressed, and latterly, in the aftermath of war, especially in their economic guises. The relationship between changes in our social structure and the proliferation of the educational system has in some respects been close. Where formerly, for instance, the upper echelons were recruited on a basis of birth and heredity, today the development of the industrial-bureaucratic state has needed many types of

expertise for its implementation, expertise which has been provided, by and large, by our system of schooling, so that 'meritocracy' has tended to replace aristocracy. Education has always,
in some degree, had an economic function to perform in that,
traditionally, it has prepared young people for their life's work.
In this, and in other senses too, it has fulfilled a social role, in
that it has always sought to induct into a way of life, the way of
life that was socially approved of.

Today, then, the fostering of individual rational self-consciousness which came about in the Protestant Liberal state and which
it is still, in large measure, the function of modern education to
encourage, has encountered the collectivist implications of more
recent developments. This raises acute problems of the relation
between education and society. More particularly, economic
pressures nourished by a predominantly business and industrial
civilization with its concern for profits, economic self-sufficiency
and a 'standard of living' in materialistic terms have produced a
demand for 'educated manpower'. The vice-chancellor of a new
university seeks to produce 'the all-round graduate of the sort
that industry requires'. It is this economic pressure more than
anything else which has stirred public and, to some extent,
governmental interest in education in recent years—the idea
that education means money. It is, of course, no new discovery.
Horace Mann, in the nineteenth century, urged that: 'Education
has a market value; that it is so far an article of merchandise,
that it can be turned to pecuniary account.' Since the Second
World War, this attitude has become more prominent and it
has had the propagandist advantage that it has introduced a note
of hard realism into a field which in the past has produced a fine
crop of vague theorizing.

But, of course, to succumb to such economic incentives is to
approve the whole tendency of a society in which the more insistent valuations raise many doubts and queries. The economic
motive is symptomatic of a set of presumed obligations which
raise important questions about the relationships between
the schools and the social order. Before, then, I examine the
more specific problems of the post-war world in education (I
shall be concerned mostly at the secondary level) it will be

necessary to probe, in general philosophic terms, what is implied by the social responsibilities of the school. Is an appeal to social 'need' a sufficient ground for the implementation of educational policies? How are we to characterize the social role of the school? A relevant witness here will be John Dewey, for he has done more, in our time, than any other educational thinker to stress the social responsibilities of the school, though his aims are political and idealistic rather than economic; he represents, indeed, the collectivist, egalitarian trend in modern social thinking about education rather than the technical, hierarchical tendency. The force of the latter will be examined in the later chapters. The roots of both are to be found in the rationalism of the eighteenth century.

II. THE SOCIAL ROLE OF THE SCHOOL

In considering the school as a social institution,[1] I may be implying either that the school is a society in itself, comprising a number of people together and forming a community for the purpose of realizing educative ends; or I may intend to stress the relationship between the school and the world outside school ('not-school'), the school, that is, as a body having a certain sort of rapport with the larger life of Society as a whole. I may, that is, intend to speak of the school as a 'society' (small 's') or of the school in relation to Society (large 'S').

The fact that it is possible to think of the school as a society on its own implies that there is some point of demarcation which enables us to distinguish where the school as a society ends and

[1] It may be urged that, in this chapter, I employ a number of phrases—'the social role of the school', 'the school as a social institution', 'education as a social process', 'education as socialization'—as if they meant much the same thing. Certainly they obviously need not mean much the same thing—the phrase 'the school as a social institution', for instance, has, to the specialist sociologist, a precise connotation. But I am referring to comparatively loose usages of these phrases as employed by educationists—like Dewey, for example—who do not carefully distinguish one from another; and I believe, therefore, that in the context of my present purpose—which is simply to examine education in its relation to society—my seemingly cavalier employment of them is justified.

17

where Society begins. The position is clarified visually and topographically by the presence, in various parts of our towns and countryside, of buildings which are known as 'schools'; we say, moreover, that the child 'goes to school', and such a way of talking would hardly arise if it were not clear that there are a large number of places where a child may be which are describable as 'not-school'.

All children, except perhaps the very sub-normal, are perfectly aware of when they are 'in' school, as we say, and when they are not. Yet the situation is not quite so simple nowadays as it once was. Even physically, to be 'in' school is not the same. When Bentham was drawing up his plans for his ideal school, he advocated windows placed high up on the wall so that children's learning would not be distracted by what they saw going on extra-murally, as it were. Yet, a little time ago *Punch* carried a cartoon showing a teacher leaning against his desk, one eye directed out of the enormous pane of glass which formed the fourth wall of the classroom, and the other balefully glaring at the Giles-like urchin in front of him; 'It's a good job for you, Atkins,' he was saying, 'that your mother is watching.' The development in school architecture implied represents, as such changes usually do, an altered conception of the relationship between 'school' and 'not-school'. Just as, visually, there is nothing like the same barrier there used to be between the two realms, so, theoretically, and to the extent that such theories are put into operation, practically, there is, and has been for some time, a move to blur the distinction between what is 'school' and what is 'not-school'—dating, in the case of a few progressive theorists from at least the eighteenth century. Let me illustrate what I am getting at by some propositions about 'What the School is' which John Dewey included in his *Pedagogic Creed* and which he published in 1897.

'—the school is primarily a social institution. Education being a social process, the school is simply that form of community life in which all those agencies are concentrated that will be most effective in bringing the child to share in the inherited resources of the race, and to use his own powers for social ends.

'—the school must represent present life—life as real and

18

vital to the child as that which he carries on in the home, in the neighbourhood, or on the playground.

'—as . . . simplified social life, the school life should grow gradually out of the home life; . . . it should take up and continue the activities with which the child is already familiar in the home.

'—much of the present education fails because it neglects this fundamental principle of the school as a form of community life. It conceives the school as a place where certain lessons are to be learned, or where certain habits are to be formed. The value of these is conceived as lying largely in the remote future; the child must do these things for the sake of something else he is to do; they are mere preparations. As a result they do not become a part of the life experience of the child and so are not truly educative.'

It will be obvious from these quotations what I meant when I mentioned above the blurring of the distinction between school and not-school. Yet even here, there are two points to notice. In the first place, Dewey finds it necessary to *recommend* that we shall look upon the schools in this way. He wishes us to take a conscious decision that we shall so organize our schools that they will meet the requirements, stated or implied, that he has laid down in these paragraphs. Now this in itself is sufficient to indicate that he was aware of a barrier between school and not-school, and that what is school is amenable to a conscious decision; so that a school is always, in a happy phrase of Mr. Lionel Elvin, a 'contrived community', and that in a sense in which Society at large is not. Though alterations in the social and political character of Society are always possible, Society itself is never the result of specific human decisions to the extent that one of its institutions is; and the set-up of authority within Society, for example, is not precisely analagous to that within a school.

Secondly, Dewey seems to recognize this difference himself, when he remarks that 'the school, as an institution, should *simplify* existing social life'. The act of conscious simplification recognizes the gulf between school and not-school in so far as it implies a standing apart from and a conceptualization of the

19

ordinary processes of social life, essential prerequisites to the act of simplification. What, even in Dewey's theory, the school child is being asked to 'live' is essentially something abstracted from the complex fulness of external, social, not-school life.

Hence the uniqueness and, in some degree (which will vary from time to time), the essential 'difference' of the school from what is not-school can never be impugned, even by those who most ardently desire to lower the barriers between them. It may seem that I am making heavy weather of a point that was obvious from the beginning. Nevertheless, I believe that even a laborious establishment of this point is by no means a waste of time, for it is necessary to confirm the identity of the school, in the sense in which we speak of someone's identity as that which marks him off from all other people.

In thus seeking to analyse what people mean when they speak of the school in these ways, I am not, as I made clear in my footnote at the beginning of the section, intending to refer to the precise connotation of the word 'institution' which the sociologist would have in mind by its use, but to a vague general usage which is becoming popular—when to speak of the school as a 'social' institution is simply a means of stressing the social responsibilities it has. We now come to see that when people talk in this way about the school they are often doing little more than attempting to focus our gaze, to persuade our attention in a particular direction. To put it another way, when people urge that the school is a 'social' institution they are not identifying the essential or unique nature of the school; they are announcing their intention to concentrate on certain aspects of the sorts of procedures that go on in schools or on certain of the undertakings relevant to the sort of institution a school is, to the exclusion (temporary, it may be) of others; yet in doing so they are acting no less arbitrarily than others before have done when these latter have stressed other functions of the school—for example, its role in the development of 'character' or, more recently, 'self-expression'. One of the things that is interesting about the way in which such people talk about the school as a social institution is the light it throws upon *their* preoccupations and, ultimately, upon their scale of values. It is reasonable to conjecture that it is because the notion of the 'social', in the sense of social responsibility, has come to carry with it a sense of approbation, as part of the general ethos of our time, that the emphasis on the social role of the school recurs so frequently in current talk about education. Of course, it is also partly descriptive and some, when challenged, might claim exclusively so. Nevertheless, the fact that more and more people want to *describe* the various ways in which it makes sense to think of the school as a social institution, even the growing sociological interest itself, with its more technical awareness, partly springs out of, and partly in its turn stimulates, an interest which very easily slips over from being simply descriptive to being covertly normative. On the whole those who interest themselves in the social aspects of education are those who, like Dewey and Mannheim, wish to encourage the 'socialization' of the school even to the extent, in Dewey's phrase, of regarding 'education . . . as the fundamental method of social progress and reform'. To put it in more specific terms, the stress on the social role of the school *may* be a means of urging the need for more scientists, not on the grounds that science is a valuable thing for the individual to study, but because the community (Society) 'needs' more scientists for increased production. In the same way, Mrs. Floud (*et al.*) in *Social Class and Educational Opportunity*, investigate the relation between educational opportunity and social class not out of abstract interest in social phenomena, but partly, at least, in order to 'throw light on the problems of providing equality of opportunity in post-war English education'. Or, again, Professor D. V. Glass, writing of *Social Mobility in Britain*, urges that 'Such problems are central to the study of social structure, they are of direct concern both for the development of sociological theory and *for the formulation of social policy*' (my italics).

The point I am making is similar to that made by Lady Wootton in a broadcast talk on 'Lions and Water Wagtails', when she pointed out the danger of our thinking about social matters being swayed by personal preferences or moral commitments: as she puts it, the danger is that 'If we think at all, we think wishfully; and the choice of hypotheses is likely to be dictated as much by personal prejudices or moral judgments as by exact observation of the relevant data'. When, therefore, Dewey says 'The school is primarily a social institution', he is smuggling in a covert value judgment.

So far I have been concerned to establish two interrelated points. The first is that the school in some degree always stands apart from not-school, that it is, in fact, a *contrived* institution or society; it can never be reduced simply to Society as it is. And, secondly, that the current emphasis on the school as a social institution may spring in part (not, of course, wholly), from an evaluative purpose, from a feeling, that is, that the school *ought* in various ways to appreciate its social role, its social 'responsibilities', whatever these may be. I want, now, to define what sorts of relationships, procedures, aims, purposes, we may have in mind when we conceptualize the notion of education as a social process: what such conceptualization reveals about our scale of values. I will begin by examining a general proposition about the social function of education and I will then go on to consider a number of particular stresses which the notion has received in recent years.

Here, then, is a general proposition derived from Durkheim: 'Education consists of a methodical socialization of the young generation'. And I will begin by examining this on its merits rather than by attempting to elucidate precisely what it was that Durkheim himself intended in the historical context of his times to imply by his statement. But, in fact, we shall reach a stage when we shall see that it is not possible to understand what is being implied unless we also come to appreciate how Durkheim understood Society.

It is not difficult to see the sorts of things which such a statement may be intending to assert. For example, in infant schools, children learn to behave in ways which are appropriate to our conventions of social behaviour—they wash before eating, restrain their bodily needs until they are in an appropriate place called a lavatory, and so on. If they are older, they are helped to acquire some of the more subtle and intangible but characteristic behaviour patterns of the society to which they belong—for example to exercise social and religious toleration. The general implication seems to be that the function of education is to enable

the child to fit himself into *current* Society, in the sense that he
acquires present social habits.[1] Moreover, it may suggest that
the acquiring of 'social' habits of a general nature—such as
learning to 'mix', to get on with one's contemporaries, to co-
operate with others—should take precedence over more solitary,
which *might* be more academic, pursuits. Certainly, children
learn a number of skills which enable them to communicate in a
variety of ways with others; particularly do they learn how to
speak and write a language which behaves as it does because of
the way it has developed at the hands of previous members of the
society. Language, in fact, it is urged, is primarily a social
phenomenon[2] and its acquirement would be regarded as one of
the quite fundamental steps illustrating the accuracy of Durkheim's proposition.

Yet it so happens that my interests are literary as well as
educational; and anyone who has received a literary education
must regard with some suspicion the unexamined proposition
that language is a social phenomenon. Certainly it is true that
our word orders, the syntax of the language, are decided a good
deal as a result of convention and usage, and this implies a social
orientation. Furthermore, the meanings which people give words
and the contexts in which they use them are in line usually with
the decisions of dictionary-makers who, in the main, report on
social usage. Nevertheless this is not the whole story. The reader
understands a good deal of what I am saying at the moment
because the meanings of the words I am using have been decided
by social convention (understood in this sense to imply the activities of makers of dictionaries). But it is still true that what he
understands is never likely to reproduce *exactly* what I mean,
even where simple discourse of this kind is involved, and that in

[1] Durkheim supports this contention when he observes that: 'Education is . . .
the means by which society prepares, within the children, the essential conditions of
its very existence . . . Its object is to arouse and to develop in the child a certain
number of physical, intellectual and moral states which are demanded of him by
both the political society as a whole and the special milieu for which he is specifically
destined.' (*Education and Sociology*.)

[2] 'It is true that language is a logical instrument, but it is, fundamentally and
primarily a social instrument. Language is the device for communication; it is the
tool through which one individual comes to share the ideas and feelings of others.'
(Dewey.)

part, at least, because the meanings of words can only be fixed within certain very broad limits by the makers of dictionaries; furthermore, one of my reasons for making this very point stems from an extensive experience of literature and of the sorts of very different interpretations critics have placed on the same work at different times or even at the same time. Thus speech, a social phenomenon admittedly to the extent that some degree of communication is usually possible on a wide range of topics, is nevertheless never simply a social phenomenon. Most collocations of words while 'making sense', as we call it—a social phenomenon—make unique sense—a private phenomenon. The only completely social languages are those of mathematics and of the scientific formula, in the sense that their meaning is unmistakable. It is such considerations which justify Dr. F. R. Leavis' contention: '. . . you can't be interested in literature and forget that the creative individual is indispensable. Without the individual talent there is no creation. While you are in touch with literature no amount of dialectic, or of materialistic inter- pretation [Dr. Leavis is explicitly concerned with Marxist notions] will obscure for long the truth that it is only in indi- viduals that society lives.' (*The Common Pursuit.*) Furthermore, language has functions other than those of communication. It is a means of exploring, privately, personal experience; and it serves egocentric purposes in young children, as Piaget points out.

If, therefore, by a process of socialization is intended an approximation of the child to the currently accepted social *mores* and conventions, or, as Dewey would have it, a means by which all members of the community shall come to share a common experience, it must be appreciated that only an approximation is even possible. The precise boundaries between social acceptance and individual autonomy cannot profitably be discussed, I think, except in concrete cases; but that such discussion is always a pre-requisite to educational activity should never be forgotten. For, of course, there is involved in such a case not only the question of what is possible in the way of 'socialization' but also of what is *desirable*. The process of formal education always raises the question of values.

But there is yet a further difficulty. Durkheim, we have said,

urges that education 'consists of a methodical socialization of
the young generation'. Karl Mannheim intends much the same
notion when he contends that 'By becoming society-conscious
we no longer formulate the needs of Youth in the abstract, but
always with reference to the needs and purposes of a given
society.' Yet when we come to examine what the two men meant
by Society we find that, despite certain similarities, there are
considerable differences in the nature of the Society they intend
to prepare the young for. These differences cannot entirely be
explained in terms of the diverse Societies within which they
were writing and which formed the background of their analyses
—though this diversity is obviously a factor. One of the great
dangers in talking about education, which involves the notion
of a process leading to the achievement of ends, is that of slipping out of a purely descriptive account of what the relations
between education and society in fact *are* into an expression of
normative opinion on what the role of education ought to be—
perhaps in bringing about a more desirable Society—and treating
the latter similarly as fact.[1] Mannheim connects the two aspects
explicitly when, in stressing the importance of the investigation
of social factors in education, he says that such knowledge can
help in assigning men to the functions most suitable for them:
'. . . knowledge, however, can have a wider function. It is not
merely a question of adapting men to a certain given level of
development, but of producing individuals capable of developing the existing form of society beyond itself to a further stage.'
('On the Nature of Economic Ambition', reprinted in *Essays in
the Sociology of Knowledge*, ed. Kecskemeti, p. 233.) An exposition, then, that begins by being factual and analytic frequently
ends by paying unconscious tribute to the purposes and intentions of the analyst (we shall see that Dewey falls into this trap
also). The concept Society easily becomes normative rather than
descriptive; and then what one has, as in these two cases, are
rival views as to what constitutes the good Society.

Though both writers are aware of the social phenomenon of
change, Durkheim tends to stress the conservative nature of

---

[1] Cf. my essay 'Fact and Value in Education', *British Journal of Educational
Studies*, November 1956.

Society. This emerges in his emphasis on the historical force which Society exerts on the growing child, on the relative difficulties of change, on the regenerative role that Society plays in a paternalistic, authoritarian fashion, substituting 'an entirely new being' for the 'egoistic and asocial' being which is man's original nature. Hence Society itself is the moral personality which lasts beyond the generations and binds them together. It is not surprising to find that, for Durkheim, education is 'essentially a matter of authority', necessary in order to 'bring us to overcome our original nature'.

Implicit, then, in Durkheim's conception is a sense of stability in terms of which Society is able to provide both security and release for human powers. By and large he approves the values of the Society of his time, though he admits to some puzzlement in relation to current changes; and such a Society becomes a matter of positive recommendation. Behind the analysis one discovers the prescription. Mannheim, however, is aware chiefly of change, of disintegration on the one side and of the need to emerge out of the 'crisis' into a 'new Society' on the other. In this sense much of his later work tends to be prophetic rather than analytic; education, in its social role, becomes almost indistinguishable from propaganda—he speaks of it as a 'social technique'. This is in part implicit in his conception of the sociology of knowledge, with its view of the intimate relationship between thought and action; but it springs also out of his own particular socio-political history and the extent to which it impressed on him the imminent decay of European Liberalism. Hence he sympathizes with those social groups like the intelligentsia and Youth whom he considers to stand apart in some degree from the current social process and to whom he looks for the regeneration of Society. Hence, too, the tendency to emphasize change rather than stability in Society and to conceive education as an instrument for bringing about a *new* social order rather than as a means of introducing children to the values implicit in present Society.[1] This is reflected in his view of

---

[1] And this, of course, ill assorts with his recommendations that we should break down the barriers between present school and not-school. Hence his use of the concept 'Society' itself shifts in meaning.

educational technique; it becomes a matter of mastery in an evolving situation rather than of the acceptance of a ready-made teacher-inspired picture. And so it is not surprising to find him writing: 'The rate of transformation can . . . be accelerated, if deliberate changes in education are planned, corresponding to the parallel social tendencies in the same direction.'

It is important, then, to realize, that the same form of words may, in fact, cloak different conceptions concerning the aims of education. Behind some such general formula that education is a process of socialization very varied practical notions about what exactly ought to be done may be involved; what one must understand is not so much the form of words as the values implicit in the concrete and practical recommendations which the implementation of such views would necessitate. Obviously, education may, in some measure, be said to serve the 'needs' of Society; but the word 'need' carries with it value implications which require very precise examination. Unless such an examination of implication is carried out, there may be considerable danger of our being rushed into the implementation of policies which a little more consideration might show were ill-advised.

Moreover, when one expresses the general notion of 'socialization' in some such terms as 'serving the needs of Society', it is important to ask, in the particular context, 'Who here represents Society?' This, at any rate, would be one way in which it might be easier to come to a decision concerning the admissibility of the 'need'. There is, in fact, no such being as 'Society' which can make demands on anyone—though writers like Durkheim refer to the 'collectivity' as if it had a personality apart from the individuals which go to make it up. Social 'needs' or demands are in fact made by individual people acting in certain social roles, and sometimes, at least, they are people pursuing their own interests as much as those of the Society in whose name they claim to speak. At the moment these individuals are often business men, to the extent at least that our Society is being increasingly geared to the economic demands of business, and therefore such men are likely to equate the satisfaction of their own interests with the public good. Whenever, then, we meet the phrase 'the needs of Society' it is always necessary to ask two questions. The first is 'Who is being referred to by the word "Society"?'[1]—which individuals or groups of individuals are, in fact, 'in need'. And when we have arrived at some quite concrete and specific answer to this, we ought to ask: 'Are the values and aims implicit in such a demand —understood as the sorts of aims and purposes the groups or individuals concerned may be said to have in mind—such as I can allow to justify? Are they, in fact, *good* aims and purposes? Or should there be times when educationists ought to resist demands made on the schools even when the people who are making the demands are socially powerful?'[2]

[1] In the next chapters I will drop the device of referring to Society with a capital 'S'.

[2] I have analysed further aspects of the relations between education and Society in an article published in *Educational Review*, June 1963.

CHAPTER TWO

John Dewey on Education

———————————◆———————————

Though Dewey was an American, his view of the social function of education has, in a wide variety of ways, become part of
the intellectual currency of our time and has affected our thinking about schooling in an industrial society very considerably.
He is not today much read: he has simply become part of our
climate of opinion; and he expresses succinctly many of the
errors and half-truths by which we are beset. Yet more fundamental is the fact that, like most influential educational thinkers,
he raises issues of general philosophic importance in making his
particular assessments of the social role of the school. It is
therefore highly relevant to our current dilemmas to consider
both his view of society and of the function of the school therein.

With Dewey, indeed, there is the closest relationship between
his specifically philosophical interests and his general theory of
education. This is not surprising, in view of the 'practicality' of
that philosophy; he regards education as the means by which his
philosophy can be implemented; and that it shall be implemented
is an inherent part of the philosophy itself: 'Unless a philosophy
is to remain symbolic—or verbal—or a sentimental indulgence
for a few, or else mere arbitrary dogma, its auditing of past
experience and its program of values must take effect in conduct.'
Hence, 'Education is the laboratory in which philosophic distinctions become concrete and are tested.' The nature and quality

29

of Dewey's educational advice is, then, very much bound up with a certain view of human life which he is concerned to reveal in his specifically philosophic work; and the clue to the adequacy and comprehensiveness of his educational ideas must be sought in an understanding of the philosophical framework within which they are designed to operate. The range and quality of an individual's views on education are always intimately related to the range and quality of his response to the nature of life in general; one seeks to educate for the type of existence that one desiderates.[1]

Like Froebel, Dewey belongs to that nineteenth-century movement which transformed 'teaching from a mechanical to a biological art'.[2] Like Froebel, too, he is much concerned to stress the continuity of man and nature. But there the likeness ends; for whereas most of Froebel's references to nature are for the purpose of illustrating some lesson that man can learn from her processes ('Men, who wander through your fields, gardens and groves, why do you not open your minds to receive what Nature in dumb speech teaches you?')—in other words, his purpose has something Wordsworthian about it—Dewey sees nature as a vehicle for the extension of man's power and control. About man's receptive side, his capacity to achieve wisdom from processes outside himself in the natural world, he is almost wholly silent; he is concerned only with the active side, what man can do with the raw material of nature. Thus, when he points out that 'Man's home is nature', he continues significantly: 'his purposes and aims are dependent for execution upon natural conditions'; in other words, nature is merely the material and the scene of man's endeavours. What is involved is what Santayana has termed 'the dominance of the foreground': 'A foreground is by definition relative to some chosen point of view, to the station assumed in the midst of nature of some creature tethered by fortune to a particular time and place . . . Some local perspective or some casual interest is set up in the place of universal nature.' Thus, for Dewey, the subject-matter

[1] One of the difficulties of discussing Dewey's work, however, lies in the unusual vagueness of his terminology. He certainly uses such abstractions as 'social', 'growth', 'democracy', etc. without any attempt to make them very precise.

[2] Cf. Graham Wallas's useful essay, 'A Criticism of Froebelian Pedagogy', reprinted in *Men and Ideas*.

of human learning only appeals as it relates itself to the social
life of man; in geography, 'the residence, pursuits, successes,
and failures of men are things that give the geographic data their
reason for inclusion in the material of instruction'. (Dewey,
Democracy and Education.) Otherwise geography 'appears as a
veritable rag-bag of intellectual odds and ends'. That the geo-
graphical structure of the world might form an order of experience independent of man's purposes and desires does not
seem to occur to Dewey: 'The educational centre of gravity
is in the cultural or humane aspects of the subject. From this
centre, any material becomes relevant insofar as it is needed to
help appreciate the significance of human activities and relations.' (*Democracy and Education.*) Again, the significance that
the past has for Dewey—the past is indeed the object of some
animus on his part; his ideal society is, in fact, a rootless one—
lies in its ability to illumine man's present condition: 'The true
starting point of history is always some present situation with
its problems . . . History deals with the past, but this past is the
history of the present.' (*Democracy and Education.*)

And what is true of history and geography is true of all
knowledge. Its significance is bound up with the present interest
and activities of man; it 'translates into concrete and detailed
terms the meanings of current social life which it is desirable to
transmit'. Even religion, in this scheme of things, merely constitutes 'the idealization of things characteristic of natural
association, which have been projected into a supernatural realm
for safekeeping and sanction'. Unless religion is reduced to this
state, 'fundamental dualism and a division of life continue'. (*A
Common Faith.*)

The last sentence gives us a clue as to the motive force behind
this specifically anthropocentric scheme. There is an unwillingness to make distinctions, 'divisions', which would in any way
detract from the effectiveness of 'practical' concerns. To distinguish is first to submit to the nature of the things distinguished
between, to bring them within the sphere of attention and to
examine their natures, not merely as they affect the here and
now of the immediately contingent, but as they are in their
own natures constituted. And such an attempt at objectivity is

indeed, in the last resort, subjectively enriching; because, in fact, objects are what they are, and to move among them with confidence—which is what successful living entails—one needs to know them for what they are, not for the way in which the fleeting moment accidentally presents them.

By contrast, Dewey's system is highly subjective. His concern is that of the practical man, who sees the world only as the sphere for his activity, and therefore only as an offshoot of himself as at the moment he conceives that self. Thus, a transcendent sphere, a world in which man can by definition exercise no control, is repudiated:

'The idea of a double and parallel manifestation of the divine, in which the latter has superior status and authenticity, brings about a condition of unstable equilibrium. It operates to distract energy, through dividing the objects to which it is directed.' (*A Common Faith.*)

Dewey is powerfully attracted by science; indeed, as we shall see, his educational recommendations comprise principally the application of its methodology to the teaching situation. Dewey's attitude towards science is Baconian—it is, that is, technological rather than descriptive. He belongs, indeed, to the tradition of which Bacon was the great 'Instaurator', and his repudiation of the classic philosophical tradition reflects Bacon's rejection of the Schoolman. He always speaks of Bacon with the greatest respect, as 'an outstanding figure of the world's intellectual life'; and he stresses, as the 'best-known aphorism' of Bacon, 'Knowledge is Power', an aphorism that not unjustly sums up Dewey's own attitude. For indeed, his pragmatism involves, on a scale unthought-of by Bacon (who at least considered it 'most wise soberly to render unto faith the things that are faith's', even if his desire to separate religious truth and scientific truth was, on the whole, in the interests of science), '. . . a change from knowing as aesthetic enjoyment of the properties of nature regarded as a work of divine art, to knowing as a means of secular control—that is, a method of purposefully introducing changes which will alter the course of events'. (*Quest for Certainty.*) The slipping in of the value judgment is interesting and altogether typical. For the moment, what is important is to note how intimately Dewey's conception of life is bound up with what he conceives to be the processes of scientific investigation. And even more important is that he often appears to misconceive the nature of what the scientist is doing. His 'science' is largely of the 'common-sense' variety; with the full contemporary philosophical implications of the scientific outlook he seems only imperfectly acquainted. Even in 1929, no good scientist would have claimed that 'scientific inquiry always starts from things of the environment experienced in our everyday life, with things we see, handle, use, enjoy and suffer from'. Furthermore, Dewey points out that one of the virtues of reducing objects to the status of data for an investigation is that it 'liberates man from subjection to the past'. Hence, 'the scientific attitude, as an attitude of interest in change instead of interest in isolated and complete fixities, is necessarily alert for problems'. (*Quest for Certainty.*)

All through his exposition Dewey seems too much to assume that the ability to recognize the presence of problems is a matter of little or no difficulty. Now, the need to recognize problems forms a significant part of his repudiation of the past; for unless problems are recognized and met, we remain the victims of habit, which involves the domination of the past. What Dewey fails to make sufficiently clear is the enormous dependence of even the modern scientist on past knowledge before the presence of a problem can be recognized and an hypothesis formulated. For as a scientific investigation implies a well-developed habituation to the modes and procedures of science, and to its characteristic undertakings, as well as a close acquaintanceship with the affiliated circumstances of the point of issue, so any 'scientific' mode of living, even within Dewey's comprehension of the term, would imply a deep appreciation and comprehension of the conventions, social mores, and modes of understanding of the society within which it was being lived. Dewey's comparative[1]

---

[1] 'Comparative' only—for in *Art as Experience* he does appreciate that '. . . there has been no great literary artist who did not feed upon the works of the masters of drama, poetry and eloquent prose. In this dependence upon tradition there is nothing peculiar to art. The scientific enquirer, the philosopher, the technologist, also derive their substance from the stream of culture.' (Chapter XI.)

In this respect, however, *Art as Experience* stands out from much of the rest of his work. The burden of his educational writings is anti-historical.

neglect of this aspect of modern scientific work, his too eager grasping after a 'progress' (largely technical), a 'future', a 'reconstruction' whose very definition should necessitate an ample appreciation of the past, makes, as we shall see, an important lack in his application of scientific ideas to his educational conceptions, as well as an attenuation in possible richness of the concept of the 'social'. He accepts too readily the notion of a perpetually changing world.

It will be becoming increasingly clear that Dewey is primarily concerned only with certain features of human experience, and that his system depends on the conscious (and assumed) isolation of a limited number of aspects only. This, of course, is true of all philosophers; what matters is the range and richness of inclusiveness within which they work. The word 'experience' is one that is very frequently encountered in modern educational writing, and its use in the sorts of contexts in which it is found partly springs from Dewey's persistent emphasis on the word. Thus, in criticizing the older education, Dewey states:

'. . . the fundamental fallacy in methods of instruction lies in supposing that experience on the part of pupils may be assumed. What is here insisted upon is the necessity of an actual empirical situation as the initiating phase of thought . . . The fallacy consists in supposing that we can begin with ready-made subject-matter of arithmetic, or geography, or whatever, irrespective of some direct personal experience of a situation.' (*Democracy and Education.*)

What, then, Dewey implies by experience is a matter of some moment, especially as most educationalists who use the word tend to make somewhat similar assumptions about its nature.

Roughly, it comprehends the world of 'practical' events: 'to realize what an experience, or empirical situation means, we have to call to mind the sort of . . . occupations that interest and engage activity in ordinary life.' (*Democracy and Education.*) Yet it is of the essence of this 'experience' that it shall be dynamic in nature; it involves the sphere within which man acts, and within which he is acted upon; '. . . the combination of what things *do* to us (not in impressing qualities on a passive mind) in modifying our actions, furthering some of them and resisting and checking others, and what we can do to *them* in producing new changes constitutes experience.' (*Democracy and Education.*) Or again: 'The nature of experience can be understood only by noting that it includes an active and a passive element peculiarly combined. On the active hand, experience is *trying*—a meaning which is made explicit in the connected term experiment. On the passive, it is *undergoing*. When we experience something we act upon it, we do something with it; then we suffer or undergo the consequences. We do something to the thing and then it does something to us in return: such as the peculiar combination. The connection of these two phases of experience measures the fruitfulness or value of the experience. Mere activity does not constitute experience. . . . When an activity is continued *into* the undergoing of consequences, when the change made by action is reflected back into a change made in us, the mere flux is loaded with significance. We learn something.' (*Democracy and Education.*) Hence the emphasis on activity; significant experience is the outgrowth of experimentation. In line with his conception of what constitutes the sciences, Dewey believes that there is 'no such thing as genuine knowledge and fruitful understanding except as the offspring of *doing*'. Such is what he terms the lesson of the 'laboratory method'; and such, he adds, is the 'lesson which all education has to learn'.

From this view of 'experience', which is always in an active state of 'reconstruction', which is contingent rather than cognitive—'knowledge how' rather than 'knowledge that'—stems his condemnation of the failure of modern philosophy to 'bring about an integration between what we know of the world and the intelligent direction of what we do'. This, he states, is the result of adhering to two ideas formulated in the conditions which, he considers, differ very considerably from those appertaining today: '. . . that knowledge is concerned with disclosure of characteristics of antecedent existences and essences, and that the properties of value found therein provide the authoritative standards for the conduct of life.' (*Quest for Certainty.*) Hence the 'quest for certainty' has misled men into the assumption of a world, ascertainable by cognitive means, anterior to, and more important than, the world of practical activity. The refinement of scientific inquiry—refinement because even scientists like Newton assumed the existence of ultimate unchangeable substances which interacted without undergoing change in themselves—has shown, he goes on to state, that it is not necessary to assume any permanent substrate; and scientific inquiry, be it remembered, 'is taken as the type and pattern of knowing since it is the most perfected of all branches of knowing'.[1]

Thus the world as Dewey conceives it is one of continuous reconstructed change, the stage for technical exploration, where 'authority' claims no precedence but what is derived from concretely tested experience, where, in fact, all beliefs, 'tenets and creeds about good and goods' are so many tools, 'guides to action', 'instrumentalities of direction', hypotheses whose value is tested as the result of active experimentation. Hence the test of value lies in consequences. For instance, the soundness and pertinence of a moral law are 'tested by what happens when it is acted upon'. How it came initially to be framed Dewey never reveals; neither does he tell us on what basis one pattern of behaviour is chosen rather than another. And, indeed, he forgets that even the contention that the moral law seeks to meet human needs depends on some anterior formulation of what constitute human needs.

Still, Dewey grants the necessity of value considerations. He admits, for instance, that 'mere activity does not constitute experience'; it must result in increased capacity for control. Thus, 'the *measure of the value* of an experience lies in the perception of relationships or continuities to which it leads up'. (*Democracy and Education.*) In other words it must work, submit to test in action; hence values are 'identical with goods that are the fruit of intelligently directed activity'.

Now it is here that the attempt to make the total human world co-extensive with the world of practical activity breaks down.

[1] Yet experience, rightly conceived, must always include the possibility of persistence and permanence: 'That beings, who are capable of action and observation, are born into, and move among, a world of persisting objects is a logical necessity and not a contingent matter of fact', and cf. the discussion of reality as 'consisting of things of different types and kinds rather than of events of different types and kinds', involving the necessity for 'points of reference or attachment, which are identifiably the same through change'. (Stuart Hampshire, *Thought and Action.*)

For indeed, any test must assume the acceptance of some standard in terms of which the test can be said to have succeeded or failed. In the world of practical activity, this is comparatively easy to provide. Thus, in the case of a doctor faced with the task of having to cure a patient (an example actually used by Dewey) the test of the diagnosis will lie in the effectiveness or otherwise of the treatment proposed, if treatment is considered possible. But what will not be tested is the antecedent assumption on which both the calling and behaviour of the doctor are based, the assumption, that the saving and preservation of life is a good thing. In a sense Dewey admits this, but in such terms, it seems to me, as to brush away the problem as irrelevant. He admits that the 'knowledge of nature' that now exists only enables us to ask 'proximate questions, not ultimate ones', but urges that in 'restricted and technical fields, men now proceed unhesitatingly along these lines . . . Increased knowledge of nature and its conditions does not raise the problem of validity of the value of health or of communication in general.' Such a problem, he seems to be saying, is irrelevant to the purposes of philosophy today.

And, certainly, closer examination of Dewey's world of practical activity goes to show that it rests on a series of implicit assumptions, only a few of which are ever brought into question, in a manner to be indicated, and yet which of necessity sustain the range of activities which he is concerned to recommend. As we have seen, he seems to assume that 'problems' presented by the data of sensory experience offer themselves for treatment, forgetting that the appreciation of the presence of a problem depends on a whole series of anterior assumptions as to what constitutes relevance and importance. In a passage quoted above, and already referred to, he speaks of nature as 'material to act upon so as to transform it into new objects which better answer our needs', without attempting to address himself specifically to the problem of what constitutes a need, and in what sense the implications of 'better' are to be taken. And such implicit value judgments are constantly encountered in Dewey's writing. Thus he speaks of 'growth' and 'development' as if the terms were self-explanatory. Moreover, his exclusion of anterior conceptions prevents him from setting up some antecedent yardstick;

he allows of no tradition in terms of which 'growth' can be measured. His naturalistic universe *appears* to seek no standard beyond itself; the end to be achieved, he is fond of asserting, is something *within* the process of attainment, not something external to it. He asserts that. 'Since education is not a means to living, but is identical with the operation of living a life which is fruitful and inherently significant, the only ultimate value which can be set up is just the process of living itself.' Hence his repudiation of the idea that there is a hierarchy of values.

But this is not the whole story. Dewey does, in fact, though careless of its implication for his metaphysic, indicate a standard in terms of which the 'process of living' is to be judged. We have already noted the extent to which he imposes a social criterion on right action and right learning; and implicit in much of his writing is the assumption that the social repercussions of man's behaviour provide the real standards by which man's acts shall be judged. He tolerates, however, only one type of social organization—the democratic, a state of society which he nowhere defines with any clarity, and the manifestations of which he does not indicate in any detail. His conception of it is partly emotional—he equates it generally with anti-authoritarianism, and sees in it a bulwark against privilege and exploitation. Perhaps the nearest he gets to definition is when he asserts that 'a democracy is more than a form of government: it is primarily a mode of associated living, of conjoint communicated experience'. The two most important elements of democracy to which he draws attention are: 'more numerous and more varied points of shared common interest (and) greater reliance upon the recognition of mutual interests as a factor in social control' and 'freer interaction between social groups . . . (and) change in social habit—its continuous readjustment through meeting the new situations produced by varied intercourse'. It is here that the two chief elements in Dewey's system meet. For it is quite obvious that however much he advocates the necessity of constant change, of continual reconstruction of experience, that change must work *within* the democratic framework, and no changes in social habit which will in any way endanger this 'mode of associated living' are to be permitted.

Thus his system really rests on the assumption of vaguely defined 'democratic' values. For, of course, his democratic state constitutes an ideal; it is not simply descriptive of any actual form of government. And we must go on to consider some of the implications of this assumption of a specifically social criterion; for though vaguely defined, the general trend of Dewey's advocacy of 'democratic' criteria has certain sinister implications which need to be explored more fully.

One of the characteristics of scientific knowledge is that it is open and public, offering itself for verification by anyone who cares to acquaint himself with the facts of the case. Implicitly, Dewey advocates this 'openness' as the criterion by which men should be judged. Indeed, just as the scientific hypothesis must allow itself to be tested in action, so, in a sense, must Dewey's social man lay himself open to inspection and examination. Self, to Dewey, only makes sense in terms of other men (the obverse side of which is, of course, that other men only make sense in terms of self). He asks, for instance, how the beliefs and aspirations of group life can be communicated to the young, and replies:

'By means of the action of the environment in calling out certain responses. The required beliefs cannot be hammered in; the needed attitudes cannot be plastered on. But the particular medium in which an individual exists leads him to see and feel one thing rather than another; it leads him to have certain plans in order that he may act successfully with others; it strengthens some beliefs and weakens others as a condition of winning the approval of others.' (*Democracy and Education.*) Furthermore Dewey repudiates the idea of imitation in education in these terms:

'One has only to consider how completely the child is dependent from his earliest days for successful execution of his purpose upon fitting his acts into those of others to see what a premium is put upon behaving as others behave . . . The pressure for likemindedness in action from this source is so great that it is quite superfluous to appeal to imitation.' (*Democracy and Education.*) Hence the main criteria which are to guide human activities are those of group approval and group contribution: 'There is always a danger that increased personal independence will decrease the social capacity of an individual.

In making him more self-reliant, it may make him more self-sufficient; it may lead to aloofness and indifference.'

In this conception of man the main emphasis is, then, on what is capable of being communicated, what in fact is open and public. A man is what he is to other people, dependent upon the 'free and equitable intercourse which springs from a variety of shared interests'. Ultimately, Dewey conceives a society where all will be able to communicate with all on a footing of equality: 'The extension in space of the number of individuals who participate in an interest so that each has to refer his own action to that of others to give point and direction to his own, is equivalent to the breaking-down of those barriers of class, race and national territory which have kept men from perceiving the full import of their activity.' Hence, perhaps, the most questionable of Dewey's conceptions, his repudiation of the 'inner':

'. . . the idea of perfecting an "inner" personality is a sure sign of social divisions. What is called inner is simply that which does not connect with others—which is not capable of free and full communication. What is termed spiritual culture has usually been futile, with something rotten about it, just because it has been conceived as a thing which a man may have internally—and therefore exclusively. What one is as a person is what one is as associated with others, in a free give and take of intercourse.' (*Democracy and Education.*) For all the apparent saving grace of 'free' in the last phrase, such a conception makes a mockery of Dewey's contention concerning the 'freedom' of democratic life; for no man is to be allowed to exist beyond other men, even in the inner recesses of his consciousness.

In the same way, in his *Art as Experience*, Dewey shows little understanding of that private self-consciousness forced upon the artist by the current cultural situation. Though there is much in that book with which I can sympathize, even appreciation of the force of such remarks as 'Instead of signifying being shut up within one's own private feelings and sensations [art] signifies active and alert commerce with the world; at its height it signifies complete interpenetration of self and the world of objects and events', (p. 19) is marred by the over-emphatic 'complete'; and in the rest of the book it is clear that Dewey's feeling against 'fine art' as an 'escape from, or an adventitious decoration of, the main activities of living' comes to demand only an equivocal assent, still question-seeking, as it were, in the light of the further statement: 'Works of art that are not remote from common life, that are widely enjoyed in a community, are signs of a unified collective life. But they are also marvellous aids in the creation of such a life. The remaking of the material of experience in the act of expression is not an isolated event confined to the artist and to a person here and there who happens to enjoy the work. In the degree in which art exercises its office, it is also a remaking of the experience of the community in the direction of greater order and unity.' (*Art as Experience*, p. 81.) However much this may represent an ideal, it shows no comprehension of the predicament of the serious artist in the twentieth-century social order about which Dewey was writing. And there are further indications of this sort of judgment in his educational writing. He appraises the Penelope in the *Odyssey*, as 'a classic in literature because the character is an adequate embodiment of a certain industrial phase of social life'. (*School and Society*.) Literature too readily becomes the hand-maiden of the practical; he sees little of its affective force. Thus he admits that, in a sense, the 'motif of American colonial history and of De Foe's *Robinson Crusoe* are the same. But when *Robinson Crusoe* supplies the material for the curriculum of the third—or fourth—grade child, are we not putting the cart before the horse? Why not give the child the reality, with its much larger sweep, its intenser forces, its more vivid and lasting value for life, using the *Robinson Crusoe* as an imaginative idealization in a particular case of the same sort of problems and activities!'[1]

II

Criticism of Dewey's concrete educational prescriptions comes under two broad headings: his substitution of 'social' for traditionally 'educational' criteria, and his changed emphasis in the

[1] After this, one feels that Soviet Realism is only just round the corner: 'Art also renders men aware of their union with one another in origin and destiny' (p. 271). This is Dewey, but it could have been a hack Soviet apologist.

subject-matter and mode of instruction. Both features are, of course, closely interrelated, and the latter may be said to spring largely from the former.

We have seen that Dewey is concerned to stress constantly the close relationship between school and life. Thus he speaks of the 'artificial gap between life in school and out'; and he insists that 'education . . . is a process of living and not a preparation for future living'. Again, 'the school itself shall be made a genuine form of active community life, instead of a place set apart in which to learn lessons'.

At the same time there is a certain discrepancy between his desire to make school as like life outside school as possible and his conception of education as having a reformatory social mission. He criticizes the traditional school as a place where 'certain information is to be given, where certain lessons are to be learned, or where certain habits are to be formed'; at the same time, in pursuit of his own ends, he is willing to assert: 'we may produce in schools a projection in type of the society we should like to realize, and by forming minds in accord with it gradually modify the larger and more recalcitrant features of adult society.' Indeed, for one so anti-authoritarian, it is surprising to find him actually using the word 'instill': 'The secondary and provisional character of national sovereignty in respect of the fuller, freer, and more fruitful association and intercourse of all human beings with one another must be instilled as a working disposition of mind.' (*Democracy and Education.*)

When, then, Dewey claims that the purpose of education lies in the 'freeing of individual capacity in a progressive growth directed to social aims', it is obvious that what matters is the 'social aim' rather than the individual growth (unless one assumes with Dewey that one is what one is to other people and that one has no identity apart from them). With Dewey, 'progressive' education moved from its individualistic to its collectivist phase, though the apparent anti-authoritarian bias remains: 'The teacher is not in the school to impose certain ideas or to form certain habits in the child, but is there as a member of the community to select the influences which shall affect the child

and to assist him in properly responding to these influences.'
(*Education Today*.) Yet it is relevant to ask what the precise
difference is between 'forming certain habits in the child' and
'selecting the influences which shall affect' and 'assisting' him
to respond to them 'properly'. At most, 'authority' has become
rather more indirect; it is none the less present, in spite of
Dewey's attempt to conceal the fact. And, indeed, in saying that
'through education society can formulate its own purposes, can
organize its own means and resources, and thus shape itself with
definiteness and economy in the direction in which it wishes to
move', the collective noun dangerously conceals the fact that in
practice only certain elements in society can be involved in this
formulation. What, in fact, has happened is that Dewey has
substituted a form of authority potentially at least as pernicious
as the one he so much dislikes; for one must judge the adequacy
of his 'authority' from the depth, extensiveness and clarity of
his view of man's nature. We have already analysed the restricted
nature of his conception of life and some of the defects in that
particular form of technocratic democracy which he desiderates.
Thus the incipient totalitarianism there revealed, characterized
by his repudiation of the 'inner' and his emphasis on social
criteria, becomes more apparent in the concrete realization of his
educational principles; the crusade against 'Un-American activities' was explicable when associated with the mental climate
induced by Deweyism over the last fifty years—though, of
course, Dewey is as much a symptom as a portent;[1] De Tocqueville actuely diagnosed the elements of the situation sixty years
before Dewey became a force:

'In the principle of equality I very clearly discern two tendencies; the one leading the mind of every man to untried
thoughts, the other inclined to prohibit him from thinking at all.
And I perceive how, under the dominion of certain laws, democracy would extinguish that liberty of the mind to which a

[1] That certain elements among the campaigners against un-American activities
turned against Deweyism (cf. 'American Vigilantes', *The Times Educational Supplement*, 1 February 1952), in no way destroys my thesis. For Dewey, like many
'revolutionaries', is caught up in the situation of his own creation; and what he has
helped to create is a population with insufficient personal integrity and 'being' to
combat attacks on that academic freedom for which ostensibly he stands.

democratic social condition is favourable; so that, after having broken all the bondage once imposed on it by ranks or by men, the human mind would be closely fettered to the general will of the greatest number.' (*Democracy in America.*)

Just as perturbing is the vastness of the claim made by Dewey for the 'socializing' power of education, and the tremendous force which those responsible for the conscious formulation of the society's purposes require to command; it is significant that those countries which so far have most closely followed Dewey's precept in this matter have been totalitarian. No such vast claims for education would have been made by the older 'authoritarian' educationalists; partly because such educationists would never have equated 'life' with the conscious formulation of social policies; and partly because they had too much respect for the past to be constantly searching after the conscious direction of the future. They appreciated human activity as something which existed within a larger framework which certainly included an element of acceptance; they did not jealously seek 'control', and they believed that there were more cogent criteria for human behaviour than the temporary ebullitions of Tom, Dick and Harry. Dewey's repudiation of the past, which contains lessons irrespective of man's immediate purposes, serves him ill.

The close correlation between Dewey's social preoccupations and his preference for practical activities in education is easily recognizable:

'Where the school work consists in simply learning lessons, mutual assistance, instead of being the most natural form of co-operation and association, becomes a clandestine effort to relieve one's neighbour of his proper duties. Where active work is going on, all this is changed . . . A spirit of free communication, of interchange of ideas, suggestions, results, both successes and failures and previous experiences, becomes the dominating note of the recitation.' We have here one of the main arguments in favour of the 'group' methods introduced into our schools. And since Dewey is the father of the 'project method', his views on 'co-operation' merit close investigation—particularly as they also have implications relevant to the arguments used for comprehensive education.

John Dewey on Education

The stress on 'co-operation' is clearly in line with other aspects of Deweyism. It is indeed worth noting how closely
Dewey's conception of co-operative school work approximates
to that free interchange of experiment and result which charac-
terizes the behaviour of scientific researchers; furthermore, his
'democracy', which he wishes to reproduce in the schools,
comes often to look like a collectivity of scientists, constantly
experimenting and interchanging hypotheses and results. Here,
indeed, we have one of the sources of the belief in a common
culture. There are, however, some unfortunate implications for
schools worth bearing in mind. In the first place, such co-operation implies that no one shall be capable of learning more than
any other, otherwise the 'spirit of free communication' will not
be able to manifest itself; for the idea of 'communication' involves both a communicator and one communicated with—and
implies that both will be equally capable of following the other.
The fact that certain concepts can be grasped by some children
and not by others means in practice that the pace and level will
be set by the others.[1] For that some should grasp ideas, processes, which are beyond the capacity of others surely comes
under Dewey's condemnation of what is not open and public.

Secondly, the precise nature of this 'co-operation' is worth
indicating. For it involves a purely arbitrary association within
the particular project undertaken, one imposed temporarily by
the nature of the problem, not that far deeper co-operation which
is only possible when working from a common background of
assumption, when in fact we say that people 'speak a common
language' because they talk of things within a common frame of
reference: in other words, the co-operation which springs from
living within an 'organic' community, not one imposed temporarily from without by the common undertaking of a problem

[1] That such is not a purely theoretic fear can be seen from Professor Boris Ford's
account of the school at the Jewish settlement at Mishmar Haemek in Palestine.
There group work is undertaken, and Professor Ford makes the following admission: 'The group works as a team, in the sense that it distributes the work among
itself and moves at the pace of the slowest member.' After a little more detail about
the working of the project, Professor Ford continues: 'This system has obvious
enough consequences. The children develop little if any desire for *self*-advancement,
they think of the *group*'s advantages and success and they accept as natural a scheme
of mutual assistance.' ('Freedom in Education', *Scrutiny*, Summer, 1948.)

45

—or the chance collection into the same building. The co-operation of the former, though it may on occasions produce valuable results—as in the co-operative undertakings of science—is thus no solution to the human problem of 'competitiveness' and differentiation, as some educationists believe it to be. Such 'competitiveness', indeed, is related to profounder aspects of the human ego than educationists are now accustomed to admit. Moreover, when working on more difficult problems which necessitate important value-judgments, such stressed need for co-operation can be dangerous. Many significant human advances have resulted from heretical opinions.

Furthermore, Dewey's constant emphasis on social gratification as the valid criterion for any educational practice introduces a very real restriction into the type of education it is possible to undertake with children. There are indeed some unfortunate implications for the range of our educational activities involved here, implications which may well be against the true interests of *some* children: 'The mere absorbing of facts and truths is so exclusively individual an affair that it tends very naturally to pass into selfishness. There is no obvious social motive for the acquirement of mere learning, there is no clear social gain in success thereat.' It is surely a matter for observation that many highly valuable forms of learning bring to the learner no immediate social access of strength and may indeed require considerable resistance to social pressures outside the school. And yet such learning may not only benefit the learner considerably, but may also make him, ultimately, more beneficial as a social being. Matthew Arnold's defence of the man of culture is relevant here. How, indeed, is one to defend by Dewey's criteria the teaching of Latin and Greek, for instance, or, ironically, the study of philosophy, or even the reading of poetry? Such disciplines transcend the world of practical activity; yet it is hardly deniable that they may have a place in helping to decide which practical activities are likely to be most beneficial.

Finally, Dewey's antagonism to the notion of 'preparation' which is fundamental to his endeavour to correlate school and 'life' has serious consequences; even at the level of activity which he posits, his attitude is dangerously restrictive. He criticizes the traditional set-up of the school because 'it conceives the school as a place where certain information is to be given, where certain lessons are to be learned or where certain habits are to be formed. The value of these is conceived as lying largely in the remote future; the child must do these things for the sake of something else he is to do; they are mere preparations. As a result they do not become a part of the life experience of the child and so are not truly educative.' But it is necessary to bear in mind the essentially limited nature of what, to Dewey, constitutes a 'life experience'. In any case, he is repudiating an element which is essential in all teaching situations. Even the most practical activities require a certain element of preparation. The child cannot absorb the experience into himself, cannot see the result until he has undertaken the total process; it merely happens that some sorts of human activities and these, often, the most valuable, need longer preparation than others—and are those whose purposes are most difficult to explain to a child.

There are, then, dangers in Dewey's formulation of the social purpose of education, though some of them it is yet safe to assume Dewey never intended. No system of education can take into account more factors of experience than enter into it; and it is obvious that Dewey's conception of life only produces an education fitted to those who share, in some degree, his mental limitations. To them it is undoubtedly true that he has brought considerable benefits. We are committed to the education of a whole community and many sections of that community are unable to benefit from the type of education traditionally considered adequate. To recognize the needs of this section of the community—roughly equivalent in this country to those who attend the secondary modern school—is a matter of vtial importance.[1] And a large part of Dewey's popularity undoubtedly derives from the fact that because his mind is open to those demands of

[1] Dewey quite explicitly recognized this: '. . . we see about us everywhere—the division into "cultured" people and "workers", the separation of theory and practice. Hardly 1 per cent of the entire school population ever attains to what we call higher education: only 5 per cent to the grade of even high school . . . The simple facts of the case are that in the great majority of human beings the distinctively intellectual interest is not dominant. They have the so-called practical impulse and disposition.' (*School and Society*.) Cf. Chapter VII, below.

practical activity with which this section of the community is most concerned, he has provided as matter for 'scholastic' treatment those aspects of experience with which this type of mind can best cope. Hence 'activity', in Dewey's school system tends to practical activity—'making and doing'. And, in so far as the child is allowed to transcend the demands for immediate doing—working in wood and metal, weaving, sewing and cooking, 'the problems and interest of the life of practice', in fact, where the result is 'obvious and tangible in form'—he is merely involved in the world of practical activity at another level; in different times, which is history, and at different places, which is geography.

Such, then, are some of the characteristics of the mind which has exercised so profound an influence on twentieth-century educational thinking. And, indeed, in this philosophy, which is supposed to concern itself so much with experience and with changing, altering, reconstructing and directing that experience, what is surprising is the extraordinary narrowness of the system within which Dewey's 'technique' for living—it amounts to that —exists and which he is prepared to *accept*. He considers much of that environment which profounder minds have questioned for so long to be adequate. He is largely at one with the tendencies of his times—an excellent example of one of Arnold's swimmers with the stream; indeed, he wishes to accelerate the current. He accepts many of the surface qualities of industrialization; thus he states that: 'a wider educational outlook would conceive industrial activities as agencies for making intellectual resources more accessible to the masses, and giving greater solidity to the culture of those having superior resources'. He points out, in *School and Society*, how learning is no longer a class matter: '. . . as a direct result of the industrial revolution . . . this has been changed. Printing was invented; it was made commercial. Books, magazines, papers were multiplied and cheapened. As a result of the locomotive and telegraph, frequent, rapid and cheap intercommunication by mails and electricity was called into being . . . The result has been an intellectual revolution. Learning has been put in circulation . . . Stimuli of an intellectual sort pour in upon us in all kinds of ways.'

If he is not completely satisfied with current society it is largely because elements of that 'spiritual', 'literary' and 'aesthetic' civilization—with which he associates aristocratic, 'dominative', static forms of society—still persist. He is so obsessed with political notions which lead him to deprecate aristocracy, authoritarianism and the dominance of the past that he is unable to see that the social structure he so much desiderates can only be bought—indeed has only been bought—at a considerable cultural cost, a cultural cost which affects *all* sections of the community. He looks upon the modern era as having brought about an enormous cultural enrichment: 'The social world in which the child now lives is so rich and full that it is not easy to see how much it cost, how much effort and thought lie back of it . . . The industrial history of man is not a materialistic or merely utilitarian affair. It is a matter of intelligence.' One bears in mind Matthew Arnold's indictment of 'our modern world of which the whole civilization is, to a much greater degree than the civilizations of Greece and Rome, mechanical and external, and tends to become more so'. Indeed, to conjure up the name of Arnold, and what Arnold stood for, in his criticism of action 'with insufficient light', is to provide a further measure of the degree to which Dewey's vision of life seems inadequate.[1]

Yet it must be made clear that in all this Dewey is sincerely concerned that there shall not merely be an increase in technical efficiency. He asserts that 'we must conceive of work in wood and metal, of weaving, sewing and cooking, as methods of living and learning, not as distinct studies'. In other words, the child must participate with his whole being in the processes learnt. Dewey does emphasize the fact that so many of the employed are now 'mere appendages to the machines which they operate', instead of having had the opportunity to develop the 'imagination and sympathetic insight as to the social and scientific values found in [their] work'. But he has no profound realization of the essential predicament of industrial man: 'The problem of the educator is to engage pupils in these activities in such ways that

---

[1] Another writer whose work implies a fundamental criticism of Deweyism is Professor Michael Oakeshott: cf. especially *Rationalism in Politics*.

while manual skill and technical efficiency are gained and immediate satisfaction found in the work, together with preparation for later usefulness, these things shall be subordinated to *education*, that is, to intellectual results and the forming of a socialized disposition.' (*Democracy and Education.*) He points out that scientific inquiry has replaced 'mere custom and routine' in most economic callings: 'The most important occupations of today represent and depend upon applied mathematics, physics and chemistry.' But this, of course, only offers educational opportunities for the technically able; and even for them, of a sort that singularly fails to nurture the affective life. What Dewey failed to realize was that in the nature of much industrial work no such educative opportunities existed for the ordinary operative. He demonstrates a typical naivety when he urges that 'The invention of machines has extended the amount of leisure which is possible even while one is at work. It is a commonplace that the mastery of skill in the form of established habits frees the mind for a higher order of thinking. Something of the same kind is true of the introduction of mechanically automatic operations in industry. They may release the mind for thought upon other topics.' (*Democracy and Education.*) The facts of the industrial situation are very different, as I shall make clear in Chapter VII. Dewey failed to realize that the intrinsic nature of the work and the sort of attention it invited were insufficient to maintain a culturally adequate environment; and that is merely another way of urging that such an environment is humanly inadequate.

Yet, to the extent to which Dewey desires to enlarge the horizons of the factory worker, his attitude deserves sympathy. His error is simply the typical rationalist one, that 'opportunity' will necessarily produce the intellectual man, the man capable of a 'higher order of thinking'. Here, Dewey is typical of an important trend of nineteenth-century thought in making the common intellectual error of neglecting powerful affective drives which perpetually tend to destroy the social harmony he desiderated.

And, of course, his picture of the world, though it may contain much that the less able or 'average' can encompass, is not adequate for the best intelligences. For them, the 'social and scientific' values will only become apparent within a framework of instruction which includes more than social and scientific modes of experience; such spheres do not in any way exhaust the actualities of man's nature. Thus, to see such significances needs a wider frame of reference than is apparent in Dewey's philosophic framework or mode of instruction; that, for instance, to see the import of man's relationship with nature it is essential to go beyond the immediacies of man's contact with nature; that, in fact, to see the significance of the immediate, the immediate must be transcended.[1]

This brings us to a matter of fundamental importance in all consideration of present-day schooling. When Dewey says: 'The child's own instincts and powers furnish the material and give the starting point for all education', he is giving further currency to a conception which has exercised a profound influence since the time of Rousseau; and, to the extent that modern educators have been led to consider much more than heretofore the natural aptitudes and abilities of the individual child—so that, for instance, those grievous blunders that George Eliot depicts in her account of the education of Tom Tulliver, can be avoided—much good has been derived. Moreover, considerable attention has been focused on the learning process, so that children's ability to learn shall be increased and facilitated. But, when we consider Dewey's conception of the nature of human existence, we find that it contains no principle of development beyond that implied by the 'child-centred', none which would help to transcend the idea of human knowledge indicated in the above quotation. We have seen that he urges that 'the true centre of correlation in the school subjects is not science, nor literature, nor history, nor geography but the child's own social activities'. Indeed, as we have noted, he regards all human learning as a mere appendage to man's immediate interests— useful as a tool in the control of his environment—but affording no standard within itself, of its own nature, with which man must

[1] The point has been made by A. N. Whitehead when he states: 'I will disclose one private conviction . . . that as a training in political imagination, the Harvard School of Politics and Government cannot hold a candle to the old-fashioned English classical education of half a century ago.'

E

come to terms if he wishes to understand the external world and consequently his own place in it. Thus what starts as child psychology turns into spoilt child psychology. It is of the nature of children that they see the world as an appendage to themselves and their own desires. Part of the difficulty in growing up comes from the necessity of transcending this egocentric system and admitting the external world. And the only aspect of this external world which Dewey permits to shape the growing child is the social aspect, whose narrowness has already been remarked. For the discipline of other people is, in the last resort, only the discipline of oneself according to the limits of 'free and full communication'. Thus, for many, even this discipline is no discipline. It inhibits, indeed, the unusual child; and it is barely adequate for the vast majority—that majority with which Dewey is specifically concerned. Certainly, they are afforded no standard outside themselves in terms of which to judge their own inadequacy, since the external world only exists in so far as it satisfies their needs and desires. And, if one appeals no further, that human history which Dewey half despises would suggest that this is not a healthy state of mind.

Dewey's exposition of what constitutes the curriculum is symptomatic of the degree to which he is willing to pander to majority interests: '. . . the curriculum must be planned with reference to placing essentials first, and refinements second. The things which are socially most fundamental, that is, which have to do with the experiences in which the widest groups share, are the essentials.' The analysis of Dewey's conception of experience set out above will indicate something of the short shrift which the 'refinements' are likely to receive. And, indeed, Dewey frequently deprecates what he terms the 'bookish' or the 'academic': 'Academic and scholastic, instead of being titles of honour are becoming terms of reproach.' And, again, where the 'academic' and the 'social' are brought into explicit conflict: '. . . when the schools depart from the educational conditions effective in the out-of-school environment, they necessarily substitute a bookish, a pseudo-intellectual spirit for a social spirit.'

Again, Dewey's philosophic emphasis on 'process' is responsible for those continual changes in the syllabus which are intended to meet the needs of the 'evolving situation'. What is taught is dependent on the flow and flux of social events. Thus we are told by another writer that 'the effectiveness of the education provided . . . should be under constant scrutiny and the results of instruction should be frequently appraised to permit adaptations to meet changing social needs'.[1] And, linked with this, an offshoot of Dewey's idea of 'instrumentality', there is the common distinction between 'useful skills' and 'inert facts': 'The importance of historical topics varies over a period of years, and it is probably more important to teach methods of study, good civic habits and useful skills than it is to teach details of past events.' Though it should indeed be the job of the school not only to encourage learning but to help children to learn how to learn, it is still necessary to ask how it is possible to teach the useful skill of historical study without involving the teaching of the details of past events. (I shall return to this problem in Chapter Five.)

In his unwillingness to consider ends apart from immediate social effectiveness, it is not surprising to find Dewey denying any hierarchy of values among subjects: 'We cannot establish a hierarchy of values among studies. It is futile to attempt to arrange them in an order, beginning with one having least worth and going on to that of maximum value. In so far as any study has a unique or irreplaceable function in experience, in so far as it marks a characteristic enrichment of life, its worth is intrinsic or incomparable. Since education is not a means to living, but is identical with living a life which is fruitful and inherently significant, the only ultimate value which can be set up is just the process of living itself.' (*Democracy and Education*.)

In this denial of difference of value as between different sorts of studies, Dewey achieves the ultimate 'democratization' of the curriculum. But such a process is full of dangers for the education of abler children—those, in fact, capable of undertaking more complex and sophisticated studies. For if any study is as 'good' as any other, then such a child would be morally justified in studying push-pin rather than poetry—to make the point in relation to an old controversy. Indeed, it attempts to deny the

[1] S. A. Rayner, *Special Vocabulary of Civics*.

morality inescapably present in all teaching situations, for it implicitly urges that any sort of conduct is the same as any other; the only words which suggest evaluation are 'irreplaceable' and 'unique' which simply suggest that uniqueness of identity is the only criterion to be appealed to. Yet, other statements of Dewey suggest that he did not, in fact, hold to his own precepts. For instance, his statement already quoted, that 'the curriculum must be planned with reference to placing essentials first, and refinements second' suggests that he has a fairly rigid hierarchy of choices. His values, that is to say, are basically quantitative; and studies are valued to the extent that they can appeal to the majority.

It is sometimes said that America has been highly successful in coping educationally with the less able, but has failed with its bright children; the opposite, it is asserted, is true of this country. One can see at least why America, under Dewey's influence, has geared her system to the 'needs' of the majority: for Deweyism springs out of the desire to discover motives for learning that will appeal to the dispossessed. There is no doubt that Dewey has a great deal to offer us in our thinking about the education of our 'average' children; though, even here, it must be remembered that his social values—the social world, that is to say, into which he wished to induct these children—were unconsciously geared to the world of work as romanticized on the frontier and the log cabin, rather than cognizant of the fully industrialized state. Where industrialization is concerned, he is still at the romantic phase of acceptance on the grossly over-simplified grounds that 'knowledge is power', thinking that a whole culture can grow from the meanings implicit in industrial activities. He failed to realize the paradox of industrialism—that it provides the means to the fuller life but, by its very nature, induces a conformist, culturally impoverished passivity.[1] The social world into which he sought to induct his less able children is barely adequate, then, to their needs, because it fails to realize their cultural plight. How much

[1] He did, however, criticize the prevalent cult of efficiency, cf. C. A. Yengo, 'John Dewey and the Cult of Efficiency', *Harvard Educational Review*, Winter, 1964.

less does it answer the requirements of the brilliant, those to whom is given the possibility of qualitative reorientation in our vulgarized cultural order. For, by introducing the ethos of 'mass-man' into the traditional curricula of the learned, Dewey represents a threat to the whole tradition of European scholarship. Whatever in the American scene may excuse or justify Deweyism—and that is a matter outside the scope of this chapter—to apply it unrefined and unexamined within the European tradition would be inexcusable. He provides a warning that all claims to serve social ends should be scrutinized and examined for the depth and validity of the social world they implicitly or explicitly reveal. Dewey's stands largely condemned for the narrow range of his egalitarianism; for to encourage only what have come to be termed 'other-directed' disciplines is to impoverish the very social process itself. Even our dullest children need to be protected from socially powerful forces which threaten to blunt and exploit their sensitivities.[1] And, further, they need to be helped at that level of decision-making which is relevant to their capacities *as individuals*, rather than remain the victims of mass pressures.

Dewey is essentially the philosopher of 'rootless', urban man; he is unable to see, as Arnold saw, that even the capacity to appreciate the extent and nature of social action depends on the quality of mind brought to the situation; that the appreciation of implication and possible contingency in social matters depends on the depth of penetration into the nature and possibilities of society to which the viewing mind has previously attained. Yet, in Dewey, one finds the refined efforts of profound minds grappling with the ultimate problems of human destiny dismissed in this way: 'Work has been onerous, toilsome, associated with a primeval curse. It has been done under compulsion and pressure of necessity, while intellectual activity is associated with leisure

---

[1] In general, some of Dewey's later books are better than his earlier ones. Thus *Experience and Education* (1938) contains some acute criticisms of the excesses of his own followers in progressive education. But the Dewey who has been influential, the one we associate with 'Deweyism', is the Dewey of the earlier period, particularly that of *School and Society* and *Democracy and Education*—with which this essay has been mostly concerned. In any case, his fundamental principles persist, if refined.

... "Safety first" has played a large role in effecting a preference for knowing over doing and making.' Thus 'understanding' becomes inferior to technical interference, a mere dilettante pleasure of the rich and idle: 'After a time, a few persons with leisure and endowed by fortune with immunity from the rougher impacts of the world, discovered the delights of thought and inquiry.' It was as easy as that!

Other aspects of his thinking are relevant to the themes to be taken up in this book. His emphasis on nature as subject for control rather than as an object of contemplation and enjoyment raises explicitly the question of the cultural role of technology; and his conception of knowledge as an instrument, related to his subjectivity and anthropocentricity, implies views on the nature of the relationship between 'liberal' and 'practical' knowledge which require further investigation. He missed the meritocratic implications of the industrial-bureaucratic state; but his egalitarian leanings still represent powerful tendencies of the modern world as instanced in the comprehensive school and the concern for social unity and the common culture. Certainly, he sees in the school an important instrument of social policy; but then, his view of the nature of man is essentially a socialized one, tending towards the dissolution of the 'inner' into a set of social attributes. This perhaps accounts for the facts that he has so little to offer the emotional life and that he is so largely innocent of the cultural awareness that is an essential prerequisite to any rounded attempt to assess the modern world and the place of education in it. In general, he approves the trend of events—more science, more industrialization, more practicality, greater equality. He has no sense of *angst*.[1] At the least, however, he represents powerful forces in the modern world and offers a challenge to a profounder analysis and diagnosis of the state of universal literacy; these I hope to contribute to in the following chapters, together with recommendations of more satisfactory educational provision and content.

[1] His optimism emerges in his statement that, whatever reforms are necessary in our industrialized society, 'the quality of social changes already accomplished lies in this direction. There are ampler resources now than ever there have been before. No insuperable obstacles, given the intelligent will for its realization, stand in the way.'

CHAPTER THREE

Some Social and Ideological Roots of Modern Education

I. IMPLICATIONS OF UNIVERSAL LITERACY

A

The nineteenth century showed the liveliest interest in education and in most of the countries of Western Europe embarked on an undertaking unique in the history of mankind—the provision of formal education intended to lead to universal literacy. We take such education so much for granted nowadays that we fail to recognize how extraordinary a manifestation it is.[1] Major influences were the ideological beliefs of the Enlightenment. Part of the pressure for universal education, indeed, sprang from the belief in a common and uniform humanity canvassed by many of the eighteenth-century *philosophes* and their nineteenth-century heirs, the philosophical radicals. Such an education stemmed from rationalist oversimplification allied to a secular ethic which saw self-perfection within the grasp of mankind: 'Men have in their own hands the instrument of their greatness and simplicity, and to be happy and powerful nothing more is requisite than to perfect the science of education.' (Quoted by Talmon.) Basically, a number of the eighteenth-century thinkers

---

[1] I am only concerned here, as the title of the chapter indicates, with *some* of the influences which led to the spread of education.

considered, men shared the same natural sentiments—their general dispositions were benevolent and similar whatever particular differences might divide them; and such differences as existed were explained in terms of an ignorance which education could cure. The anti-historical bent of the *philosophes* led them greatly to over-estimate what a rationally devised environment could stimulate in the way of human betterment: 'L'éducation peut tout', the dictum of Helvetius, was a means of denying history both in social terms and in those of heredity. And such a view was echoed by James Mill when he urged that 'all the difference which exists, or can ever be made to exist, between one class of men, and another, is wholly owing to education'.

This was a profoundly important statement, for it pointed to the replacement of an aristocracy of birth by a 'democracy' of the educated. Thus, although the earlier nineteenth century decidedly produced its theorists of 'individual spontaneity' (the phrase is J. S. Mills'), in the later years especially this was accompanied by a contrary pressure, in part due to the prevailing Hegelianism,[1] in the direction of universality and uniformity (within limits, of course) of provision. The demand for equality of opportunity, growing during the nineteenth century, destroyed finally in our own century, the earlier class basis of education.[2] And the social fact of uniformity implicit in these tendencies of the age reflected the conscious policies of the *idéologues*. Saint-Simon's idea of the scientific and industrial system, for instance, rested on 'uniformity of teaching': 'The strongest link that could unite the members of a society consists in the similarity of their principles and their knowledge; and that similarity cannot be established except by uniformity of teaching.'

Even in the more 'liberal' countries, what Professor Talmon has termed Messianic Totalitarian Democracy has exerted its influence. As 'reason' has taken 'the place of tradition and drift as the determining factor in history', the advocates of uniformity

[1] Cf. W. S. Fowler, 'The Influence of Idealism upon State Provision of Education' (*Victorian Studies*, June 1961).

[2] Except, of course, for the persistence of the public school system, which is now again under attack from the Labour Party. Otherwise, technically speaking at least, an educational career is today open to talent.

have done much to create an image of social man living in harmony and unity with his neighbours, a vision which in our own
time has produced the cry for parity of prestige, secondary
education for all, the comprehensive school, and the ideal of the
common culture. In education the ideal of self-expression has
persisted as a facet of 'progressivism', and as a perpetuation of
nineteenth-century individualistic liberalism manifest, for example, in so influential a work as Sir Percy Nunn's *Education:
Its Data and First Principles*; and the need for differentiation has
been imposed by the demands of the economic and social structure, as we shall see. Yet a statement like that of D. H. Lawrence:
'Is not radical unlearnedness just as true a form of self-expression, and just as desirable a state, for many natures (even the
bulk), as learnedness?' would seem wildly perverse and 'retro-
gressive';[1] the checks on self-realization in *these* terms have
been the three R's, the Acts of 1870 to 1880 and, latterly, the
common core curriculum.

A modern sociological-historical account of the development of
the elementary school in the nineteenth century has yet to be
written; but C. Birchenough chronicled, in his *History of
Elementary Education*, a change from diversity to a considerable
measure of uniformity in structure and syllabus: '. . . the conception of an elementary education more or less common to all
classes was non-existent at the close of the eighteenth century.
Equality of educational opportunity was undreamt of, and . . .
the nature and scope of even an elementary schooling depended
upon the social grade to which the individual belonged. The
charity school had one ideal, the common school quite a different
one. Not that the schools which fell into one or other of these
two classes were uniform in type; on the contrary they presented
wide differences in organization and curricula. Thus the "school
of industry" had a motive very different from that of the ordinary
parochial charity school. The Sunday school, again, had features

---

[1] Certainly, in nations where literacy is by no means universal, 'unlearnedness' can
obviously accompany great force of character. In a recent lecture, Dr. Leakey drew
attention to the regrettable preference for the literate in current elections among
the Africans; this leads to the advancement of petty clerks in preference to men who,
though they have the necessary personal qualities for leadership, and, indeed, constitute the natural leaders of the area, are illiterate.

peculiar to itself. Similarly, the term "common school" conveniently denotes the great number of private adventure schools resorted to by the working and lower middle classes, lying between the dame schools on the one hand and the academies for young ladies and for young gentlemen on the other.' (p. 184.) This diversity carried on well into the nineteenth century: 'Between 1833 and 1862 the reforms in organization, staffing, curriculum, and method that had appeared during the two previous decades slowly made their way into general practice. These years present a picture of extraordinary diversity between schools. Some were good, others were poor, but it is doubtful whether such a thing as an "average" school can properly be said to have existed.' (p. 250.)

Among the instruments of uniformity was Robert Lowe's Revised Code: 'The school in a poor neighbourhood was to reach exactly the same standard as the comfortable school attended by a good class of children. If it did not, it was to be penalized. Six cast-iron annual standards were applied to the whole country.' (p. 281.) Uniformity had been implicit, too, in the mechanical device of the monitorial system. Thus Thomas Bernard, writing in 1807, compared Adam Smith's use of the division of labour in industry to Bell's application of this principle to 'intellectual operations'. The possibility of mental uniformity, moreover, is inherent in the major psychological doctrine of the times—that based on the association of ideas; for it implied that all should be capable of forming the same associations. It is little wonder that Bernard urges that 'The principles in manufactories and in schools are the same.' Certainly, the levelling process which has ensued has included a great deal of levelling *up*; that is clear. Granted the prior requisite of literacy, both in width of curriculum and in teaching efficiency the schools of today represent a great and manifest improvement on the standards implicit in this diversity of the eighteenth century. Nevertheless, the very notion of *universal* education involved, in some degree, a pressure to similarity of accomplishment. And it was a version of that offspring of rationalist politics, 'abstract man', who, in the era of the Codes, was forced into the schools and who, in spite of all the diversity which appears to exist in later, twentieth-century provision, still oddly dominates our thinking about curricula.[1]

On the one hand, then, there was a move towards uniformity of provision and equality of opportunity within what was provided. But the notion of the 'ladder of opportunity' developing rapidly during the century represents a contrary tendency, so that equality of opportunity comes to mean, for many, the equal chance of all to become unequal.[2] This tension between the principles of diversity and uniformity reflects the basic split, in democratic ideology, between liberalism and collectivism, a split which Professor Talmon has analysed and which de Tocqueville noted as implicit in the 'principle of equality' well over a hundred years ago; his words I have quoted in my essay on Dewey.

'Diversity', indeed, is implied in the social stratification necessitated by the development of the industrial-bureaucratic state of the nineteenth century; and the instrument of differentiation has been the examination. Max Weber noted the trend of events: 'The development of the diploma from universities, and business and engineering colleges, and the universal clamour for the creation of educational certificates in all fields make for the formation of a privileged stratum in bureaux and in offices. Such certificates support their holders' claims for intermarriages with notable families . . . claims for a "respectable" remuneration for work done, claims for assured advancement and old-age insurance, and, above all, claims to monopolize socially and economically advantageous positions.' What he saw, indeed, is

---

[1] Relevant, here, is Mr. T. S. Eliot's comment: '. . . "half-education" is a modern phenomenon. In earlier ages the majority could not be said to have been "half-educated" or less: people had the education necessary for the functions they were called upon to perform . . . *Education* in the modern sense implies a disintegrated society, in which it has come to be assumed that there must be one measure of education according to which everyone is educated simply more or less. Hence Education has become an abstraction.' (*Notes*, p. 105.) Another aspect of 'uniformity' has recently been demonstrated by G. E. Davie in his account of the gradual Anglicizing of the Scottish University tradition of education by the substitution of English specialization for Scottish general education; cf. *The Democratic Intellect*.

[2] Cf. Professor T. H. Marshall on the ambiguities inherent in the notion as enshrined in the 1944 Act: 'Its aim is to eliminate hereditary privilege. In essence it is the equal right to display and develop differences, and inequalities; the equal right to be recognized as unequal.'

what has recently been popularized under the title of the Rise of the Meritocracy.[1]

The nineteenth and twentieth centuries have seen, to all intents and purposes, the final dissolution of the old hierarchical society based on birth and inheritance of the land; though 'Establishments' of a sort persist (the plural represents the reality more fully than the singular), they are of a more fluctuating character than that of the old aristocracy. Industrialization has demanded technical expertise, and commercial enterprise has led to the evolution of the business corporation, with its opportunities of management and its need for skilled clerical and technical assistance; the day of even the gifted amateur is largely over. The professional society has arrived.[2] In government, the spreading demands of bureaucracy have likewise made calls for a higher standard of education, of a certain sort, and at the same time provided incentives to seek further qualifications in the general struggle for higher status. There has been a coincidence between the working and lower middle classes' realization of the potentialities of qualifications in terms of better jobs, and what has come to be called the 'need for educated manpower'—revolting phrase![3] (Of course, there was at all times a considerable measure of social idealism,[4] which created an atmosphere favourable to the spread of education; but this affected a comparative minority of 'thinkers'.)

Implicit in both an administrative bureaucracy and an indus-

---

[1] Of course, there are a number of checks on any full working of the merit system —particularly the functioning of what might be termed the 'old boy' code. This is likely to work particularly strongly in fields where the criteria of selection are less certain and dependent more on individual taste. Personal patronage of an indirect sort has only been radically modified, not excluded, in the bureaucratic state. Another check that is increasingly operating is what I will call the criterion of 'personalism'—the need to be good 'on the personal side', which is assessed at interviews and through the private reference system.

[2] 'Largely' is perhaps still the operative word; Mr. Anthony Sampson's *Anatomy of Britain* points to a considerable.element of amateurism in the 'cluster of interlocking circles' which go to form the Establishments.

[3] 'The nineteen twenties saw a tremendous public demand for secondary education. This was based on a realistic appreciation of its advantage in the struggle for better jobs and social advancement.' (*Social Class and Educational Opportunity*, Floud, Halsey and Martin.)

[4] In both senses of the word.

trialized economy are the principles of the division of labour
based on some degree of specialization—the need, that is, for
the 'expert' in the sense at least of the functionally specialized.
No one has characterized the nature of modern bureaucracy more
clearly than Max Weber. He points out how bureaucratic organization has come into being partly as a result of a levelling
of social differences: 'Bureaucracy inevitably accompanies modern mass democracy in contrast to the democratic self-govern-
ment of small homogeneous units. This results from the characteristic principle of bureaucracy: the abstract regularity of the
execution of authority, which is a result of a demand for "equality
before the law" in the personal and functional sense—hence of
the horror of "privilege" . . .' (*From Max Weber*, ed. Gerth
and Mills, p. 224.) Its effect is to put 'paid professional labour in
place of the historically inherited avocational administration by
notables'. (p. 225.) Bureaucracy, indeed, has a ' "rational"
character: rules, means, ends, and matter-of-factness dominate
its bearing'. (p. 244.) Considered in exclusively 'rational' terms,
it demonstrates a 'purely technical form of superiority over any
other forms of organization': 'Precision, speed, unambiguity,
knowledge of the files, continuity, discretion, unity, strict subordination, reduction of friction and of material and personal
costs—these are raised to the optimum point in the strictly
bureaucratic administration.' (op. cit., p. 214.) And Weber
concludes that 'The fully developed bureaucratic mechanism
compares with other organizations exactly as does the machine
with the non-mechanical modes of production.' (p. 214.) As such,
it 'offers . . . the optimum possibility for carrying through the
principle of specializing administrative functions according to
purely objective considerations . . . The "objective" discharge
of business means primarily a discharge of business according to
calculable rules and "without regard for persons".'

The effect on the personality and nature of the 'official' is
explained in terms that help us to understand characteristic
features of modern education and of the cultural situation that
accompanies it: 'The individual bureaucrat cannot squirm out of
the apparatus in which he is harnessed . . . [He] is chained to
his activity by his entire material and ideal existence. In the great

majority of cases, he is only a single cog in an ever-moving mechanism which prescribes to him an essentially fixed move of march. The official is entrusted with specialized tasks and normally the mechanism cannot be put into motion or arrested by him, but only from the very top. The individual bureaucrat is thus forged to the community of all the functionaries who are integrated into the mechanism.' (p. 228.) Thus, the personality type of the official functions within comparatively narrow limits; the area of decision-making is prescribed by rules and law; his expertise is of the interpretative kind and his affective life is likely to be cramped by the network of rationally interpreted legal dogma within which he finds himself: 'the bureaucratization of all domination very strongly furthers the development of "rational matter-of-factness" and the personality type of the professional expert.' (p. 240.)

Thus it is not surprising to find that our educational divisions exist in more purely intellectual—because rational—terms, where the distinctions become ever wider, as specialisms proliferate; yet this intellectual diversity of our times is also accompanied by the phenomenon of a growing similarity of social 'tone'—a 'bourgeoisification', for instance, which is patently affecting the working classes in this country, so that a working-class 'culture' can barely be said to exist and certainly not in such terms as existed among the pre-literate folk.[1]

Hence the conflicts of our age are ideological; we tend increasingly to wear identical protective social clothing and our affective life is guarded all too often by a set of similar stereo-

---

[1] '. . . Young workers, coming out of their factories at Paris, Frankfurt or Milan are likely to see the same cinema or television programmes, hear on the radio the same variety shows, songs and jazz records, and look at the same magazines as the son (or daughter) of their foreman, engineer, overseer and middle-class adolescents in general. Workers are to be found more and more often, during their holidays with pay, frequenting the same organized holiday clubs, sunbathing on the same beaches as the middle classes. It is true of course that, in office and factory, the social relations and even the tensions and conflicts created by their job-states still persist; but outside the place of work, mass media tend to dispel "proletarian" culture and class consciousness.' Thus 'whole societies are being drawn towards identical leisure occupations'. (Georges Friedmann, 'Leisure and Technological Civilization', *International Science Journal*, vol. xii, No. 3, 1960.) This, indeed, may involve a move towards a 'common' culture; but the nature of that culture is largely unacceptable. Cf. Chapter IV.

types. What vitality there is goes on in the world of rational thought; feelingly, we are being emasculated by the very proliferation of mass cultural substitutes and a working life which rests more and more on what is rationally determined in accordance with legal or administrative decision or the demands of 'scientific management'. And this, as Max Weber points out, is implicit in the social organization of the modern beaureaucratic state: '[The calculability of decision-making] and with it its appropriateness for capitalism . . . [is] the more fully realized the more bureaucracy "depersonalizes" itself, i.e., the more completely it succeeds in achieving the exclusion of love, hatred, and every purely personal, especially irrational and incalculable, feeling from the execution of official tasks. In the place of the old-type ruler who is moved by sympathy, favour, grace, and gratitude,[1] modern culture requires for its sustaining external apparatus the emotionally detached, and hence rigorously "professional" expert.'

B

The evolution of the modern 'expert' would be a study of some interest: by 'expert', I imply specialized functions at a variety of intellectual and social levels, such as are largely provided by our technical and grammar-type education and, at a more elevated level, by the universities.[2] In the mid-nineteenth century,

[1] And hatred too, of course!

[2] The influence of German universities and the particular success of their natural science faculties inspired a view of the function of a University education which stressed the need for the advancement of knowledge through specialization: 'The true measure of academic progress is the share which the university takes in the advancement of knowledge, and the part which it plays in training its alumni in original investigation', as the authority on medieval history, Tout, expressed it. The move towards specialization had already been assisted by the notion of the 'division of labour' and the advance of knowledge. The evolution of the modern Honours course, with its emphasis on the single subject, followed: 'The man who emerges from it, the man with the trained university mind, will be "the expert".' (Gallie, *A New University* p. 75.) Such an aim, was usually not utilitarian; vocational applications were to follow later. In the German university, the general tendency in all faculties had been for the work to become, according to Paulsen, more and more 'purely theoretical'. And this had been accompanied by a rapidly

where the public schools were concerned, one of the main needs in the rapidly expanding economy of Empire was for rulers and administrators—a very particular sort of 'expertise' which could be nurtured on what was apparently remote, the classics. Though the reasons for studying the classics themselves changed—it was no longer a style or an elegance which was sought, but a training in accuracy and precision—the doctrine of mental training combined with the notion of 'transfer' did a great deal to preserve the apparently unvocational nature of a classical education;[1] it was also fortunate that the classics provided a political literature and one, therefore, at least relevant to the demands of Empire— they had been regarded as appropriate training for the vocation of ruling since the eighteenth century. Furthermore, a new conception of the teacher of classics was encountered in the later nineteenth century: 'their teachers were no longer "pure" scholars, linguistic servants or literary "appreciators", but *politici*, men deeply concerned with the social and political problem of contemporary life, steeped in philosophy and well able to generalize the mature thought of the ancient world in terms of contemporary necessity. The Oxford of the days of Jowett and T. H. Green and the establishment of a rigorous system of selection for the higher civil service belong to the same phase

growing specialization, and a proliferation of Chairs as 'subjects' that had been integral subdivided. The same manifestation is characteristic of English specialization, during the nineteenth century, in mathematics and classics. Cf. G. E. Davie, op. cit., and the suggestions for the reform of Scottish education on partly English models by the setting up of post-graduate specialized research schools and the founding of new chairs.

[1] Another reason for the persistence of an apparently vocationally remote education among the upper classes in the nineteenth century has been suggested by the late Sir Fred Clarke: '. . . the plea for a classical education as the "real thing", a purely humanist training unsullied by technical taints, is relatively modern. It owes much to Newman and there is, perhaps, some justification for Professor Mac-Murray's suggestion (in *The Boundaries of Science*) that the cult of "knowledge for its own sake" tends to arise in a society which is quite ready to accept the techniques of a new order, but not ready to accept any essential change in the structure of an existing order . . . If that is so, then the plea for knowledge for its own sake, becomes socially suspect as the dress of an interested ideology . . . the ideal of a disinterested student pursuing knowledge "for its own sake" may express the interest of a regime which has the strongest reasons for not wishing to see new knowledge used instrumentally all along the line—that is, in social and political reconstruction as well as in the provision of scientific techniques.' (*Education and Social Change*, p. 20.)

of social-cultural history.'[1] (F. Clarke, *Education and Social Change.*) Thus, to some extent at least, a classical education 'for culture' was '*re-assimilated* to the needs and conditions of a complex industrial and imperial society' (op. cit., p. 25) in the 'production of professional public servants who were at once cultivated and efficient' (p. 27). There were, however, limits to the process; and a classical education has had an appeal precisely on the grounds of its uselessness.[2]

The training here was still, then, in some respects,'amateur' —the ideal was the 'gentleman', and the gentleman it was who could best cope with the 'lesser breeds'. Thomas Arnold 'believed that it was the duty of the morally superior English state to be helpful to weaker or less civilized states' (Mack, *Public Schools and British Opinion* (1780–1860), p. 380). The public schools, in any case, encouraged 'character' more than brains;[3] and business, at the level at which it produced the demand for 'experts', clerical and otherwise, was largely a middle-class occupation until the end of the century and thus affected the public schools comparatively little. Nevertheless, there were already signs of a change—the beginnings of a concern for 'qualifications' rather than family connections and the ability to quote Latin or Greek tags. Diplomas gradually began to supplement 'character'. The Civil Service examination instituted in 1854 introduced a 'professional' note. The criterion of superior fitness was to become an educational one rather than one derived from birth; as Horace Mann expressed it, in a paper to the Social Science Association in 1858: 'The not unreasonable argument for competition is that, in the absence of any other criterion, superiority of education affords a fair presumption of superior fitness for official labours.' (*Transactions*, p. 202 (1858).) A demand for the scientific and the technical, too, was heard

[1] The view of Jowett implict here, however, needs to be modified to some degree —cf. Geoffrey Faber, *Jowett*, particularly pp. 357–9. Nevertheless, it is broadly true.

[2] Cf. the quotation from T. H. Green on p. 69.

[3] 'Shall I tell him to mind his work, and say he's sent to school to make himself a good scholar? Well, he isn't sent to school for that—at any rate, for that mainly. I don't care a straw for Greek particles, or the digamma; no more does his mother. If he'll only turn out a brave, helpful, truth-telling Englishman, and a Christian, that's all I want.' (Squire Brown in *Tom Brown's Schooldays*.)

F

powerfully on many occasions during the century[1] and gradually brought about the development of night school technical education and the call for the reorganization of secondary schooling. And in the worlds of pure and applied science, at least, the lesson of this century has been that of the final replacement of the amateur by the purely professional.[2]

This demand for a trainable expertise, then, rather than for those qualities which come from having been nurtured within a certain environment, has done a great deal to bring about the educational revolution of our times. The need for experts, in this sense, has meant that anyone of the necessary *intellectual* capacity can achieve both a high degree of 'expertness' and the success which our competitive society so esteems. The rootless, socially mobile intellectual is the prototype of the new man of the technological age. For it is partly the nature of the 'job' which has necessitated the sifting of ability we now witness. The 'job', that is to say, has become something *sui generis*, abstracted as a nine-to-five phenomenon (or whatever hours are worked), largely detached from the 'before' and 'after' of home and family—indeed, usually opposed to 'leisure'.[3] In this, modern education produces, and is intended to produce, something quite different from that nurtured, say, by the medieval institution of

---

[1] Dr. Cardwell points out how unsystematic was the evolution of the applied scientist and technologist in industry, and of the educational system which he considers a prerequisite to their appearance: '. . . the process was one of fits and starts. There was, in fact, no kind of settled policy for orderly, evolutionary development; there was only a series of responses to awkward situations.' (*The Organisation of Science in England*, p. 175.)

[2] 'There has occurred, over the last seventy years, the virtual exclusion (from the Royal Society) of all not engaged in the physical and biological sciences in a professional capacity—the excision of the amateur element has been surgical in its neatness.' (D. S. L. Cardwell, op. cit., p. 176.)

[3] Georges Friedmann, in an essay on 'Leisure and Technological Civilization' points out how unusual, in the history of civilization, this distinction between work and leisure is. In pre-machine societies 'there was no sharp dividing line between the interminable working hours and those not devoted to work. In the absence of any definite criterion, the length of the working day was not fixed in advance. In essentially peasant societies, which pay no attention to time-by-the-clock, spare time is dependent upon the slow cycles of cultural seasonal and social rhythms that have been established gradually over many years.' Occasionally this attitude is still found among old craftsmen; I was recently told of a highly skilled wood-carver who works twenty to twenty-four hours and then disappears for a couple of days.

apprenticeship, the monastic school or the renaissance training in 'courtesy' provided in the great house. Such institutions existed, it may be urged, for 'professional' training. But it was a professional training wider than that implied by modern schooling in that the 'profession' concerned catered for much more of the whole man. As Weber points out, 'the point of gravity in Hellenic, in medieval, as well as in Chinese education, has rested upon educational elements that were entirely different from what was "useful" in one's speciality'. The 'cultivated' man had previously been the ideal type preferred.

This, then, is the other great characteristic of modern education we need to examine—education as a route to increased status, with its consequences for social mobility, and its requirement of diversity *in the terms posed by this sort of professional stratification*.[1] There has been a growing demand for clerks, managers, technologists and other recruits to the world of industry and business—recruits to 'superior' white collar jobs. Even in 1868 we find Mr. T. H. Green, of the School Enquiry Commissioners, criticizing the provisions made at King Edward's School, Birmingham, on the grounds that 'as a rule the business of Birmingham can and must absorb the boys of Birmingham' (vol. 8, 132); and, in his General Report, Green urges that a compromise solution to the problem of adapting the classical curriculum to the growing commercial needs of the times lies in the postponement of Greek and the substitution of arithmetic: 'The words "arithmetic" and "Latin" should be graven on the heart of every grammar-school master. The one represents the primary condition of popularity with the commercial class; the other the wicket-gate through which must pass every boy, not endowed with special gifts or the subject of some unconvenanted mercies, who is to attain an appreciation of anything high and remote in the intellectual world.' (*Reports*, vol. 8, 191.)

[1] Many people (like Professor Donald Macrae and Mr. Anthony Sampson) urge that professionalism still has not gone far enough and that our society lags in the modern competitive world market because of our adherence to outmoded attitudes and procedures. The urge to increased professionalism will undoubtedly have its educational consequences in the years to come.

C

The development of the examination system is closely connected with the implementation of the modern rationally administered state, as I have briefly noted. The examination itself in its modern guise fits in well with the rational and impersonal ethos nurtured by bureaucracy and industrialization. The candidate often becomes a number rather than a name; he is given the same set of questions permitting the same varieties of choice as his companions up and down the country. Thus the demands of democratic egalitarianism are served, and a genuine uniformity achieved. The marking is impersonally assessed by remote figures whose prerogative extends only to the facts in the shape of answers placed before them and who judge in accordance with rationally assessed prearranged criteria of relevance and correctness. In some examinations elaborate 'scaling' devices produce the predetermined percentages of distinctions, passes, etc. Examination administration, we are assured by an expert, is an 'exceedingly complicated technical problem'.[1]

In spite of all the high-sounding aims and claims of educationists, the history of twentieth-century education is, in considerable measure, the history of certain examinations; and, in an age of still rising expectation emerging from the widespread acceptance of a norm of social mobility and the status-seeking it engenders, diploma hunting is likely to increase rather than to diminish.[2] Now, of course, it is possible to become 'cultivated' in the course of preparing to pass an examination; the two things are not necessarily mutually exclusive, even though there exists a degree of tension between them. Nevertheless, it must be faced that a diploma-grabbing ethos is not one in which the wider benefits of 'general culture' are likely to be convincingly diffused. It is remarkable that, when education has become so

[1] Cf. J. L. Brereton, *The Case for Examinations*, p. 11. Relevant, too, is Mr. Brereton's picture of the examiners: 'In a properly conducted examination they are only agents for classifying the results of previous education. They should be as powerless to affect the result as an apple grading machine is to alter the sizes of the apples that pass through it.'

[2] Thus, recently, the C.S.E. has been announced.

universally distributed among the population, there should be signs of cultural decline, of the sort of situation which for twenty years *Scrutiny* diagnosed. A diffusion of education, indeed, seems to have had, paradoxically, a deleterious effect on the highest cultural standards; it may be that, to the extent that the educational system reflects what is socially acceptable, the peculiar demands made on it by the bureaucratic-industrial state are inimical to a high standard of culture in the *Scrutiny* sense of the term. The effect of examinations, for instance, is likely to be a concentration of those aspects of the discipline which are thought to be susceptible to treatment within the temporal and ideological restrictions of the forty-minute question and the three-hour stretch. And this is bound up, too, with the expectations created in the mind of the student as to the conditions relevant to question answering; these can be summed up as the need for a journalistic fluency—the temporal requirement—and a state of booklessness—the reliance on memory. For one of the peculiar features of the examination is its essential artificiality in face of the normal requirements of the intellectual life, which usually demands tentativeness (at least in the early stages) and a piecemeal building up and perhaps revision or testing. The impact of examination requirements is one which is likely to induce a certain sort of 'technical' competence in the field rather than to encourage the more delicate awarenesses or the subtler manipulations of the relevant data. Furthermore, as Dr. D. S. L. Cardwell has pointed out in his *The Organisation of Science in England*, there is a close connection between the development of examinations and the incidence of specialization: 'Experience shows that increasing specialization is characteristic of written examinations; educational authority tends to "rationalize" them.' (p. 114.) For one thing, people who are good at a subject stand a better chance when the examination is confined to the subject concerned than if they are expected to be examined in what is not their specialism—a fact which early removed extraneous text material from examinations in mathematics. Indeed, Dr. Cardwell concludes: '. . . the proliferation of specialization is accounted for rather by the nature of academical systems than by concrete external demand. Examination stimulates study and, as the London examiners pointed out, the student who usually has a preference, or an aptitude, for one branch of knowledge would naturally prefer to be examined solely in that branch than to be compelled to study other branches as well.' So long, in fact, as the examination is the avenue to advancement, so the pressure for status will tend to contradict attempts to 'liberalize' the curriculum.

The criticism of examinations has been a favoured but unavailing pursuit of those involved in the business of education for the last hundred years at least. Thus J. G. Fitch complained to the Social Science Association in 1858: 'Now, the character of the examinations will always determine the character of the teaching; . . . the introduction of written tests into our lower schools tends to discourage the more intelligent and laborious methods of promoting mental activity, and to drive teachers back upon the adoption of mechanical instruments. . . . The descent to the "Avernus" of routine and memory-work is facile enough . . . We may see already, from advertisements in the newspapers, what has been the effect of the great increase of competitive examinations on the education of older students. The task of preparing men to pass such examinations has become a trade.' (*Transactions*, pp. 223–4 (1858).) And, in 1873, Todhunter was exclaiming that 'The excessive cultivation for examination purposes of one department of knowledge to the exclusion of others seems to me one of the great evils of our modern system of bribing students by great prizes and rewards to go through our competitive struggles.' (Quoted Cardwell, op. cit.) Many other voices were raised to the same effect; a distaste for the implications of examinations is in no way a prerogative of 'progressive' thinkers in education; many of the educationally conventional in the nineteenth century expressed disgust. [In view of recent criticisms of research it is interesting to note that many who had come under the influence of the highly praised German universities of the period much preferred the implications, for education, of the research thesis to the restrictions imposed by the examination. As Dr. Cardwell puts it, summarizing a contemporary account, 'examinations suit the acquisitive mind, while thesis suits the creative mind' (p. 119);

72

Mark Pattison, for instance, at a meeting called to discuss the function of research in 1872, proposed the first motion: 'That to have a class of men whose lives are devoted to research is a national object.' (p. 120).]¹

There is, however, another aspect of the examination system which deserves attention. Many of the attributes tested by these examinations are curiously irrelevant in face of the actual demands which are later to be made on the employees who are awarded their posts on the strength of their achievements. Though it is broadly true, as Wright Mills puts it, that 'Formal requirements for entry into different jobs and expectations of ascent tend to become fixed by educational levels' (*White Collar*, p. 266), it is still noteworthy that a good deal of what is learnt at the various levels has no further significance where the 'job' is concerned. Particularly is this true of a good deal of recent white-collar work, which may require for entry a necessary combination of 'ordinary' or even 'advanced' subjects in G.C.E., but which may make little or no use of the knowledge or skills thus acquired. As 'white-collar work is rationalized the time needed to acquire the necessary skills decreases. Some 80 per cent of the people at work, it is frequently estimated, now perform work that can be learned in less than three months.' (*White Collar*, p. 245.) Even in 1868, one of the Assistant Commissioners on the Taunton Commission could write, of the English School, part of King Edward's School, Birmingham: '. . . the business of Birmingham absorbs nearly all the boys who pass through the English School, and . . . this business is not of a kind which requires any preliminary education but the most elementary'. Again, '. . . though the prospect of practical availability may not be altogether without influence, it cannot at Birmingham be relied on as a general incentive to any study beyond the region of the simplest elementary knowledge . . .

¹ A major piece of research which needs to be undertaken is a history of the examination system together with an assessment, by highly skilled subject specialists, of the particular expectations, within their specialism, which the great national examinations foster. For instance, what conception of what it means to read a novel, a play, a poem is implicit in the sort of questions which normally appear in the G.C.E. literature papers; what is being tested by such questions, and how adequate a view of the nature of literature do they imply?

the English department, therefore in its promotion of "general culture", has very little to appeal to but the genuine desire for knowledge'.[1]

Now that modern psychology has shown how important the question of motivation is, here surely is a clue to many of our troubles. In general, education will have some appeal when it leads to an examination; but its effects are likely to be short-lived after the examination is over because much incentive for learning is gone. *The fact of the matter is that much modern work —even at 'white collar' and managerial level—is of too trivial a nature to nurture a fully literate and cultivated population.* On the one hand, because so small an area of the work done in schools has any real relevance for many to the life's work, the curriculum tends to be treated simply as a means to examination success; on the other hand the fact of so treating it destroys a great deal of the 'educative' value—in the wider sense—it might have. The various subjects, for instance, are not treated as complex means through which we can come to some understanding of ourselves, our society and our world. They do not, that is to say, afford a range of such possible modes of inquiry except perhaps for the best minds, and a selection only among these pursue their 'subjects' to university level. For the rest, it still all too frequently provides simply a collection of unstructured facts whose only relevance lies in the ability to reproduce a sufficient number to meet the temporary exigencies of examiners; what results in the mind usually has little relevance to the ordered structure implicit in the material.

The excuses made by the nineteenth century for a classical syllabus which was in part socially irrelevant were those of 'mental discipline' and 'learning for its own sake'. Indeed, the commonest virtue to be derived from learning was thought to be the mental training and discipline of the faculties it afforded, irrespective often of the nature of the material on which the mind was to be exercised. Thus, Mr. Kazamias, in a recent article in the *Harvard Educational Review*[2], has pointed out that

---

[1] Mr. T. H. Green's Report, Taunton Commission, vol. 8, pp. 128–9.

[2] A. M. Kazamias, 'What Knowledge is of Most Worth?' (*Harvard Educational Review*, vol. 30, No. 4, Fall 1960, p. 317).

the Public Schools Commission plumped exclusively for mental discipline; and the Taunton Commission only accepted the acquisition of knowledge 'which bore upon and could be practically useful in business, several professions, manufactories and so on' as inferior to what trained the mind. Both the defenders of the classics and the advocates of science employed the mental gymnastics argument. The mental gymnastics argument is still used quite extensively by Grammar school teachers, as Miss Stevens shows in *The Living Tradition*, though, of course, it has been supplemented by other views as to the purpose of the syllabus.

In a sense, there may here exist a notion of education as a preparation for life, in that such mental agility may have its relevance to future needs and social necessities. But it exists at least one remove from current and actual social requirements. Its finest fruit has been the ability to inquire further, and in a relevant manner within a chosen subject field out of the number provided—to specialize in fact, untrammelled by vocational concerns, with due deference to the *nature* of the discipline involved—'for its own sake', as it were. In this way it has produced good scholars and original thinkers, whose work has, paradoxically, often borne much social fruit. And it is of inestimable value. It is not too much to urge that the future of our civilization depends on a comparatively few people who pursue the established disciplines in this way. (I shall examine the notion of learning for its own sake in Chapter Five.) But for those who do not get so far, the apparently broad syllabus has afforded little more than the means, through examinations, of entering minor bureaucratic or industrial posts often demanding a type of expertise which, as I have pointed out, has only a very restricted relevance to what has been studied. In such cases, the sheer wastage of educational effort has been considerable unless the mental gymnastics argument is allowed more effectiveness than most psychologists today would allow.[1]

---

[1] Where learning is carried out in terms of the fundamental nature and structure of the subject, some psychologists would allow the possibility of considerable transfer: 'Virtually all the evidence of the last two decades on the nature of learning and transfer has indicated that, while the original theory of formal discipline was poorly stated in terms of the nature of faculties, it is indeed a fact that massive

The question, then, arises as to the extent to which the syllabus—which over the whole range of our schools is too much dominated by that rightly provided for the Grammar schools—can be expected to provide rewards for leisure, when the notion of learning 'for its own sake' would bear fruit. The sad conclusion, borne even out of university experience, is that the number who will be prepared to tackle complex disciplines simply for the satisfaction to be got out of them is likely to be restricted. Even among those who attend a university, the 'disinterested' love of ideas is sorely limited. The universities, indeed, are not so very far from becoming what Mr. A. P. Rowe, the former Vice-Chancellor of Adelaide University, called 'factories' for producing 'professional men and women'; only a certain percentage—and that smaller than is often assumed—are interested in ideas, or knowledge 'for its own sake'.[1]

Where the population as a whole is concerned, then, there is a considerable number of people who at present require neither for their jobs nor for their leisure time activities much more than

general transfer can be achieved by appropriate learning, even to the degree that learning properly under optimum conditions leads one to "learn how to learn". These studies have stimulated a renewed interest in complex learning of a kind that one finds in schools, learning designed to produce general understanding of the structure of a subject matter. Interest in curricular problems at large has, in consequence, been rekindled among psychologists concerned with the learning process.' (J. S. Bruner, *The Process of Education*, p. 6.) But, of course, most learning necessitated by school examinations is not of this sort. Only learning designed with deference to the nature of the subject material produces this possibility of extensive transfer.

[1] These statements are based partly on my own experience in an Education Department. An Education Department, indeed, is a peculiarly favourable position from which to assess the appeal of 'knowledge for its own sake'. (Few fail and the incentive of examination-passing is therefore negligible.) The work of such a Department *appears* to be divided into two fairly separate parts. There is practical work in schools, the social and vocational importance of which is immediately obvious; and there is the theoretical work some of which seems vocationally almost irrelevant. Despite every effort to link the two (legitimate in one view of the function of theory) it cannot be said that the majority of students look for much more than classroom tips and subject method. To the wider educational issues, so fascinating at least to the intellectual student and by no means irrelevant to a teaching career, the majority remain obstinately indifferent—and this in an atmosphere (such as I am accustomed to teach in) which deliberately encourages the following of personal interests and enthusiasms.

bare literacy. Furthermore, the culture which accompanies literacy is foreign to them and has few roots in the social groups to which they belong, whose culture patterns involve little acquaintanceship with the great academic disciplines. Indeed, the oddity and *narrowness* of the requirement of literacy should not be overlooked[1]—narrowness, that is, from the point of view of the folk. (Even their spelling has to be uniform, in a way which no educated person of the sixteenth or seventeenth centuries would have tolerated.) It has meant the imposition on the 'folk' of a quite alien civilization. In the face of something so bewildering and unpalatable it is hardly surprising that the folk —now the 'masses'—have reacted in favour of a piped, commercial culture, brought to them by men clever enough to realize that there is money to be made out of this bewilderment and resentment; that there are, indeed, whole great areas of interest, particularly at the affective level, almost untouched by the 'rational' education presented by the idealists of the Education Acts and the successive Boards. When the *Daily Mail* was described at its inception by its detractors as a journal written for office boys by office boys, the nature of the person chosen to represent the new exploitable literate was interesting. The office boy, indeed, stands as a symbol of the new 'emancipated' white-collar classes, socially superior in his own eyes to those who labour with their hands, but, in reality, merely spawned at the behest of the industrial-bureaucratic state as a necessary element in its implementation. What such boys and their peers have made of the literacy into which they have been inducted can be guessed at from the history of popular journalism in this century.

If many of the white-collar classes have failed to make much of the 'culture' into which they have been inducted, what of George Bourne's coal carter, lacking the rich complexity of the old village way of life, and failing lamentably in the new ways of book learning? George Bourne, indeed, makes quite explicit the

[1] Many skills practised by the non-literate folk have been lost—so that, as Dr. Hodgson realized in the passage quoted below, the modern working man is often less stretched as far as creative possibilities go than his illiterate predecessor. Cf. p. 192–3. See also Lambert and Marx, *English Popular Art*, for some indication of skills previously exercised by the folk.

dilemma which, in many respects, is still with us; on the one hand: 'One would have thought that at least in a man's own parish and his own private concerns illiteracy would be no disadvantage; yet, in fact, it hampers him on every side. Whether he would join a benefit society, or obtain poor-law relief, or insure the lives of his children, or bury his dead, or take up a small holding, he finds that he must follow a nationalized or standardized procedure, set forth in language which his forefathers never heard spoken and never learned to read. Even in the things that are really of the village the same conditions prevail. The slate-club is managed upon lines as businesslike as those of the national benefit society. The "Institute" has its secretary, and treasurer, and balance-sheet, and printed rules; the very cricket club is controlled by resolutions proposed and seconded at formal committee meetings, and duly entered in minute-books. But all this is a new thing in the village, and no guidance for it is found in the lingering peasant traditions.' (*Change in the Village*, pp. 255–6.) On the other hand: 'In the education of their children . . . they [the folk] have no voice at all. It is administered in a standardized form by a committee of middle-class people appointed in the neighbouring town, who carry out provisions which originate from unapproachable permanent officials at Whitehall. The County Council may modify the programme a little; His Majesty's Inspectors—strangers to the people, and ignorant of their needs—issue fiats in the form of advice to the school teachers; and meanwhile the parents of the children acquiesce, not always approving what is done, but accepting it as if it were a law of fate that all such things must be arranged over their heads by the classes who have book learning.' (p. 257.) And, of course, there is D. H. Lawrence's challenge, derived from his experience of Jimmy and Nancy Shepherd and the local bottle factory and laundry: 'Drag a lad who has no capacity for true learning or understanding through the processes of education and what do you produce in him, in the end? A profound contempt for education and for all educated people. It has meant nothing to him but irritation and disgust. And that which a man finds irritating and disgusting he finds odious and contemptible.' (*Phoenix*, p. 596.)

D

In what image, indeed, did the nineteenth-century Establishment, which imposed the requirement of universal literacy, seek to form the new denizens of the schools? What was this 'understanding' they sought to promote? A picture of an 'excellent school' in 1882, derived from the Instructions to Inspectors, affords a clue to the answer. The time-table, we are told, is to provide 'a proper variety of mental employment'; reading is to be 'fluent and expressive', arithmetic to involve not only accuracy but an understanding of 'processes'; when higher subjects are attempted, memory work must give way to a 'clear knowledge of facts' in order to 'train the learner in the practice of thinking and observing'. Above all, character is to be affected and, in general, the children are to be infused with a 'love of reading and such an interest in their own mental improvement as may reasonably be expected to last beyond the period of school life'. This notion of mental and intellectual improvement, indeed, is fundamental. Arnold, pleading for a wider curriculum in face of the restrictions of the revised code, states that the aim of the school should be 'the animation of mind, the multiplying of ideas, the promptness to connect, in the thoughts, one thing by another'. (*Reports*, p. 155.) The advanced educational thought of the time looked upon the developing of the mental powers[1] in contrast to the acquisition of knowledge—inert knowledge, Whitehead would have called it —as what was to be most sought after: thus, the Reverend James Fraser, one of the Assistant Commissioners who investigated the state of Popular Education, criticized the education of his area on the grounds that 'the children's minds . . . are

[1] The Assistant Commissioners asked a number of the local dignitaries whether, in their opinion, the subject-matter of education in the schools helped to 'develop mental powers'. One reply criticized the 'cramming and repetition of words'and commented that 'the child is not regarded as a "thinking being"'. Gradually, the influence of Froebel made itself felt (cf. Bramwell, *Elementary School Work*, 1900-25), but the emphasis on the 'thinking being' has persisted if in a form modified by the decay of the faculty theory of mental structure and the challenge of utility and self-expressive activity.

"reservoirs, not fountains", receiving what is poured into them from without . . . not bubbling up and flowing over with fresh springs of thought from within. I do not mean that there are not schools . . . which have the power of awakening children to the pleasurable sensation that they possess *minds* as well as memories; but I am quite certain that in the majority of the schools that have come under my observation there is very little attempt made to cultivate the intellect as a living, organic, reproductive power.' (*Reports*, II, p. 102.)

This emphasis on intellect issuing in rational thought, then, is symptomatic; the contrast to the rightly criticized rote learning is 'intellectual training' (*Reports*, III, p. 296); and teachers themselves are rebuked for their inability to exercise 'their own reasoning powers' (ibid.). It is interesting to note that the Crowther Report reasserts the ideal in almost identical terms: 'The proper test of an education is whether it teaches the pupil to think, and whether it awakens his interest in applying his brains to the various problems and opportunities that life presents.' (*Crowther Report*, p. 262.) What the pupils were to exercise their minds on were not the immediacies of conduct and behaviour with which they were likely to be faced—the problems of domestic life, marriage and so on—but the, to them, abstractions derived from some at least of the orthodox subjects. How often in educational exposition the precise nature of what the 'thinking' is to be exercised on is left vague and ill-defined, as if the ability 'to think' exists *tout court* apart from concrete situations and specific realities; or else it is vaguely associated with the politically inspired aim of 'thinking' as a concomitant of democratic citizenship where again the thinking required is necessarily on a highly abstract level.

Towards the end of the nineteenth century, indeed, certain novel features—echoes of eighteenth-century progressivism—became more widely canvassed. In his last Report of 1882, Arnold strikes a more 'progressive' note by suggesting 'the aim of calling forth, by some means or other, in every pupil a sense of pleasurable activity and of creation'[1] and Sadler and

[1] Yet, of course, modern 'creativity' as it manifests itself, largely, in infant schools, is a purely hothouse phenomenon, having no roots whatsoever in the life

Edwards sought to develop the 'whole nature of the child and to foster the harmonious growth of its moral, physical and intellectual powers'.[1] There are increasing references to the need to relate the subject-matter of school instruction to what is done outside: Deweyism raises its head. There are vocational emphases of a practical or technical nature made also, from time to time; but what continues, to my mind, to characterize a great deal of the aims and purposes implicit in the practice of the elementary school in the nineteenth and early twentieth centuries—practice apart from 'advanced' theory—is its almost complete abstraction from any full and coherent way of *folk* life in terms of which what is done can take on significance in a mode the folk can be expected to comprehend.[2] It was a 'rational' education to fit a figure abstracted from the real pressures of the age as they affected the classes to which it was to be applied; and the child who entered the elementary school encountered disciplines which, beyond the basic skills of literacy, made practically no sense in relation to the satisfactions the folk had traditionally sought, and little enough to the life outside school which an industrialized society had to offer him.[3] 'Mental improvement' might in a limited number of cases lead to declassification, higher status and the discovery of an environment where the improved mind could perhaps find an adequate milieu; but, for the majority, what went on in the schools was largely unrelated to what could be expected to happen to them outside.[4] The mere achievement of literacy produced the 'benefits' I have indicated

of the community in general: child art, for all its virtues, exists largely in a vacuum. Nevertheless it exists as a possible means through which the school might initiate change.

[1] *Special Reports on Educational Subjects*, 1896–7. Cf. too, for a detailed account of the effects of new approaches, Bramwell, op. cit.

[2] The very concept of 'self-expression', when it arrived, is one derived from 'high' culture of the liberal romantic variety. Most folk art and behaviour has existed in terms of a strong binding tradition which allowed little scope for self-expressive 'originality'.

[3] Only D. H. Lawrence, in *The Education of the People*, has really had the guts to say this. I shall argue in Chapter VII, that the characteristic mind-movements of the less able are quite unnurtured by the sort of 'mental discipline' the curriculum, in general, imposes on them.

[4] Other than what was afforded by a very limited provision of technical, commercial and domestic subjects.

—the necessities imposed by the modern state have made the ability to read, write and calculate essential. But the extension of the curriculum to the mass of the people, until today it constitutes largely a pale imitation of what goes on in the grammar schools, has simply produced, in many minds, at best a bewilderment, at worst a repugnance for school and all it stands for.[1] The theme of moral regeneration, with its implication of making a difference to the whole outlook of the educand and of saving him from his indigenous social influences—'their gin and their fun', as Arnold put it—did not for nothing influence the nineteenth-century concern for educating its new masters; for the morality imposed was, again, an abstract one, apart from the real stresses of the poor. Education, indeed, stepped in as the folk environment collapsed—and failed precisely because it neglected what the folk environment had provided in moral and cultural strength. Furthermore, the very aims it set itself paid tribute to a socio-political ideal of abstract man with its implication of uniformity, rather than asked concretely what, in terms of a particular set of environmental stresses, and a particular set of mental restrictions, might be within reasonable grasp to attain. Literacy for the 'masses' has followed too much what John Morley considered its aim: 'an instrument by which [a man] may know how the world fares outside his narrow penfold';[2] for such an aim has the less to be said for it if the penfold fails to afford the basic securities, as the modern environment does (very largely) so fail. Amidst the bewildering complexity of modern urban existence, the sources of traditional wisdom implicit in folk song, folk tale and conventional religious practice have dried up. The justification of Morley's attitude lies in the narrowness, for the gifted, such tradition could imply;[3] the condemnation lies in the lack of direction and certainty which the breakdown of the traditional order has induced, and which Richard Hoggart has finely and intuitively realized in much of its complexity of gain and loss in *The Uses of Literacy*.

[1] Ameliorated only by the fact that schools are much less harsh and more 'human' places than they used to be.

[2] *Struggle for National Education* (1873), pp. 119–20.

[3] Though, at certain times, the gifted have made much use of folk modes—cf. Purcell and Bunyan in the later seventeenth century.

E

The lesson of modern education, then, as it has evolved in the nineteenth and twentieth centuries, is the lesson of a confusion of principles leading both to uniformity and diversity. The levelling tendencies of the times have secured the one; the needs of the technological-bureaucratic state have promoted the other. But the diversity which has inevitably followed from such needs has tended more and more to exist only in terms of those needs—of differences in degrees of expertness, that is, rather than in a rich diversity springing from widely different ways of life, mutually enriching as much of the history of English culture shows it to have been in pre-industrial days. At its best, our modern education produces a largely disinterested love of learning which has made possible the finest thought of our age; or it has produced a lively awareness of some of the complexities behind practical decisions. But this caters only for a comparatively few—some part of the grammar school and technical school population, whose assimilation of the curriculum bears this kind of fruit. For the rest, subject as we know from modern social psychology to a wide variety of group pressures where such learning appears quite irrelevant, most of what is learnt in school beyond the practical benefits of literacy itself—that ability simply to read and write the modern world demands—appears an unnecessary burden. Above all, the very nature of modern 'expertness'—that sort of expertness which is in most social demand, exerts most pressure as a 'need' at least—goes far to explain the comparative neglect, in our educational system, of what will feed the affective life; for such 'expertness' springs from the rationalizing demands of the industrial-bureaucratic state, whose main educational instrument is the examination and whose criteria of differentiation are bound up with the particular demands of that sort of technical and bureaucratic requirement Max Weber has characterized as the ' "objective" discharge of business'.

Along with this increasing concentration on professionalization and the restricted expertness which is its fruit (with the cultural consequences of standardization I have noted) have gone important changes concerning the *quality* of our civilization. Arnold noted the dangers a hundred years ago. For Arnold, the fundamental educational dilemma of his times which he saw, though not, naturally, with the urgency it has assumed in our own day, was how, in the new democratic society, the sense of quality which the English aristocracy, whatever its faults, had provided, was to be preserved. Here lies the importance of his introduction to his survey of 'Popular Education in France'—an essay which gave him a good deal of trouble to write and which the editor of a recent reprint, Mr. R. H. Super, rightly considers to be 'in many ways . . . the keystone of his thinking about politics and education'. The aristocracy which had, in the past, wielded power was not remarkable for its quickness of intelligence or its openness to ideas; but it had been in the 'grand style'. A governing class imbued with such a style 'may not be capable of intelligently leading the masses of a people to the highest pitch of welfare for them; but it sets them an invaluable example of qualities without which no really high welfare can exist'. For the *noblesse oblige* of the aristocracy, then, Arnold hoped to substitute the light generated by the benevolent State —the spirit of the Best Self; for the 'immaterial chivalrous ideal of high descent and honour' he hoped to substitute the 'immaterial modern ideal of spiritual and intellectual perfection through culture.' ('A French Eton'). What was basic was the need to preserve 'superiorities'; and he criticizes the 'dominant tendency of modern Swiss democracy', which he regards with some disquietude: 'It is socialistic, in the sense in which that word expresses a principle hostile to the interests of true society —*the elimination of superiorities.*' ('Popular Education of Switzerland.')

Education, then, to Arnold was a moral force productive of that excellence which would ensure that in the inevitable transfer of power the nineteenth century was to witness, the characteristic aristocratic virtues were to be preserved—indeed supplemented by that openness to fresh ideas, that concern for intelligent action, which 'culture' could foster. His ideal is basically that of Plato—a pursuit of the best that had been thought and said

(Plato's concern for 'philosophy') with the aim, ultimately, not of contemplation but of the refining of our social life, though he concedes much more to the notion of *general* equality than the Greek would have done. At root, his problem was ours: 'The difficulty for democracy is, how to find and keep high ideals . . . Nations are not truly great solely because the individuals composing them are numerous, free, and active; but they are great when these numbers, this freedom and this activity are employed in the service of an ideal higher than that of an ordinary man, taken by himself. Our society is probably destined to become much more democratic; who or what will give a high tone to the nation then? That is the grave question.' ('Democracy.') He combines, indeed, a generous desire to see that expansion of spirit in the oppressed which a more equal state of society can bring about with a concern for the maintenance of standards in the process of activation. In the intervening years, the problem has only become more acute.

CHAPTER FOUR

Some Social and Ideological Roots of Modern Education

---◈---

II. PRESENT PROBLEMS OF ORGANIZATION

The very organization of the school system has also been deeply affected by the rationalizing tendencies of the modern official. It is symptomatic of such a mind that the solution of educational problems should be thought of so much in organizational terms, rather as if the educational structure can be rationalized in much the same way as a business. Indeed, the recent appearance of what are admittedly valuable socio-economic studies of the educational system and of its place in an expanding national economy involves a disquieting use of language and terminology in referring to education. Education is spoken of as a social service, or, worse still, as a commodity with much of the same ability to attract purchasing power as the washing machine or the television set; it is reduced to the level of a function of the economic state.[1] We are told, by Mr. John Vaizey, that a rising tide of affluence is not only going to produce an increased demand for educational 'goods', but that the mere ability to provide more money for educational purposes will be followed by higher educational standards. People who talk in such terms

---

[1] Symptomatically, when *The Observer* recently printed a much publicized article on the future of education, it was entitled 'Education: Our Untapped Wealth'. Cf. also pp. 187–189.

forget to ask what sort of 'education' is likely to be purchased by those who conceive of it in this manner. What will their expectations be? Almost inevitably, they will regard education as an 'investment' (another word, incidentally, which is employed in this very context by people of Mr. Vaizey's persuasion) and will expect the same sort of return from it which people who invest normally do; that is to say, they will look to it simply as a means to better paid posts and higher status.[1] And the discovery that education truly conceived in fact is not a 'commodity' in the same sense that a washing machine is may prove unpalatable to those ignorant of its subtler requirements.[2]

It is in such times of national expanding economy, indeed, that the concern for secondary reorganization has arisen. In so far as the two events coincide, the principles behind the outcry which we have witnessed in recent years are of more than temporary interest. They reveal, indeed, important assumptions about the nature and role of education in our society; and they pose with a peculiar clarity the dilemma of diversity and uniformity in education, the historical roots of which were examined in the last chapter.

[1] This, of course it is—and, in some degree, always has been. The accusation that people 'use' education to achieve higher status looks like becoming one of the accepted stereotypes in the mid-twentieth century catalogue of crimes. Nevertheless, one's objections persist—even though they need to be formulated with more care than they usually are. It has to be recognized that some higher status posts offer more in the nature of intellectual opportunities, more possibilities (when grasped) of cultural satisfactions. But in the industrial-bureaucratic state this is not by any means invariably so. Status-seeking often becomes an end in itself, for the inflation of ego it encourages rather than for the opportunities it affords. One's objections are not so much to the way in which the 'right' people ('right' in moral, cultural and intellectual terms) can find their just places in the inevitable hierarchy; but to the elevation of certain sorts of 'smart alecism' with a gift for examination passing and the degradation of education this involves. The education which ends simply and exclusively in the passport to the next stage on the journey upwards is not an education worthy of the name. For it leaves untouched much that is fundamental in the human being.

[2] Thus, it is interesting to note that in recommending the two-tier system of education, a specific point is made of the way in which existing 'plant' can be adapted to its requirements. It is not therefore surprising to find the industrial metaphor applied to the school itself—it now becomes a 'factory'. Cf. *The Times Educational Supplement* (27 January 1961) which carries a reproduction of a mural at Manor Park Grammar School, Nuneaton, depicting the 'School as Factory'.

A

Though schemes for reform betray differences of organizational stress, they all seem to manifest a common desire to promote 'comprehensiveness' at some stage of post-eleven development. Moreover, their promoters seem to be actuated by a fairly homogeneous set of assumptions. They share a common faith in the power of structural changes, in *organization*, to promote their ends.

In this sense, they are environmentalists. Their ends, too, are not by any means exclusively scholastic. In the main, they aim to fulfil the traditional purposes of the school in the learning of 'subjects' and skills; but, often as important, they are concerned to use the school as an instrument of social policy, in order to promote a 'juster' (by which they usually mean a more egalitarian) social order (here Dewey raises his head).[1] Thus they are secular moralists, having inherited something of that easy optimism concerning man's nature and his power to shape his own destiny which stems from the rationalists of the eighteenth century and to which I referred at the beginning of the last chapter. The particular nature of their rationalism has been admirably characterized by Professor Michael Oakeshott (though Professor Oakeshott is speaking of political rationalists):

'Much of his [i.e. the rationalist's] political activity consists in bringing the social, political, legal and institutional inheritance of his society before the tribunal of his intellect; and the rest is rational administration, reason exercising an uncontrolled jurisdiction over the circumstances of the case. To the Rationalist nothing is of value merely because it exists (and certainly not because it has existed for many generations), and nothing is to

---

[1] 'The desirability of educating adolescent boys and girls in an environment planned to encourage social unity through mutual understanding, respect and shared experiences, and the urgent importance of establishing schools where staff, facilities and equipment made possible the provision of a diversity of courses, both academic and practical, which would realize the full potential of the whole secondary school population, formed the foundation of the case for the comprehensive school.' (H. R. Chatwynd, *Comprehensive School: The Story of Woodbury Down*.)

be left standing for want of scrutiny.' (*Rationalism in Politics*, p. 4.)

The grasp which such rationalists maintain, in education and elsewhere, on current procedures is often not very acute; for deeply, though to some extent unconsciously, imbued with the rationalist sense of human perfectibility, they constantly strain after the as yet unattained in the fond faith that it is bound to prove superior to what already is. Because they rely to a great extent on a *restricted* use of the intellect, they have a great tendency towards abstraction. Their difficulties they call problems and their solutions, plans.

Now, it is a necessary preliminary, in the recognition of a problem, that it be formulated; and any formulation is a means of focusing the attention. Before attention can be focused, however, it is necessary to become blind to circumambient conditions, to shut out all half-lights and shadows. It is usually true that what one sees is very much bound up with what one wants to see, or what one is looking for; and the particular persistence of a problem, with its implication of definition, its belonging to the ranks of the noted and the assessed, the set down and the formulated, renders it peculiarly susceptible to a halting of attention to what does not enter into its purview. The very process of definition involves a sloughing off of inessentials, inessentials, that is, considered in terms of the problem to be defined. The man who is concerned with right-angled triangles and their congruence must forget about pentagons; the doctor who diagnoses measles may remain indifferent to appendixes. And with problems of this kind it is right that it should be so.

But not all human affairs can so profitably be dealt with by the process of Cartesian isolation as can the concerns of the doctor and the geometrician. Levin, in Tolstoy's *Anna Karenina*, discovered that, however admirable schemes for the reform of Russian agriculture might seem to be in the abstract, they were so much wasted effort if they failed to take into account the historical situation within which they were to be applied. For the results of 'reforms' turned out, in concrete fact, very differently from what their promoters had hoped for, simply because of the imponderables inherent in the historic consciousness of the Russian people.

One of the major arguments used by these promoters of educational reorganization lies in the unreliability of selection at eleven-plus. As, admittedly, we are never likely to achieve one hundred per cent success in our selection, the reformer, irked by the stubborn imperfectibility of human institutions, proposes a new *system*; and this in part at least because he is so obsessed by the nature of the problem he is concerned with that he has not the time nor patient application to examine his difficulty in relation to a wider context. His concern, we may admit, is a serious one, and he deserves some credit for drawing attention to it. But he does not stop to ask just how serious it is, because to seek an answer to this would necessitate his being able to step outside the confines of his immediate problem, to appreciate that his problem is something abstracted from a highly complex situation within which it admittedly forms a somewhat unhappy anomaly.

He does not, that is to say, attempt to assess the admitted evils of the difficulty he is facing in relation to the total balance of good and evil inherent in the situation he is concerned with. The question as to whether a great institution has outlived itself is a delicate and difficult one; it involves much careful balancing of possibilities, and an imaginative projection into the complexities of the posited new as well as an awareness of the nuances of the criticized old. And when an institution is as old as our grammar schools are,[1] has played as important a part in the intellectual and cultural life of our nation as they have, and has shown so remarkable an adaptability to changing circumstances, there would seem to be reasons for considering their abolition as a matter of some moment, not lightly to be entered on.

There is, for instance, the 'psychology' of the people who have to work the posited new to consider. When one finds an advocate of the county college urging that 'it could be staffed mainly by the able and experienced teachers of the existing grammar schools who would thus have the great opportunity, in ideal conditions, of concentrating on the higher education of all

---

[1] I know, of course, that many date from only 1902, but many are much older. As a boy I attended one of the latter, and even as children we were aware of a sense of historical continuity.

full-time pupils over the compulsory school age', one notes the insensitive disregard of the possible wishes of the staff concerned, of their 'psychology' in the sense of their developed professional awareness of function which cannot suddenly and arbitrarily be switched into very different channels. It is one of the nuances of the situation to which the reformer is blind.

Now, it is precisely in this matter of subtleties that reformers are often most unaware; for, to be susceptible to a nuance in this context involves an historical consciousness which is aware that human institutions of proved value are the work of the generations, each of which has contributed its tithe of reinterpretation and reassessment. Yet your reformer is perpetually indignant with the past because it has provided problems; he remains insensitive to atmospheres, because his focus of attention is too narrow to allow for them. In any case, he is so heavily orientated to the future, to the new, to what might, in his limited conception, be, that he is too frequently unaware of the virtues of what is.

He fails then to see that there is any virtue in the fact that an institution like the grammar school has a particular ethos, or that the common pursuit of a particular purpose may engender a pervasive atmosphere, not easily definable in particulars but, nevertheless, strong enough to create its own sanctions and subtly to affect the quality of the living that it surrounds and interpenetrates. For the grammar school, however much, in individual instances, it may fall down in its task, nevertheless is an institution with a developed purpose and a particular awareness of certain values. It is informed, at its best, by the notion of scholarship; it maintains contact with the idea of a liberal education; it is concerned about standards of learning. Its link with the universities—a link which these schools have maintained since medieval times—ensures an attention, at a particular and appropriate level, to important academic disciplines. It would be as silly to idealize the grammar schools as it is to fall into denigration; nevertheless, however much it may fall short of a desired disinterested love of learning, the grammar school, in an imperfect world, maintains some corner of respect for the things of the mind.

Now, it is in this problem of academic standards that the re-organizer finds himself on the horns of a dilemma. He usually realizes that his particular brand of reorganization will only find favour with the public at large, if it delivers the goods. And an important section of the goods in this case is academic, at least to the extent that it implies the normal academic prizes in terms of G.C.E.s and university scholarships. And so, of course, he must present his scheme as offering an even more efficient means of selecting the best brains than the old tripartite system. Only in this way can the great Industrial and Economic Machine be adequately fed. He makes much play, as we have noted, with the inefficiency of selection, with the present system's denial to promising 'material' of a chance to proceed to the grammar school because of local inadequacies; he will animadvert on the problem of the late developer . . . and so on. (That some measure of selection within the comprehensive school is necessary he omits to mention; that the other problems can at least be alleviated within the tripartite system, he conveniently forgets.)

Yet, one often wonders to what extent his heart is really in his work; for his concern is equally social in character. He is deeply imbued with a sense of the importance of the classless society, that curious will-o'-the-wisp which has so haunted the imagination of the more vacuous social theorists of our day. He is offended by the snobbery—intellectual as well as social—which he thinks is induced by the tripartite system. And here indeed comes the rub; for the admission of the importance of intellectual abilities cannot so very easily be harmonized with the expressed desire for an egalitarian social order. The admission of intellectual inequality implicit in the whole problem of maintaining intellectual standards is not easily reconciled with an ethic which seeks to deny any real difference between people. Diversity and uniformity in these terms are not, in fact, compatible aims.

The dilemma can be illustrated from the work of Dr. R. Pedley. On the one hand Dr. Pedley desires to promote social togetherness, relating 'all our activities in a harmonious, purposeful whole', '. . . it would be invaluable for [the liberal scholar] to understand the minds and outlook of scientists and technicians—and indeed of craftsmen and shop assistants and unskilled workers—through meeting them in the same environment of college clubs and societies; on the games field and in the students' council'. (*Comprehensive Education*, pp. 165–6.) On the other, he sees in education an instrument of national prosperity; he speaks of the consequences of putting his plan into operation in these terms: 'Thereby we shall use not only our material resources but our human resources (pupils and teachers) to the full, eliminate waste and frustration, and take a giant stride towards the achievement of national prosperity and individual happiness.' One can only comment that the sort of diversity and power structure necessitated by economic and industrial progress is not likely to be compatible with dreams of a unified and harmonious society—at least in the terms envisaged by Dr. Pedley.

The dilemma, indeed, affects the internal organization of the schools; often I have discovered uncertainties over streaming and the allocation of staff in schools I have visited—an uncertainty which betrays the confusion in the minds of headmasters and mistresses. On the one hand, there is the desire in the name of equality to furnish a common curriculum; on the other, the necessity of streaming is thought to be imposed[1] by the varying rates of academic advance manifested at different intellectual levels. Again, should the abler teachers be allocated to the more academically able forms, on the grounds that they represent a more important educational 'investment'; or ought the more backward children to receive their due attention from the more capable members of staff? Education of the sort that we formally impose is willy-nilly a divisive phenomenon unless the curriculum is so arranged that the brighter children are not academically pressed on, as seems to have happened in America.[2] There,

[1] The need of this has, of course, recently been much disputed.

[2] There are disquieting indications in some of the published work on the comprehensive school of a desire to obfuscate the issues. Thus, in a recent compilation, *Inside the Comprehensive School*, a headmaster writes: 'We are learning that perhaps there are not such great differences in the quality of children's minds as in the nature of them, and that before we begin to adjust the content of their education in quality we must explore different ways of adjusting manner of presentation and time allocation.'

Now, there is surely some disingenuous juggling, in the context, in this distinction between 'nature' and 'quality'. It may spring, in part, from an unwillingness

93

the social divisions, which persist, exist within the school in other terms.

B

The notion of 'social unity' can, in fact, refer to very different ideal social structures. In Plato it involved a class society in which each fulfilled the function his nature allowed him to perform; in modern usage it implies an egalitarian classless society which seeks to promote widespread mutual understanding between people of very different intellectual and cultural levels— 'conjoint, communicated experience', in Dewey's ugly phrase.

In these terms, the notion of 'social unity' is one which I find extremely difficult to grasp. I can only think of social relationships in terms of particular communications made between individuals or between people acting on behalf of corporate bodies and individuals or between people acting on behalf of corporate bodies one with another. When I think of these communications to recognize that different human activities do represent different levels of value. If the nineteenth century went far in the direction of denying importance to anything except mathematics and classical studies, the twentieth century is tempted to accept all studies as being of equal value. It is significant that some of the advocates of comprehensiveness are also the enemies of streaming; and the terms in which some talk of the mutual esteem to be generated between the academic child who wins a scholarship and the duller child who turns out to be, say, a champion swimmer would seem to suggest that in their hearts they esteem the two sorts of prowess as being of equal significance. It is indeed possibly some attempt to imply this that lies behind this distinction between 'quality' and 'nature'. The implication seems to be that children's minds are of equal quality but that they manifest themselves in terms of different subject-matter: this is their 'nature'. We have seen that Dewey is quite explicit in his repudiation of any hierarchy of subject matter.

In effect, it is the old dilemma of push pin and poetry translated into twentieth-century terms. It is not difficult to show that the study of poetry involves a higher and more delicate degree of brain organization, affects more aspects of the personality and produces more valuable consequences—the utilitarian criterion—than the study of push pin. The modification that might need to be introduced is that certain types of subnormals might well benefit as much from push pin; in other words, the general principle might need to be modified in relation to the individual case, when other factors of defective or slow mentality entered in; in the vast majority of cases, however, this would not be true, and as a general principle, the fact that, in such terms as I have mentioned, some subjects make more demands on human beings, require, for their mastery, a more complex human organization and finally produce more valuable consequences, is inescapable.

I can see that even when they lead to perfect understanding (and this, in view of the complexity of language and of the different intelligence ranges which exist as social facts and which necessarily affect the level of meaning comprehensible to the different sections of the community, is impossible over the whole range of possible—and actual—communication), there is no guarantee whatsoever that understanding will lead to agreement: the temperance worker and the innkeeper, for instance, just do not share compatible ends, and this situation reproduces itself many times. Furthermore, in any large-scale community—whatever happens on the South Sea Islands—there must inevitably arise a power structure. Within such a structure, there must inevitably be occasions when communication cannot even be open and frank. As Professor G. P. Meredith puts it when speaking of the responsibilities of leadership in any organization: '. . . only the leader can see the whole pattern. Often the reason for asking one man to undertake a particular duty concerns the weaknesses or private tragedies of others and cannot be stated.' This seems to me an unavoidable concomitant of that structuring of social life which all complicated societies inevitably undergo—for they could not be carried on in other terms. Even the social unity brought about by a common religious faith, though it permits the binding force of a common set of symbols, is more apparent than real; heresies arise and are often dealt with by persecution and death. The modern world, outside the totalitarian communities, where 'heresy' may exist in different terms, has abandoned these devices. We must, therefore, be prepared to accept the consequences of such abandonment—diversity and disagreement But perhaps, in the last resort, 'social unity' simply implies that people at different levels of the power structure or of different intellectual abilities should be polite to one another. With this I would agree.

The question arises, indeed, as to the extent to which the school can be expected to foster social cohesiveness of the kind which is in question. The evidence available that it can is not particularly convincing. In a recently published monograph, for instance, *Values in the Comprehensive School*, Dr. T. W. G. Miller attempts to assess the degree of cultural and social unity fostered in the comprehensive school by a series of tests which compare the attitudes of a number of comprehensive school boys with those found among children who attend separate grammar and secondary modern schools in the same areas. Tests designed to demonstrate the nature of leisure interests, occupation ratings and school subject assessments made by the children, attitude-to-schooling tests, etc., given in 'three well separated localities', seem to show that, in Dr. Miller's careful exposition, 'the comprehensive secondary schools have beneficial effects in regard to certain cultural, social and educational phenomena'; they appear to indicate, for instance, a tendency for comprehensive 'grammar' and 'secondary modern' school children to rate the sorts of occupations each is likely to be destined for higher, to be more appreciative of the subjects each is likely to study, etc., than are children drawn from separate grammar and secondary modern schools.

It must be emphasized that Dr. Miller is extremely cautious and circumspect in presenting his findings; and, indeed, even taken at their face value, they should in no way suggest to those who emphasize the importance of social and cultural unity that their case is proved. For instance, Dr. Miller points to the superior equipment and facilities of the comprehensive schools as important factors which might well have affected the issue. He might also have drawn attention to the importance of the subjective image framed in the minds of the teachers in these various types of school which could well have affected the quality of what was being done: morale is likely to be relatively high in a school which finds itself the focus of public attention as the comprehensive schools still are, on the analogy of the famous Hawthorne experiment. This, for instance, might account for the superior quality and number of the comprehensive 'secondary modern school' children's leisure interests. Furthermore, although he assures us that all schools of the various categories were either 'good' or the 'best available' or 'fairly typical', such vague assessments merely draw attention to the vast complexities involved in comparing schools, and go far to destroy any claim to scientific validity the thesis may be considered to have, especially as no indication is given as to what is considered to be a good school of the varying types. Such vagueness at such a crucial point, indeed, undermines his whole case. Also, some of the tests used are educationally suspect; if an important educational aim is to bring children to a true appreciation of relative value, the fact that, as a result of attending the comprehensive school, children of differing intellectual abilities come to rate occupations more homogeneously is no test of the educational worth of the establishment; some people do, in fact, fulfil more important roles than others, and the worth of the school would be better judged by the nature of the discriminations it enabled the children to make than by the fact that it led them to attribute superior status to those whose occupations did not warrant it—a form of inverted snobbery as reprehensible as its uninverted form. (Children should also be taught to appreciate the human quality of the people so occupied, so that they will come to see that a good dustman is a better human being than a bad doctor; but that is not the matter at issue; we are simply concerned with the status of occupations in Dr. Miller's analysis.[1])

C

Associated with the call for social unity is that for a common culture. The cry for a 'common culture'[2] might seem a futile one, at the very time when the difference between levels of attainment is growing owing to the specialization which goes along with the 'division of labour' in the intellectual field. Partly, of course, the cry is itself a reaction against such specialization, an attempt to lay down a common 'experience' agreeable to the unifying tendencies in modern democracy, so that members of the community shall have a 'shared' understanding of their cultural heritage. Yet the aim is not as incapable of realization, in admittedly unacceptable terms, as at

[1] I have examined other aspects of the concern for social unity in an article on 'Tripartite Reform' in *The Times Educational Supplement* March 7th and 14th, 1958.

[2] The term 'culture' can be used in two senses: either to refer to the whole way of life of a people or to refer to a range of intellectual and artistic experiences which result from the general cultivation of the individual. I am using the word in its second sense here.

first sight it appears to be; and the reason for this is again bound up with the specialized, 'expert' nature of modern knowledge. It is in so far as the modern 'educated' man is not also a 'cultivated' man that what at first sight appears a futile quest takes on an air of feasibility. For a high degree of expertise in one direction is usually obtained in some degree at the expense of general culture. Furthermore, the agencies of general culture are themselves subject to the specializing tendencies of the time; so that, for instance, such an apparently straightforward task as the reading of a novel implies, in relation to modern criticism at its best, a good deal of training and experience. What have previously been the general agencies of cultivation are themselves coming to take on some of the marks of an esoteric procedure. Without, then, some degree of specialization in these fields, an acceptable 'taste' is not readily obtainable. This, of course, must not be blamed on the artist; in a 'much-divided' civilization, it is to be expected that literature, which takes cognizance of this complexity, will be 'difficult'.

To some extent this has always been so; it is a purely romantic notion that the spontaneous and untutored response is superior to the considered judgment. The very notion of 'cultivation' suggests more than simply spontaneous rapture. But the situation has been further complicated by the fact that social prestige has flown from cultivation in the arts to expertise in other fields. A century of 'rational' education ('To teach children to *think*') has gone a good way to destroy the traditions of artistic education—for example, those of the renaissance painter —and, at the same time, by its comparative neglect of the refinement of the feelings, has destroyed the roots of 'spontaneous' artistic creation in the popular mode. D. H. Lawrence has pointed to the extent to which elementary education as it existed in his day contributed to the drying up of the affective centres, through the imposition of an alien and 'genteel' culture upon the native resources of the people or 'folk' who had had their own traditions. And, affectively adrift, the folk have been an easy prey for the mass media.

But not only the folk. The split, broadly speaking, between the intellectual and affective—the emphasis on the 'thinking being'

in the schools and the neglect of the 'very culture of the feelings'
—has meant that the intelligentsia, too, have been found victims,
to a less marked, though significant, degree. Partly this has been
a reaction against the specialization in literary and artistic
creation, not readily acceptable to the non-expert, to which I
referred above; for writing and art, too, have developed their
own mystique. The works of James, Eliot, Joyce and W. B. Yeats,
the offsprings, in some measure, of consciously formulated policies in a developing tradition of theory, are not as immediately
intelligible as the ordinary 'educated' man, appreciative of his
own expertise but unwilling to concede it in a 'cultural' field,
would like or expects. Furthermore, the dominant scientific
technologies, as we shall see, tend to develop the 'will', the
desire to control and the expectation of a 'rational' simplicity.
Faced by the complexity of the best modern literature and art
and by the fact that there is little social prestige to be gained by
mastery in this field and none to be lost by the acceptance of the
common standard as put forward through the mass media, he
succumbs, and the tastes of tycoon (whether business, administrative or even academic), clerk and labourer tend to become
assimilated, as we have noted. The high official, even the university academic,[1] listens to the TV banality without loss of status.[2]
The situation has been affected, too, by the sort of recruitment
to the power elite which is characteristic of a bureaucracy where
authority is closely regulated by rules; this creates an atmosphere of psychological homogeneity and encourages the employment of the 'safe' person, even in high office, someone
without the arbitrary and 'surprising' quality which often accompanies greatness. In this way, standardization of power—
within the compass indicated—is the concomitant of a standardization of cultural outlook. There has been a considerable 'affective' drawing together of classes, though in other,

[1] Particularly those whose academic discipline involves a high degree of what I
might term 'technical' competence without in any way refining the sensibilities;
and such disciplines certainly exist—indeed, all disciplines can be practised in this
way, even the study of literature as Eng. Lit.

[2] Thus, the defenders of traditional culture should no longer think of it in terms
of 'class' against 'mass', but of quality against vulgarity which is to be found
amongst all classes.

intellectual, respects there is greater diversity than ever before between the specialist and the layman.

Nevertheless, the notion of a 'common culture', in so far as it works in these terms, is vicious, witnessing simply to the self-indulgent laziness of the intellectual, and in so far as it does not, is unobtainable. For as soon as the 'cultivated' assert themselves —as, in coteries, they do—the chasm yawns; and this chasm exists as a quite different qualitative response to the nature of our common life. To the further examination of the concept of a 'common culture', then, as it manifests itself among educationists and apologists today, I must devote some space.

The notion of a common culture *vis-à-vis* the educationist rests on presumptions which are themselves highly debatable. As we have seen, the struggle for status demands that the principle of equality of opportunity shall be manifest in the provision of a common curriculum or syllabus in schools so that opportunities of advancement shall not be cut off until the last possible moment; and at the same time, the egalitarian implications of democracy demand the maximum of shared experience, of 'conjoint communicated experience', among the members of the community. This common culture is not, that is to say, to be based on the universal acceptance by high and low of a particular view of the nature of man and of the universe which he inhabits, which enabled the medieval church, for instance, to translate the same basic conception into a number of different forms, from the pictorial narrative version of church fresco and cathedral carving to the highly sophisticated speculations, theological and philosophical, of the schoolmen;[1] but imposes instead a 'scientific' view of sameness—that is a view which atomizes experience into a set of chopped-up fragments of experience, each of which ideally must be conveyed in as near its entirety as possible so that each unit of individuality shall share as nearly as possible what every other unit has apprehended.[2] Part of our difficulty today, of course, resides in the fact that there is no universally

---

[1] Though, even then, no medieval man of learning would have imagined, for one moment, that he lived in a common culture in the modern sense.

[2] Cf. John Dewey: 'to have the same ideas about things which others have, to be like-minded with them, and thus to be really members of a social group, is to attach the same meanings to things and to acts which others attach.'

accepted metaphysical picture of our world to be adapted to the varying capacities of the different elements of our population. The result is that we have to fall back on the attempt, doomed to failure from the start, to convey experiences just as they are said to exist, not poetically translated into symbols or intellectually analysed in accordance with the level of understanding.

This business of shared experience in cultural matters is, indeed, a purely intellectual abstraction, in no way associated with social intercourse as we know it—or, indeed, as we can reasonably expect it to become. It is only necessary to ask, in concrete terms, what experiences exactly one does expect to be shared, for this to be demonstrable. A cultured man, let us agree, is a man who, among other qualities, has acquired certain elaborate, civilized techniques, or who has read ('read' implying with full imaginative response) certain complex works of literature or who has disciplined himself in certain modes of advanced inquiry —and so on; the list is not exhaustive. I mean only to indicate the sort of disciplined attention within a variety of advanced modes of 'mental' and 'affective' cultivation which in some measure would be a required accomplishment before the claim to be a 'cultured' individual could be sustained.

Now, even allowing the pretension of those who maintain that there is still a good deal of undiscovered talent in our society, can it seriously be maintained that there is an unlimited supply of individuals who are capable of cultivation in the sense indicated above? To be more specific still, is there an unlimited supply of people who can respond to Eliot, Pope, Plato, Wittgenstein, Namier, Gibbon, Leavis, Coleridge—or any of these, who consitute a fairly arbitrary selection—no more than an evocative offering—of names within a limited number of disciplines but who represent the sort of level of understanding which the claim to be cultured in the sense that the nineteenth century was rightly concerned about would need for substantiation? But, it may be argued, if people differ in their ability to respond to certain sophisticated disciplines, this merely implies the distinction that admittedly exists between 'experts'. That people differ in intellectual capacities is fairly obvious; no one disputes the superiority of some people's scientific understanding. That

101

they differ too in emotional and moral sensitivities—the capacity for sympathy or moral insight and courage—appears to be much less acceptable—though such sensitivities also form an essential part of the 'cultured' individual. Our cultural differences indeed do not exist solely in intellectual terms—though they certainly do so exist; they crop up in a whole range of other awarenesses —awarenesses cultivated in part through other disciplines—and these awarenesses lead inevitably to incompatibilities of behaviour and action based on different levels of insight. The expectation that people can come to share the same experiences could only be achieved by the deliberate fostering of a low level of response over whole fields of human endeavour.

The notion of a common culture, indeed, involves an attempt to bring all sections of the population to a similar level of consciousness—the assumption, to be fair, is that it will be a high one. The general ethos of our times condemns 'narrowness' and looks to 'broadening horizons', 'widening experiences' without realizing that where many natures are concerned narrowness may prove a strength. When I speak of 'bringing to consciousness' I imply two related phenomena: on the one hand, a stimulus to self-consciousness, self-awareness, a quality of inwardness which in the past seems to have been on the whole the product of a certain level of sophistication; on the other, an extension of awareness to a whole set of relationships and concepts which in various ways transcend immediate face-to-face contact, and the ability to utilize such abstractions in coming to decisions. Here many people are being asked to make a range of contacts very different from that which their ancestors enjoyed. Perhaps I can make my point clearer by quoting from an account by George Bourne of the countryman's primitive range of awareness:

'It was largely this simplicity of their mental processes that made the older people so companionable. They were unaccustomed to using certain powers of the brain which modern people use; nay, they were so unaware of that use as to be utterly unsuspicious of such a thing. To be as little psychological as possible, we may say that a modern man's thought goes on habitually on two main levels. On the surface are the subjects of the moment—that endless procession of things seen and heard or spoken of which make up the outer world; and here is where intercourse with the old type of villager was easy and agreeable. But below that surface the modern mind has a habit of interpreting these phenomena by general ideas or abstract principle, and referring them to imaginations all out of sight and unmentioned; and into this region of thought the peasant's attention hardly penetrated at all. Given a knowledge of the neighbourhood, therefore, it was easy to keep conversation going with a man of this kind. If you could find out the set of superficial or practical subjects in which he was interested and chatter solely on that plane, all went well. But if you dipped underneath it amongst fancies or generalizations, difficulties arose. The old people had no experience there and were out of their depth in a moment. And yet—I must repeat it—we should be entirely wrong to infer that they were naturally stupid, unless a man is to be called stupid because he does not cultivate every one of his inborn faculties. In that sense we all have our portion of stupidity, and the peasant was no worse than the rest of us. His particular deficiency was as I have described it, and may be fully explained by his mode of life. For in cow stall or garden or cottage, or in the fields or on the heaths, the claim of the moment was all absorbing; and as he hurried to thatch his rick before the rain came, or get his turfs home by nightfall, the ideas which thronged about his doings crowded out ideas of any other sort. Or if, not hurrying, his mind went dreamy, it was still of peasant things that he dreamed. Of what he had been told when he was a child or what he had seen for himself in after-life, his memory was full; and every stroke of reap-hook or thrust of spade had power to entice his intellect along the familiar grooves of thought—grooves which lie on the surface and are unconnected with any systematized channels of idea-work underneath.' (*Change in the Village.*)

Given that this is still a fair characterization of what the modern folk can best cope with—the concentration on the immediacies of direct contact, specific relationships responded to at a feeling rather than an intellectual level ('for the mass of people,' said Lawrence, 'knowledge *must* be symbolical, mythical, dynamic')[1]—one is continually struck by the unreality of notions of a common culture, their existing as abstractions in the minds of committees or individuals who formulate them apart from any recognizable social experience to which they are supposed to refer. For instance the Committee which drew up the *Harvard Report* on *General Education* considered that the various phases of a high-school education 'must be bound to-gether by common purposes if they are to exert a rounded, unifying influence'. The expression of the need, in a democracy, to depend 'on the binding ties of common standards' for fear of the divisive forces implicit in the democratic process recurs in the *Report* over and over again.

A glance at the means which in the eyes of the Harvard com-mittee is to bring about this uniformity reveals the emptiness of the wish. Again, the emphasis is on 'understanding'—and in-volves a high degree of self-consciousness: 'Democracy is the view that not only the few but that all are free, in that everyone governs his own life and shares in the responsibility for the management of the community. This being the case, it follows that all human beings stand in need of an ampler and rounded education. The task of modern democracy is to preserve the ancient ideal of liberal education and to extend it as far as possible to all the members of the community. . . . To believe in the equality of human beings is to believe that the good life, and the education which trains the citizen for the good life, are equally the privilege of all.' (p. 53.) Two necessities noted are the capacities for living the self-examined life and for a univer-sality in sympathies: 'for the civilized man is a citizen of the entire universe.' These characteristics are to be fostered by four traits of mind: the abilities 'to think effectively, to communicate thought, to make relevant judgments, to discriminate among values'. (p. 65.) Despite some lip service to the need to consider 'the whole man', and a gesture in the direction of the emotions and the imagination, the ultimate aim is the self-directive, rational human being: 'Intelligence is that leaven of awareness and reflection which, operating upon the native powers of men, raises them from the animal level and makes them truly human.

[1] Cf. also p. 215.

By reason, we mean, not an activity apart but rational guidance of all human activity. Thus the fruit of education is intelligence in action.'

Here, again, we are back in the rationalist tradition of education—that model of human behaviour which among other traits accompanies a high prudential morality and a careful calculation about ends, a model which, whatever its virtues, affects a comparatively small section of our population. Though written in America this might as easily have come from an English official document, so little informed is the prose with personal pressure or any association with the spirit of place. It betrays little concrete realization of human motive or appreciation of the forces of human conduct; the sentiments are the standardized uplift which serves anywhere—the Africans will be writing it next.

All such sentiments invoke the comment that W. B. Yeats made on the plays of Bernard Shaw: 'I listened to *Arms and the Man* with admiration and hatred. It seemed to me inorganic, logical straightness and not the crooked path of life . . . Presently I had a nightmare that I was haunted by a sewing machine, that clicked and shone, but the incredible thing was that the machine smiled, smiled perpetually.' (*Autobiographies*, pp. 348–9.) The relevant gloss on this particular view of education is the comment of Mr. Richard Hoggart on certain television programmes; their emphasis, well-meant no doubt, on 'citizenship' in the same terms as are implicit in the Report, fails utterly to touch the vital affective centres—the imaginative core—in people of the type they are intending to bring into the fold: Mr. Hoggart is speaking of the relative effectiveness of what might be termed 'rational' social comment and advertisements on TV. He states: 'Television—and most forms of mass communication—raises new and difficult questions. There is for instance the matter of imaginative commitment. Think of the great number of earnest documentaries on both television channels: on the "colour problem", "nuclear warfare", "the problem of youth", and so on. We can guess why there are so many; they are transparent yet heavy with intelligent good intentions. Yet they are almost always fundamentally off-key, irrelevant to the pressure and depth and grotesqueness of "problems" as we meet them in life. Most of them give as nearly as they can a "balanced" and "objective" picture, one that represents a "fair cross section" of the "typical people" involved in the problem. I wonder what effect they have at the level at which we say "bloody niggers" or "those damn teenagers ought to be horsewhipped". They recall those surveys of television programmes which decide that *this* programme is "wholesome" because virtue triumphs in the end and there is little violence, whereas *that* is "less wholesome" because virtue is killed or goes mad and violence abounds. By these criteria the latest improving novelette is more "wholesome" than *King Lear.*' It is odd that we ignore the methods of those who have most touched the 'masses' in our times—the advertisers, the political dictators, and the purveyors of cheap art in its various forms. These people sell a myth, a symbol, a dream. We must seek the sources of their strength—which are affective; and we must seek to direct the powers they have unleashed into better channels. We may, of course, fail in our efforts, for what is needed is a refinement of feeling, not a mere exploitation. There are standards of emotional education as of rational and intellectual; the two, indeed, are never quite as distinct as our modes of speech imply. Prescription for the education of the 'average' needs to be rooted in sociological and psychological awareness—and awareness of an order usually unknown or unsuspected to the sort of people who sit on committees for educational provision. Our commitment to 'more consciousness' (and in some degree we are so committed) must come to terms with the inherent limitations of consciousness many people show. We must seek to educate them for that level of decision-making which will best foster their individuality, and this will necessitate considering their capacity for abstraction and generalization.

D

An opponent of the 'Minority' principle is Mr. Raymond Williams, whose *Culture and Society* enjoyed a certain *succès d'estime*. There he urges, in his comments on Dr. Leavis, that

'The concept of a cultivated minority, set over against a "decreated" mass, tends, in its assertions, to a damaging arrogance and scepticism.' The positive nature of Mr. Williams' view of society, as set out in that book, deserves, therefore, some comment.

Mr. Williams makes the useful point that in considering the people we should cease to think of them in terms of 'masses': 'What we see neutrally, is other people, many others, people unknown to us.' (p. 300.) He fails, however, to maintain even this level of particularity. Thus, in considering the conditions within which the culture he has in mind can grow he asserts that we should lose the 'dominative habit' and concede the 'practice of democracy'; this involves communication, an attempt to 'achieve reception and response'. To explain manifest differences between people he posits a not over-clear distinction between 'equality of being' and 'inequality in the various aspects of man' which seems to introduce in the former a somewhat doubtful metaphysical entity. What precisely is to be understood by the 'common culture' which is to emerge as the concrete realization of some of these ideas is never really clear. We are told, for instance, that we 'lack a genuinely common experience', though what is to enter into this 'experience' remains obscure.

Perhaps relevant to the difficulty is a shift that Williams makes at a crucial point in his argument from one sense of the word 'culture' to another. He makes it clear that the word is in fact used in two different senses. It can refer to certain bodies of human achievement ('a body of intellectual and imaginative work') selected from the whole range of human activities and may therefore imply a standard of moral or aesthetic excellence over against the depredations of the 'market' or of industrialism —the study of our total perfection, as Arnold called it. This is largely, though not exclusively, the sense in which it is employed by his nineteenth-century witnesses. Or it may be employed in the anthropological sense of a whole way of life, where its usage is morally neutral and purely descriptive.

At a crucial passage in his book, Williams shifts from the former to the latter meaning overtly, and then reintroduces the evaluative note surreptitiously. What he achieves is the blurring of the fact that the lower classes in our own time have produced no sizeable body of 'culture' in the first sense of the word. Let me clarify by quoting the vital passages. He is discussing the relevance of thinking in terms of class at all in the modern world. He begins by agreeing that, in some measure, culture as a body of imaginative and intellectual work is becoming more widely distributed and is now 'being addressed to a public wider than a single class'. There are a lot of questions to be asked even here, but we will let them pass. He continues: 'Yet a culture is not only a body of intellectual and imaginative work; it is also and essentially a whole way of life. The basis of a distinction between bourgeois and working-class culture is only secondarily in the field of intellectual and imaginative work . . . The primary distinction is to be sought in the whole way of life . . . The crucial distinguishing element in English life since the Industrial Revolution is not language, not dress, not leisure . . . The crucial distinction is between alternative ideas of the nature of social relationship.'

What is happening here becomes clear. Mr. Williams is obviously unable to deny that different sections of the community have, in fact, made very different contributions to the quality of our imaginative and intellectual life. He therefore blurs the issue by asserting that this is a matter of secondary importance and that the crucial difference lies in the *whole* ways of life implicit in the outlooks of the two classes. He then *selects* from these two ways of life, in the totality of which the difference is supposed to lie, one aspect of them, their differing views of social relationships, and makes of this the vital distinction; he contrasts bourgeois individualism—which admittedly has produced the body of 'intellectual and imaginative' work—and the 'basic collective idea'—glossed as the 'collective democratic institution'—which is the product of working-class 'culture'. It would not be unreasonable to conjecture that this is because he is emotionally attached to the working classes and desires to recommend, positively, that solidarity which he considers to have been their unique 'cultural' contribution and which he wishes to extend to all classes. (The romanticizing of working-class life is a peculiar feature of our times.) The effect of this is to contrast two different evaluations, for the practice of solidarity is just as much an abstraction from a whole way of life as is a 'culture' in the restricted sense of 'intellectual and imaginative work'.

Even if we allow his diagnoses of the unique nature of working-class solidarity to be correct—and, before doing so, one would need to ask whether such solidarity is anything more of a reality than that of, say, public school boys—he is side-stepping the problem which worried his nineteenth-century witnesses and which is still with us today: the concern about the quality of our lives as they are affected by the nature of many of our imaginative and intellectual productions. The effect of his diagnosis, though he may not intend it quite so blatantly, is to suggest that it is the social relationships that matter and that the quality of our 'culture' in the other restricted sense is of minor importance; though he is careful to want to protect the working classes, on no stated evidence,[1] from any imputation of indifference or hostility to education or art. It is, at any rate, with the 'social' note that he ends. In his final reference in the 'Development of a Common Culture', the notion of community is emphasized in a paean of generalized uplift: 'In its definition of the common interest as true self-interest, in its finding of individual verification primarily in the community, the idea of solidarity is potentially the real basis of society.' (p. 332.) And if this seems over rude, let me ask the reader to study these last few pages and ask what, in concrete and specific terms some of the phrases used *mean*. For example, one of the main difficulties—increased specialization in the common culture—is glossed in this way: it is 'only soluble', we are told, 'in a context of material community and by the full democratic process'. So far as one can judge, the solution is conceived in terms of a split in the personality between adeptness in a speciality on the one hand, with a consequent respect for the skills of others, and a communal self ('common resources') on the other—the 'practice of neighbourhood', whatever that may mean. This, of course, is to disguise

[1] It is interesting to see, historically, on what grounds the working classes or their articulate members have defended education. Mostly, it has been as a weapon in the struggle for social authority—the Baconian ground that 'knowledge is power' rather than Arnold's conception of education as a process of 'humanization'. Cf. Brian Simon, *Studies in the History of Education, 1780–1870*.

the fact that the development of certain skills and awarenesses so affects the personality as to make the practice of neighbourhood in many environments difficult, if not impossible[1] . . . unless the neighbourhood is a congenial one; then it will be other neighbourhoods that are uncongenial, and what happens to the spirit of community then? Some inkling of this seems to reach Mr. Williams, for he asserts that 'It is necessary to make room for, not only variation, but even dissidence, within the common loyalty.' What constitute the boundaries of the common loyalty—what things precisely are taboo—remains unrevealed. But unless we know, this sort of writing which says, in effect, nothing more precise than can be summed up in the sentence: 'We must all be together but, of course, we must allow everyone to be different', carries little significance except the revelation of a curious mental blockage—one inclines to think of emotional origin. The crucial dilemma, which our age funks and funks in the sort of verbiage of which Mr. Williams is guilty, is that if 'culture' in the restrictive sense is really to mean something and is not simply to be reduced to the level of a 'skill', if it becomes part of one's being as the practice of the novel became to Henry James, then the danger one may have to face is that which James mooted to Logan Pearsall Smith: 'There is one word—let me impress upon you—which you must inscribe upon your banner, and that word is Loneliness'; at least in the sense that some feeling of apartness from broad majority tastes must be the lot of such people even as they regret the isolation involved. Basically, this necessitates a reassertion of the 'Minority' principle, with the rider that the Minority should assert its case even against the hostility of the general public. For, just as Mr. Williams rightly attacks the stereotype of the masses, so it is necessary to attack his stereotype of the

---

[1] It is a pity that people do not more frequently take account of real situations in this respect. Consider, for instance, one's plight in a neighbourhood where the neighbours persist in playing their wirelesses loudly with windows open, thus imposing what they wish to listen to on others—and such cases exist in great numbers. Or the way in which one's peace can be disturbed by the modern curse, the transistor radio. Even the sweetest reasonableness is no weapon against such crudities; they persist in spite of protest. A trivial example perhaps—but it is in terms of such 'trivialities' that the stuff of our daily lives and relationships is made up, not in those of Mr. Williams' abstract generalities.

'Minority'. There are various sorts of minorities; that which clustered round Bloomsbury showed a significantly less sense of social responsibility than that which contributed to *Scrutiny*.[1]

In our present cultural plight, the important contribution is surely that of a Leavis, who has produced a body of specific criticism, supported by detailed analysis, clarifying as it asserts the minority principle. Such particularized judgments support and sustain our cultural life in a manner which Mr. Williams' generalities fail to do, despite the fact that Dr. Leavis, in the honesty and forthrightness with which his criticism has been expressed, would hardly seem to have sustained the 'practice of neighbourhood' in any recognizable meaning that could be assigned to that phrase. Nevertheless, a way of summing up what I am saying here is to assert the superiority, in contribution to the future of the human spirit, of a Leavis to that of a Williams.

I suspect, then, in general, that the notion of social unity in its modern sense, whether cultural or in the power structure or whatever else is intended by the phrase, is a mirage. Varied social groupings of some sort are inevitable in any large-scale society; and it is absurd to think that all such groups are likely to share compatible ends, as I have indicated above. We have probably gone as far as we can, in the Welfare State, to alleviate social tensions, unless we are willing to reduce our population to a hypnotized, muzak-doped apathetic mass. The harmonious society remains a pipe-dream of humanity. What we *need* in the way of social harmony is an agreement not to cut each other's throats, not to use the police and the concentration camps as methods of political persuasion and to see that all have the basic means of subsistence and freedom of opinion in the sense that we can tolerate the expression of different views.[2] It is as well to remember that fullness of life arises out of conflict as well as out of harmony: that if we had no one on whom to sharpen our

[1] It is, in fact, part of the *Scrutiny* case—specifically that of Dr. Leavis—that literary culture is not just a 'skill' but a leaven to the whole personality, sensitizing and strengthening, so that it at once provides the insight to understand and the moral courage to differ (and cp. Bloomsbury and *Scrutiny* minorities).

[2] This rough collection of requirements is intended to reassert the superiority of 'liberal' democracy over its collectivist successor.

wits, our minds would soon atrophy. As Mr. Eliot has pointed out, *friction* is an essential element in a cultured society.

E

But that does not mean that one can be happy about the way in which the meritocracy—the obverse principle of diversity—is evolving. For the pressure towards higher education exists here, too, at least as much in social terms at it does in terms of cultural opportunities. It constitutes part of the movement for 'educated manpower'—and the conception of social need implicit in this is by no means wholly acceptable. It is tempting, indeed, to see the emphasis on selection and the desire to afford opportunity to all who can benefit as a reassertion of the liberty of the individual to develop himself as he will against the conformity of the state. In fact, it comes to look perilously like a conflict between two sorts of social conformity, between pressure to conform to the demand for common likeness and pressure to conform to the hierarchical demands implicit in the functioning of the technicized and bureaucratic state. The latter, of course, does involve more diversity; but the pressure for the spread of higher education has to be seen as a moral imperative which has the good of the state at heart at least as strongly as the desire to afford 'chances' to individuals. It is a weapon in a battle of international rivalries, economic and political, as much as a concern for the private person. It is perhaps some realization of this that has made Mr. T. S. Eliot, working from a very different set of assumptions, utter the warning: 'Any educational system aiming at a complete adjustment between education and society will tend both to restrict education to what will lead to success in the world, and to restrict success in the world to those persons who have been good pupils of the system. The prospect of a society ruled and directed only by those who have passed certain examinations or satisfied tests devised by psychologists is not reassuring: while it might give scope to talents hitherto obscured, it would probably obscure others, and reduce to impotence some who should have rendered high service.' (*Notes towards the Definition of Culture*, p. 101.) In saying this, however, I would still be understood to prefer 'diversity' to 'uniformity'; even such diversity as is being encouraged contains within it more of the possibilities of richness and fullness of being than do the trends towards uniformity.

My diagnosis is, I think, illustrated, albeit in part unconsciously, by the outlook of the Crowther Report. The attempt to interpret our educational needs in a 'liberal' spirit, as such liberalism is understood by the 'establishment' mind, is strongly marked. Nevertheless, the dominance of socio-political and economic interests, as those interests also are so understood, is everywhere patent. The Crowther Report suggests two reasons why education is important, reasons it considers closely bound up one with the other. Education is a social service—a matter of human rights—provided to enable individuals to come to their personal fulfilment; at the same time, it is also a social investment, a means in a technological civilization of meeting the social requirements of certain skills to promote a higher living standard through 'increased efficiency in production and distribution at all levels'. Self-fulfilment and social need, then, are the twin pillars on which the Crowther committee sustains its edifice of educational recommendations. Is it unfair to the committee, however, and indeed to some of its very explicit injunctions (such as its categorical statement: '. . . children are not the "supply" that meets any "demand" however urgent. They are individual human beings, and the primary concern of the schools should not be with the living they will earn but with the life they will lead (p. 53)) to suggest that it is the latter of the two views of the purpose of education—that of social investment—which ranks most forcibly in its eyes?[1] Though there are constant warnings, of which the one quoted is perhaps the most categorical, lest education should be regarded as a way of providing machine fodder for prosperity, it is social need in

[1] The very ambivalence is, of course, of considerable interest in that it betokens the vestigial strength of the concept of 'cultivation' as an educational ideal. Yet the comments of the committee are always highly abstract here. The sap really flows on the other side.

roughly these terms which bulks most largely in the recommendations. Though there is a good deal of talk about the importance of considering 'the developing needs of the whole
man', it is usually at the highest level of generality so that it
appears as a recurrent itch rather than a focusing point of attention. The impression one carries away from a reading is that it
is this need for 'educated manpower' in terms relevant to the
continuation of the 'affluent society' and its further implementation, rather than a deep concern for the human predicament in a
materialistic and mechanical age, that the committee consciously
or unconsciously felt to be the really important aspect of its
work. There are passing references to the impact of the mass
media of communication, to the decline of received authority, to
the need 'to find a faith to live by' . . . and so on. But the
Report is finally a good deal less specific on how these highly
desirable ends are to be achieved than it is on such matters as to
how technical education is to be reoriented to the new demands
for technicians due to the 'growth in the proportion of highly
skilled jobs', which implies a 're-assessment of what must be
attempted by people of only average intelligence'. The concern
expressed in such a categorical way by the Spens committee
only twenty years before for 'creative' activities has to all
intents and purposes disappeared—there is a passing reference
to the place of the non-verbal arts in the education of sixth
formers, but little besides. The Spens report certainly opened
the door to vocationalism and stressed the need for the curriculum to make contact with 'practical life and needs', and the importance of the young growing up 'in conformity with the
national ethos'; but by and large its emphases lay in the promotion of the individual life and the need to 'humanize', with
all the implications that Matthew Arnold's word conjures up.
One's feeling about the Crowther Report is that the needs of
the practical life and of vocationalism have taken up their abode
unashamedly and that it is the element of humanization which
has been forced into a corner of the living room, though the
need to recognize its presence there has not been forgotten.

F

The emphasis on organization, the escape into the generalities of the common culture merely avoids the very specific and concrete task which faces the educationist and which is bound up with particularities of curricula—of what to teach in this or that context. For instance, instead of facing the fundamental problem: 'What ought we to teach the less bright child?' which the secondary modern school forced upon us, we have sidestepped the issue at the behest of the comprehensive idea by trying to pretend that all children are nearly the same, or ought to be nearly the same, even if they palpably are not—or different in 'nature' but not in 'quality', or whatever other formula can be found to disguise the realities of the situation. Had a satisfactory solution to the problem of the average and below average child been found, there might have been much less interest in comprehensiveness. The Secondary Modern School has never been given a chance; for what is fifteen years in the life of an institution of such complexity?

Indeed, in none of the schemes of secondary reorganization I have examined do I find any real attempt to ask the fundamental questions raised by universal literacy, to assess the way our society is going or to query the values on which that 'progress', largely technical, is based; and this despite the fact that many of the greatest minds of our times have felt themselves profoundly out of step with the whole trend of our civilization. There is a certain pretentiousness about what the school can do, and sometimes an inflated sense of its importance in the social revolution of our times; there is an almost universal acceptance of the more superficial values of our society concerning what constitutes educational success. But there is little appreciation of the tremendous problems brought about by the death of the old folk culture, killed by industrialization, and of the consequence that our people are spiritually and morally adrift in that 'candy-floss' world of commercial values so ably analysed by Richard Hoggart in *The Uses of Literacy*. I see little sign in any of these schemes of any understanding of the problems which are likely to face us

115

J

as we move into C. P. Snow's brave new world of 'electronics, atomic energy, automation', a world geared to what Lawrence called the 'plausible ethics of productivity'—except an interpretation of 'social needs' in largely those terms. To put it another way, our present trends in secondary schooling seem to involve largely an education for efficiency as that efficiency is understood in the affluent society, not a training for life as the great poets and artists and religious leaders have understood that word. (Of course, they don't agree in the pictures they offer us; but collectively they represent a standard beyond that implicit in the modern 'standard of living'.)

Nor is this anything like the whole of the problem of what to teach. For the brighter children, for instance, there is that dichotomy symbolized by C. P. Snow's *Two Cultures*, the most recent of a stream of writings which during the nineteenth and twentieth centuries have asked questions about the fragmentation of our culture and have faced us with the challenge of the scientific revolution to the traditional curriculum; and here I think of science not only in terms of technological applications, but also in terms of thought, providing us with some picture of what is. At the same time, the claims of the new technological humanism to the virtues of which, in their various ways, Sir Eric Ashby and Georges Friedmann have drawn attention, need examination. When such profound issues are at stake, it is sad to see quite so much money and energy spent on the organizational aspects, and the philosophy of the matter concerned with such comparatively superficial social strivings as I have touched on in this chapter. (Though seemingly so parochial, in reality the conflict over compulsory Latin at Oxford and Cambridge, because it faced us with the whole problem of content, raised issues inherently more profound and serious than the whole comprehensive movement.) It is perhaps partly because of an oversimplified conception of the power of organizations to affect our lives, that the organizational aspect has received the attention it has. I would not suggest that the organizational aspect is a matter of total indifference; it may, indeed, affect to some extent the quality of what goes on—radical changes, for instance, may possibly destroy what of good has only with difficulty been built up; adjustments may possibly better what exists. But thinking at the administrative level involves too high a degree of abstraction from the real business of education, which is finally a matter of what happens in the class-room.

The challenge of our times is 'what to teach'—particularly to the less able children, those who suffer the real deficiencies of the industrial age with its all too frequent degradation of personal skill and satisfying work, or its cultural impoverishment and its encouragement of a debilitating indulgence in an 'entertainment' of fantasy—a compensation culture, in fact. The real question is, 'Can we in the schools do anything towards the evolving of a new folk-culture?' The most disappointing feature of 'comprehensiveness' lies in its failure to ask fundamental curricular questions; it offers little except a modified grammar school curriculum with a wider range of vocational choices. *In general* there is little reason to think it has achieved much more than the substitution of a new set of problems for the old ones.

In conclusion, it must be conceded to the exponents of reorganization that they have brought out certain difficulties within the present system—or what must appear as difficulties to those who work within the present framework of assumptions. My point has been, not that there are no strains but that the sort of naivety too easily betrayed by those who would reorganize our whole secondary system constitutes a danger to what has been laboriously built up. Nor would I necessarily advocate any one solution as a panacea; local communities must work out their own salvations with the minimum of stress, on the principle that what is wanted is evolution rather than revolution.[1] Instead of this total revision of the whole system, then, with all the perils of the imponderables, there is no reason why the characteristic English process of patching, of local attack on specific problems within particular areas, should not be tried within a system designed to provide diversity of provision. This would serve to

[1] My own preference is for the sort of scheme to be found in Chesterfield and Southampton. Reasons for this are set out in my lecture to the British Association in 1959, reprinted in *The Advancement of Science*, July 1960—'The Reorganization of Secondary Education'.

preserve what has had a reasonable success—the grammar school, and, at the same time, recognize the force of Mr. T. S. Eliot's dictum that 'tradition cannot mean standing still'.

My 'plan', then, has none of the heroic proportions of the others. It involves achievement by means of 'small adjustments and readjustments which can be continually improved upon'.[1] The sorts of reform I have in mind can be briefly, but not of course fully or adequately, listed: (i) The improvement of selection techniques. It would seem that here refinements only are possible. (ii) Greater flexibility of moving between schools. (iii) The fuller development of technical education in areas where such education is inadequate or non-existent. (iv) The development in certain areas of secondary modern schools with many different biases, after the Southampton and Chesterfield plans. (v) The provision of comprehensive schools, in a limited number of rural areas, where the grammar schools are of an insufficient size to provide an adequate range of subjects (as in parts of Anglesey, for example), or experimentally in areas where good grammar school education did not exist. (vi) Where grammar school provision is inadequate, the building of more such schools. (vii) A willingness, in appropriate areas, to soften the outlines of the tripartite system by the setting up of grammar-technical or intermediate (technical-modern) schools. (viii) The mixing of schools for certain sixth-form classes, to make up for local deficiencies—a device often used during the war. (ix) The willingness of the grammar school to pay more and a different sort of attention to its lower streams, to give a measured hearing, at least, to some of the new techniques of teaching which the 'progressives' have developed.

The great virtue of this sort of approach is that it allows particular problems to be attacked in particular localities, with full recognition of the importance of local traditions and of local needs. It would also mean that existing good schools would remain untouched. In thus recognizing the virtues of 'piecemeal' rather than 'utopian' engineering I cannot help recalling the dictum of Matthew Arnold: 'Culture is always assigning to system-makers and systems a smaller share in the bent of

[1] K. Popper, *The Poverty of Historicism.*

118

human destiny than their friends like.' And, indeed, the quotation serves to remind us that the basic problem of our age is the 'cultural' one—our concern for quality of life—and that these wholesale alterations advocated by the utopians are only distractions from the graver issues. Furthermore, such alterations may, through devices like the common curriculum which are implicit in the very nature of the arguments used to sustain them, obfuscate what is fundamental to any solution of our educational problems: the appreciation that the egalitarianism which is implicit in our political life is quite inapplicable in our educational; for very different natures need very different sorts of educational treatment.

G

I ought to conclude this analysis of 'socialized' education by making my own position clear, the general position concerning the function of the school to which I shall be holding in this book.

Each statement of social 'need' must be analysed on its merits. One of the problems of this book will be the extent to which the school—and university, for that matter—ought to become a function of the technological society, which is what in large measure threatens it. That the social pressures in this direction are strong is undoubted—and they will increase. An important role for the school, then, will be that of the preservation of 'minority' interests, 'minority' in the sense at least that such interests serve tendencies against the main stream.

But the more one considers the particular learning processes that ought to go on in particular schools, the more one becomes convinced that the proposition 'the school is a social institution' requires analysis, not only from the point of view of what is intended by 'social institution' and its various implications, but also as to what is intended by the concept of 'the school'. Apart from the fact that it is an institution in some way cut off from Society as a whole, I become convinced that there is less and less justification for talking in terms of 'the function of the school' at all. What we have, indeed, is a variety of establishments which we should conceive of in terms of broad categories of purposes, the categories concerned being controlled by the intelligence range of the pupils and by a variety of local opportunities and conditions. 'The school', indeed, is not a simple, monolithic institution; it ought to be conceived of as fulfilling a variety of social functions which at one end of the scale will involve the inculcation of the bare minimum of social conformity[1] and at the other end will permit the preservation and conservation of highly sophisticated minority interests, not only for the good of the individuals concerned but for the cultural leavening which such individuals can provide within Society.

This raises the question as to the extent to which 'the school' can conceivably be expected to help initiate desirable changes in society as it exists; how far, in fact, it can be conceived of as an instrument of social 'progress'. In a review of a recent reprint of Durkheim's *Education and Sociology*, Mr. Philip Rieff has asserted: 'Rousseau and his sort of enthusiast for education are revolutionaries manqués, children are their proletariat, love is their ideology, and the schoolroom is the good society in microcosm. Durkheim had the sense to see microcosms are never the models of macrocosms; on the contrary, in social life, it is the macrocosm which serves as a model for the microcosm.' (*American Sociological Review*, vol. 22, No. 2, April 1957, p. 233.) This is not quite true, though I am convinced that it is truer than those theories which regard the school as a revolutionary device for the changing of societies. Nevertheless when we come to think of particular individuals in particular schools, we see that whereas some will need to be brought to a basic level of social competence, there will almost certainly exist, in relation to a variety of cultural levels, those who, in good part at least through the instruction they receive in school, may become initiators of valuable changes. Another way of making my point would be to say that 'the school' as such is neither the preserver of social values nor the promoter of social changes. What it has is a number of varied effects on different children; as a result some children will be encouraged to conserve *certain* majority social values and others will awaken to values other than those of the

[1] Teaching children how to wash and dress themselves, for instance, in the special schools for educationally sub-normal children.

conforming majority. It becomes obvious, then, that the role of the school is incapable of summation into a formula; it will, in fact, be immensely varied in relation to the capabilities of children in responding and the brilliance of the teachers in initiating.

This, then, would suggest that, because what goes on in schools is always the result of individual decisions taken consciously or unconsciously about what *ought* to be done, the attempt I shall make to suggest, at a variety of levels, certain desirable changes in curriculum or in the method of treating it is not an entirely futile undertaking—if only because certain individuals may be affected in particular contexts by what I have to say. It *was* Durkheim's contribution to see how immensely the schools do in fact reflect current values, or, to put it another way, how immensely strong are the forces of conservatism in scholastic institutions. Nevertheless, as the teaching situation remains inviolately a moral one, it always remains subject to human choice; and when the analytical philosopher becomes the prescribing educationist, his excuse must be that to think again what ought to be is the assertion of a basic human right in a world which poses perennially the question: 'What ought we to do?' For this is a question the teacher can never avoid, from the logic of his situation; even if he does simply what his predecessor did or what his children decide they want to do, it is only at his volition, once the teaching situation exists at all.

There is a final point in considering the relation of school and Society. There is no doubt that social pressures outside the school do in fact exert a powerful influence on the expectations and responses of the children; it is only a comparatively small number of children who, in any generation, are likely seriously to challenge the basic assumptions of the majority, or who are not going to find their main *raison d'être* for what they do more from the approval of the primary groups to which they belong (family and peers) than from what teachers tell them—unless the teacher is a fairly unusual sort of person with that touch of the charismatic which enables him or her to attract and persuade. This means that with the majority of children, social utility is likely to remain the most powerful incentive to which it is possible to appeal—at least it is from such an appeal that we must start. What is offered must appear to have social relevance, to take into consideration the true facts about work and leisure.

No appeal to learning for its own sake is likely to evoke much response in our non-academic children—and a syllabus which is socially irrelevant to them, like the watered-down grammar school one at present in use, is bound to have little appeal and less effect. This does not remove from the teacher the necessity for moral choice, so that he succumbs, for instance, to the more vulgar manifestations of the mass media simply because these are what his children accept and want; but it does mean that he must work from the appeals, recognize their potency and make his bid for improvement in terms that such children can critically grasp; and this means abandoning much of what is at present taught to them and re-thinking the syllabus. To present the normal academic disciplines to children to whom they lack all significance is simply to invite disaster. Even where abler children are concerned, it will be as well to recognize that it is examination success (because it has a social repercussion in terms of revised status) that matters to many of them rather than any intrinsic interest in or care for the disciplines they have been studying. To only a comparative few will the intellectual life the grammar school is supposed to foster make any intrinsic appeal. That may well mean that, educationally speaking, such children are the most valuable individuals we have; though, even in the act of saying this one recognizes and supports the intrinsic right of every child to receive that enlargement of his 'nature' which a variety of schools adapted to different needs and abilities can provide.

Obviously, in the nature of the case, one's recommendations will be subject to dispute and controversy—they will belong to the world of values not of facts. This controversy is, above all, what is needed today. There is too supine an acquiescence in the trend of events; too many educationists are concerned simply to implement the supposed 'needs' of the industrial-bureaucratic state; and indeed, the general level of educational discussion in this country is a national disgrace—it exists far too much in terms of means; fundamental questions concerning ends are sadly neglected.

CHAPTER FIVE

Some Problems in the Provision of Academic Education

---◈---

The sort of education that is implicit in the curriculum for our able children needs some preliminary definition; it stems from a particular type of civilization which has reached a certain stage of social and intellectual development. For, when we come to analyse the nature of academic learning, we see that it is essentially urban in character, the offshoot of a level of social development which aims well beyond mere subsistence. Furthermore, its nature is largely abstract and mental. Both these characteristics meet in the notion of the 'academic'. The academy is essentially the product of a society in which some individuals are released, through an advanced degree of division of labour, from the immediate cares of food-hunting and agriculture; and this tends to happen most clearly in the urban conglomeration. Again, the 'academy' suggests precisely that cutoff, enclosed and remote quality which is characteristic of certain sophisticated social groups who lift themselves beyond the immediate cares and pressures of everyday life in order to contemplate the deeper realities of human existence—those realities, that is, which do not press immediately on the consciousness but take into consideration something of man's ultimate position of strangeness in the universe or of that curious imbalance in his nature which sets him over against his environment and enables him to detach himself from it. Such contemplation may indeed emerge out of the empirical—the facts of 'birth, and copulation, and death'—but it emerges as discursive thinking *about* these situations (and 'about' implies 'round about') rather than as being directly concerned with their material attributes.

The essence of the notion of the academic, then, is that it shall be reflection on experience rather than experience itself. It belongs essentially to the notion of the ordered and arranged rather than to the spontaneous, the sophisticated rather than the 'natural', the wrought up and created rather than the given and accepted. It arises out of man's ability to stand aside from his experience and make 'sense' of it; and it represents an advanced and complex stage of even this characteristic, in that the making sense involves ever increasing consciousness of self, of one's fellows and of 'nature'.

The whole notion of the present academic curriculum, indeed, implies certain capacities of mental organization which are only to be found in advanced societies and only among certain sections even of them. For the variety of ways of ordering experience implicit in the academic undertaking require mental qualities—such as the ability to perceive relationships, to correlate phenomena, to imagine and pattern what is remote in space and time, to develop concepts and descriptions, and so on—which can only be the product of a considerable measure of 'mental' training and organization. Furthermore, the immediate social relevance of the results of this hard mental sophistication are in many cases by no means apparent. The fact that much of what is taken for granted in the way of social amenities has only resulted from these particular types of dedication is, as Ortega y Gasset pointed out, not by any means apparent to the ordinary (what he terms 'mass') man; and the even remoter rewards of 'disinterested' mental activity are such as only to appeal to the few with the imagination to foretaste the benefits and pleasures to come and who find their pursuit immediately interesting—or, perhaps, possess the self-discipline to resist more immediate social satisfactions.

There is a still further consideration. These modes of arranging

our experience develop complex techniques and modes of procedure which, as I have indicated, imply a long training before
they yield their rewards. The position is further complicated by
the fact that the very nature of these disciplines is in constant
dispute. The theoretical accounts which could be given of their
incidence and of the conceptual apparatus which forms an essential element in their techniques of management and discovery are
themselves the subjects of controversy and discussion; so that
what constitutes 'history', or 'science' is not agreed. Some
accounts of 'science', for instance, may stress its relevance to
immediate problems; others may urge that its aim is simply
'description' or even 'truth' (though this, at the moment, is
rather out of fashion). At any one time, one view may be more
popular than another and become an orthodoxy (as, for instance,
current views on the nature of philosophy itself, which differ
considerably from the account that nineteenth-century philosophers would have given of their undertaking).

The implications of all this are essentially meritocratic, involving the minority principle. It is unreasonable to expect that
the qualities of imagination, intellectual ability and perseverance
needed for success in these disciplines will be encountered often
in the one person. There is, moreover, a further characteristic of
modern knowledge which demands a constantly increasing
sophistication—its dynamic nature. In the past, certain sorts of
knowledge have provided an illusion of being fully known, of
being completely enclosed within a dogmatic system which, once
mastered, was understood for all time. Modern knowledge is
essentially contingent, subject not only to extensions of awareness within orthodox conceptualizations but also open to continual possibilities of conceptual rearrangement in pursuit of
refinements of understanding. It is of the essence of modern
knowledge at its most typical that it shall only be imperfectly
known, and that it shall, therefore, lie open to modification and
extension. (Furthermore, it is 'open' knowledge: there is
nothing that is forbidden or regarded in any way as 'demonic'.)
This is as true of the humanities[1] as it is of the sciences and social

[1] This is shown, for example, by the history of criticism. It is obvious that, for
instance, *The Merchant of Venice* was a very different play to the early eighteenth-

sciences. Whereas, then, modern learning depends enormously on techniques and methodologies hammered out by the great in the past, it demands also a peculiar flexibility in the face of new combinations of awareness, new sensibilities, new modes of conceptual arrangement.

Furthermore, such a learning is basically rootless—at least in the wider, social sense. In certain of its manifestations it may indeed provide some sense of 'belonging' in that it brings people together within the framework of a common professional understanding. But outside the common pursuit individuals may be so divided as to share nothing but this understanding with their fellows; and, even within, different views about the true nature of expert procedures stemming from philosophical quarrels concerning underlying characteristics may introduce disagreement and even rancour. Nevertheless, among the intellectual classes, one of the most characteristic of social groupings in the modern world is that based on a common academic interest.

The nature of such learning is, indeed, profoundly significant for the future of our culture. I shall go on to argue that, given the conditions, cultural and social, of the modern world, the great disciplines form satisfying and accessible sources for the education of our able children. Nevertheless, the peculiarly mental nature of the education so offered, the fact that it is only in an indirect way rooted in any moral way of life, any Tao, carries with it certain possible consequences for our culture. Traditionally, the education of the sophisticated has often been taken up with the study and elucidation of classical texts, usually of supposedly sacred origin, as I have just indicated.[1] These texts have frequently been a source of revelation regarding the moral and social virtues; they have thus formed the basis of a 'culture' in the narrower, Arnoldian sense of the term: the arts and crafts which have characterized the way of life have often

century audience from what it is to a modern one. Again, different ways of writing history strew the historical development of historical writing.

[1] 'The Han scholar was concerned to discover what the classic had actually said and meant, and he was in large measure motivated by the belief that the way to right government, to truth, and to the moral life was the way that had already been discovered and stated in the classics.' (E. D. Myers, *Education in the Perspective of History*, p. 47.)

found their stay and strength in the stability and coherence which such writings have afforded the 'culture' in the wider, anthropological sense of the term. Sometimes it has arisen directly out of these very texts, as much medieval art sprang from the biblical story.

The advantage of such a tradition lies in its coherence and centrality; its danger resides in petrifaction and trivial exegesis. No modern discipline has a comparable centrality, though all, by the very nature of modern knowledge which, as I have said, is essentially dynamic, offer continual challenges to reconstructuring. The former queen, Theology, has fallen from her high estate; in the schools, imposed as 'religious instruction', the impact made by religion on the majority is at best peripheral, at worst leads to repugnance. Many of the other disciplines reveal no more of a 'way' than is inherent in the pursuit of them. The moral training here implicit is not negligible—but it is hardly co-extensive with the total moral life.

The issue I am raising is that mooted by Aristotle when he asserts that it is not clear 'whether education is more concerned with intellectual or with moral virtue'. The western world has, for a long time, as I have noted, been increasingly reluctant to impose any moral restraints on the expansion of knowledge. The modern ideal has been profoundly affected by the dynamic and 'open' quality of science, in which most things have become lawful—even, under the Nazis, experiments on human beings. Whereas in the past knowledge has often had a moral connotation—as in the famous Socratic dictum 'Virtue is Knowledge'—the tendency has been for modern knowledge, in its most typical, scientific manifestation, to become ethically neutral.

It is partly because of this development that modern culture has failed to play the role assigned to it by Arnold in keeping up 'superiorities'; for Arnold's 'superiorities' are ethical in implication. His ideal of culture is ultimately Greek in origin; it stems from the notions of *arete* and *paideia*. Behind the Greek idea was usually an ideal of conduct to which 'knowledge', in the sense of positive knowledge, should be subordinate; certainly, after Democritus, 'pure' scientific speculation becomes in Socrates and Plato subordinate to ethical considerations: 'I have nothing to do with physical speculations', Socrates says in the *Apology*. When, then, Socrates urged that Virtue is Knowledge, he had a particular view of knowledge in mind; it was not the positive knowledge which predominates in modern thought, but a 'way' of behaviour which included an understanding of principle, an apprehension, part intellectual, of the nature of the Good,[1] and an awareness of the means to action. Thus action constantly comes under the scrutiny of the Good; indeed, properly conceived, it sprang out of the prior achieved contemplation of the Form of the Good. 'It is not being alive that one should value most, but making a proper *use* of being alive.' In Socrates, Homeric mimesis is replaced by the consciously shaped *Bios*, the life self-consciously arranged in relation to the good end to be achieved. In the modern world, much knowledge has ceased to be moralized. The tendency is even to reduce morality itself to the role of a datum—an object of investigation. Distinctions of value falter before widespread pressure simply to know and to report the findings of knowledge. The empirical world has taken its subtle revenge on the 'superiority' of the knowledge of the Good. For the modern conception of the knowledge of the Good has itself become a process of endless questioning, not an assured and accepted set of beliefs.

Hence the emphasis, even in the education of the majority, has changed. An important Ideal Type of the modern educational system has become the 'autonomous type of character': 'The ideal is that the individual will develop as Kant put it "as a law-making member of a kingdom of ends". He must not only come to know what is in general right and wrong; he must also go beyond the level of what Plato called *orthodoxa*, so that he sees why such rules are right and wrong and can revise rules and make new ones in the light of new knowledge and new

---

[1] The nature of Socratic 'Knowledge' in the aphorism 'Virtue is Knowledge' has been interestingly argued by John Gould in *The Development of Plato's Ethics*. Mr. Gould makes out an interesting case for the knowledge concerned to be 'knowledge how' rather than 'knowledge that' and draws attention to the way in which Socratic *episteme* comes in part to be subserved under the heading of a *techne*: he finds the fundamental aim of Socrates in the search for 'certainty and assurance, not wholly of logic, but a principle of action, firmly founded upon an idealized competence'. (p. 66.) At the same time, it is clear that the Socratic conception did involve an intellectual aspect.

circumstances.' (R. S. Peters, 'Moral Education' in *Philosophy*, January 1962.) (Even in the midst of our growing collectivism, ethically we maintain a liberal stance.) Thus the ideal of the modern world exists at the opposite extreme to the Platonic attempt to induce fixed and settled forms, departure from which would mark the progress of decay. The educational effort in Plato's Magnesia was, where the mass of the people were concerned, one of *habituation*. A modern ideal is precisely the opposite—it is essentially one of flexibility, of adaptability. (To some extent, of course, this marks a difference of moral climate; the Greeks had not developed the notion of individual responsibility to the extent that the post-Christian world has.)

Yet the danger remains that the disappearance of any ethical authority can lead to the substitution of inferior models of behaviour. To transcend *orthodoxa*, a great deal of moral insight is needed; and such moral insight can only spring from a realization of the world and its ways young people cannot be expected to have. Life necessarily revolts against the petrifaction implicit in Platonic habituation; but if life is wise, it first seeks to understand what it is revolting against. A distaste for convention can itself become the most boring of conventions.

There arises, then, the question of the justification of this sort of learning, the reason why one insists that, whatever its inadequacies may be, the most able children must spend their time pursuing it. For one thing, such learning 'for its own sake' represents a very obvious extension of mental awareness which constitutes a value—and few institutions in our society are devoted to the fostering of it. Furthermore, the qualities of mind and personality needed for academic pursuits, rightly conceived, can have their own character training qualities which emerge in the very act and consequence of tackling complex disciplines (though the possibility that the knowledge gained might be put to bad ends should not be lost sight of). This, indeed, represents something more *morally* reputable—and certainly something more intelligent—than what usually passes for 'character' training in our English schools, which often emerges as a set of crude and insensitive attitudes related to the superiority of one herd

129

over another.[1] Furthermore, as we shall see later, some of the humanist disciplines are ethically relevant. They do not offer moral imperatives, backed by social or divine authority; but literature, for example, offers psychologically penetrating accounts of human behaviour and reveals, through the disposition of incidents and in the concrete clash of opposing wills and desires, the relative moral stress of the author. Such writings can, at the least, sensitize to the complexity of moral dilemmas and, in the hands of great authors, can help to build up criteria of acceptable moral behaviour. But again, great literature is only possible as a source-book to the sophisticated minority.

Perhaps the fundamental justification for modern learning lies in the enrichment of personality it can engender. The major disciplines (I refer to those studied in our English universities) rightly conceived, involve an expansion of the human being through his submission to what lies outside the self or to what truly lies within—this, indeed, is the answer to Dewey's subjectivism. Such disciplines, creations as they are of the human spirit at its most refined, exist as an order independent, in large measure, of man's wishes and desires; to come to terms with the reality implicit in them, to see their objects of attention as in themselves they really are (whether those objects are external in society or nature or internal in one's own being)[2] comprehend some of the most enriching experiences of which the human mind is capable.

There is, however, a further point to be made. In general, in this book, I am implying that the philosophy of education in so far as it is concerned with the question 'What ought our aims in education to be?' is a branch of moral philosophy. If I were forced to produce some all-embracing ethical principle in order to sustain the educational recommendations I am concerned to make

[1] This, of course, does raise the very difficult question of the role of loyalty in the education of the young; and were I here concerned with the education of the whole intelligence range, I would have to admit the inadequacy, partial at least, of what I have implied by my use of the word 'herd'. But here I am concerned only with the highly intelligent, those from whom we can expect responses in terms of individual moral judgments rather than through an appeal to group loyalties.

[2] To the extent, for instance, that the writing and reading of literature is a means to the discovery and ordering of the self: cf. the passage from D. H. Lawrence, quoted on p. 164.

here, I would have to assert that I was propounding a doctrine of self-realization in terms of that excellence which is proper to a human being. Such a view would have been much influenced by Aristotle and the Greek notion of *arete*.

Recently, however, moral philosophers have shown a good deal of scepticism concerning the usefulness of propounding some all-inclusive high level moral principle of this type. Thus Mr. J. C. Rees in speaking of 'The Relation between Political Theory and Political Practice' has urged that 'High level assertions concerning the nature of man, the good he should pursue and the goal that government should seek to attain cannot be applied to practice for the simple reason that they either say nothing or too much'. In the same way, the late Susan Stebbing also protested against too much abstraction from the actual concrete facts of the moral life and the consequent creation of 'unfruitful isolates'. For myself, I would not regard the proposition of some general ethical aim like that of self-realization as a complete waste of time. What, it seems to me, such a proposition represents is a gesture, a sign-post pointing in one direction rather than another. What, in effect, such a notion as self-realization warns us of is the need to consider, in concrete instances where educational decisions have to be taken, whether the possibilities inherent in the individual are being sufficiently considered—*vis-à-vis* the state, for instance—or whether there is a danger of 'social need' distorting the range of possibilities open to young people at any one time. (This, of course, is not to forget—and it is an indication of the complexity of the issues that such a high level principle needs to subsume under its general direction—that some people have found the highest form of self-fulfilment through obedience to the state; it is in realizing such complexities that one appreciates the ambiguities and vaguenesses inherent in such wholesale offerings.)

What, indeed, I prefer to do is what I am doing in this book— proffering a number of particular value judgments concerning what I think desirable in education. The higher the level of generality, the less concrete guidance is given and the more indeterminate the significance of what is said becomes. The attempt to state educational aims in the past has suffered

131

K

because, when such admittedly high-level terms as 'self-realization', 'good citizenship' and the like have been used to set them
forth, these have been left *too* vague and *too* open to misunder-
standing and misrepresentation and have thus offered little
guidance in concrete cases. In general, it can be said that a
curriculum is usually preferable to a general principle, a syllabus
preferable to a curriculum, and perhaps a set of suggestions to
read this book rather than that, listen to this piece of music
rather than that etc. is preferable to a syllabus. Nevertheless, in
a work of this sort, a certain level of generality must obviously
be allowed for.

So much, then, to characterize and justify—in general terms—
the nature of modern learning in its most sophisticated guise.
What problems arise out of the initiation of the able young into
this heritage of learning?

The greatest difficulty in writing of the education of able
children nowadays is that no one person knows enough to assess
such an education *as a whole*. For its main instrument is the
specialism; and one can only refer to such specialisms—and
they must inevitably be few—into which one has oneself some
insight and from which one can draw one's examples. The rest
must inevitably be tentative conjecture.

This must explain why, in commenting on the education of
such children, much must be in the form of suggestion of enterprises to be undertaken, of clarifications sought rather than of
defined syllabuses or concrete policy. Such policy could only be
the collaborative result of a number of specialists working
together.[1] It also explains why, in what follows, I call so frequently on illustrations drawn from literature—for that is the
discipline, practised in schools, of which I know most.

The problems of the able, as I see them, are of two kinds.
There are those which exist within the present framework of the
established disciplines, due to demands made on them by the

[1] The great difficulty here, of course, would be the egotism which inevitably
attaches itself to human endeavours and which tends to claim more for its chosen
specialism than it can sometimes bear. Thus the adjustment of the range and nature
of different specialisms one to another, the delineation and delimitation of educative
possibilities implicit in the sorts of mental and emotional demands the 'subjects'
made, would be matters of some delicacy.

nature of our technological society. These I take to be chiefly the question of the relationship between the so-called 'liberal' and the 'practical', and that of specialization. Associated is the more general problem of the 'two cultures', and the relative worth to be assigned to a humanist or scientific training. Secondly, there are certain social and personal issues which arise out of the selective policy on which the education of the able is based— particularly the problems which arise as a result of recent refine- ments of the creaming process and the cry for educational ex- pansion. In general, however, it can be said that the education of able children is, by and large, in a less unsatisfactory state than that of the 'average' child; at least, the avenues to available knowledge, broadly speaking, lie open—even if the intellectual climate in England is not propitious for their too zealous ex- ploration.

I will begin with a brief comment on specialization and then I will consider the relation of the 'liberal' to the practical.

I

The controversy over the relative merits of specialization and general education in sixth forms and universities proceeds; and, as is not unusual in educational discussion, it proceeds in a fug of imprecise terminology and unexamined assumptions. I would like, therefore, to make one or two suggestions which might enable us to think about the problem a little more clearly.

The first question to be asked is what precisely we mean when we talk of specialization. For instance, the word is commonly used to cover at least three broad areas of study. We may be referring to the study of a small number of either arts or science subjects; or we may intend a reference to the concentration on a particular subject, whether it belongs either to the arts or to the sciences; or we may have in mind a particular study within a subject-field, a study which may contain within it important intellectual possibilities (e.g. 'The Novels of Henry James'), or which may be characterized by a distressing triviality (e.g. 'An Examination of John Keats' Grocery Lists and their Implications for the Study of his Poetry'). For, of course, there is no such activity as 'specialization'; there are only particular concentrations on particular areas of knowledge; and these areas of knowledge are so distinguishable in educational value that to carry on the discussion in terms of generalities concerning the advisability of specialization or non-specialization as such is of little significance.

However, it may be argued that the discussion at sixth-form level at least is not in much doubt; what is intended here is usually a criticism of the exclusive concentration on either arts or science subjects. It is suggested that we must 'bridge the gap' by providing some balance within the non-specialist area; and controversy seems to concentrate mostly on how this is to be done, either through the provision of an examinable extra subject or through non-examinable 'half' or 'quarter' subjects or what have you.

The introduction of the quantitative note, frequently to be observed, serves as an index of the unfortunate level at which the discussion is being carried on; as if by some arithmetical process, irrespective of what the integers or fractions refer to, it is possible to produce an adequate educative experience. I would suggest, then, that to begin with we need some analysis of what is involved in the study of particular 'subjects'. For instance, when we talk about studying history, what do we imply? What does it *mean* to investigate the past? What I have in mind would constitute a philosophical examination, though at a fairly simple level. Furthermore, what do we imply by the study of the past at a particular stage of student development, that of the average sixth former? Only by some such sort of investigation spread over the whole field of sixth-form study can we begin to form some estimate of the educative possibilities implicit in any particular set of fields of human inquiry. And we shall have something more precise to go on than is provided by Mr. Peterson's 'four main categories of mental experience',[1] as well as some idea of what inter-linkings are advisable or possible.

In this sort of way, it might be possible to build up some notion of what the varied sets of specialisms we find in our

[1] Cf. A. D. C. Peterson, 'Arts and Science Sides in the Sixth Form', p. 15.

sixth-form syllabuses provide in the way of academic experience. What 'powers of the mind' are being extended, what sensitivities developed in this, that or the other combination of subjects ? In what do the lacks consist ? Can these lacks be supplied—and how ?[1] In addition, we could begin to form some estimate of what the ability to 'think' within the various subject fields really does necessitate. My own estimate, based on some insight into the four 'subjects' which at various times in my academic career of twenty-five years I have studied—some history, English literature, 'education' and a little philosophy—is that it normally implies a great deal, and that to move with any confidence within a particular subject-field—to 'think' within it—is, as I have stressed, a long and involved process. Indeed, it could be argued that one of the main objects of a mere three-year honours course is to reveal to undergraduates the extent of their ignorance.[2]

It is this as much as anything which makes me view any attempt to extend the sixth-form programme—e.g. to the extent of taking four, rather than three advanced subjects—and the new enthusiasm for the general degree in universities with some suspicion. I suspect that, except with the most exceptional student, what will be acquired over so wide a spread will be little more than an 'informational' knowledge in the pejorative sense of the word. Indeed, I regard the present pattern of general degrees, with their pyramidal structure, broad based and leading

[1] Such an analysis, too, would assist in the answering of the fundamental Socratic question, 'Which knowledge is most worth ?'

[2] The difficulty here, it will be urged, lies in the fact that, as I have already made clear above, experts differ in their views as to the nature of their chosen disciplines. This, of course, is true—and incidentally invigorating. But that does not mean that it is not possible to arrive at broad areas of agreement, so that even the disagreements exist within their framework; and so that we can arrive at a general picture of what was inevitably involved in the study of a particular discipline and of the boundaries within which its pursuit could legitimately be carried on. Furthermore, the very effort of analysis would be almost certainly widening and enriching, would open up possibilities of restructuring not before thought of. In my own experience, I am convinced that much bad teaching of literature arises out of the fact that most teachers have no real understanding of its nature—and therefore simply do not know what to do with a poem or a novel when they face a class. In training English teachers, I have found some such preliminary exploration a basic necessity. Nor need one confine oneself to one view of its nature.

to a narrowing at the top, as the wrong way to do things. There is a good case to be made out for intensive study to be followed by extensive study, rather than the other way round. The student at University, at least, would branch out *from* a specialism rather than move towards one. For, as one comes to acquire more confidence within a particular subject field, to see more of what it implies, the tendency should be to see its linkages and correlations with other subjects and to be led inevitably outwards rather than inwards. Here again, I speak from personal experience for this has been precisely my own academic development. Paradoxically, I believe that the cause of general education can best be served by a proper education in a specialism— and by 'proper' I mean one which goes deeply into the *nature* of the specialism; for to do this necessitates an appreciation of boundaries, and boundaries can only be drawn in terms of what lies over the wall as well as of what lies within. What indeed is wrong with current specialisms is not the fact of concentration on particular areas of study—which can be immensely rewarding intellectually and morally—but the way in which very often the speciality is treated; not, that is, as a mode of apprehension in our complex life, not with regard to the fundamental structure and nature of the subject, but all too often as a collocation of factual material which reveals, to the interested mind, nothing of its philosophic nature.

II

When, as a result of social and intellectual pressures, the curriculum for the 'secondary' stage broadened out in the later nineteenth century, it is feasible to argue that a now discredited psychological theory helped to preserve the notion of a 'liberal' rather than a utilitarian-vocational—which often implied a 'practical'—emphasis in studies. Even the study of the classics, under fire from progressive thinkers of the seventeenth and eighteenth centuries, received a new *raison d'être* at the hands of the inter-related theories of faculty psychology, mental discipline and the transfer of training. With the assistance of these theories, it was possible to combine both the notions of liberality and utility. By assisting 'general cultivation', the classics, it was argued, were also preparing the grounds for specific understanding; once the mind had been trained, it could apply itself to the particular without difficulty.

The pressure for direct vocationalism, indeed, might have proved stronger if this disguised form of utility had not protected the wider curriculum; or if the classical syllabus had not provided a reasonable if somewhat disguised form of training for rulers. But, for a variety of reasons, in recent years, the overt division between the 'liberal' and the 'practical' (or 'useful' in some of its manifestations) has been wearing thin; partly this is because it is obvious that certain sorts of 'practical' work—the application of science to industry, for instance—in fact make severe, if narrow, intellectual demands. Thus, though the Spens committee advocated the notion of 'mental discipline', it also urged that there is 'no educational heresy so serious as the belief that culture and practical utility are mutually exclusive' (p. 161). In this view, the committee may have been influenced by Whitehead's contention:

'The insistence in the Platonic culture on disinterested intellectual appreciation is a psychological error.[1] Action and our implication in the transition of events amid the inevitable bond of cause to effect are fundamental. An education which strives to divorce intellectual or aesthetic life from those fundamental facts carries with it the decadence of civilization. Essentially culture should be for action, and its effect should be to divest labour from the association of aimless toil.'[2] (*Aims of Education*, pp. 73–74.)

[1] And, of course, by Dewey; cf. *The Quest for Certainty*, when the notion of 'Thought' as a 'mode of directed, overt action' is put forward. In *Democracy and Education* the technical and the cultural are brought together quite explicitly.

[2] Whitehead, of course, is mistaken in suggesting that the ultimate aim of Platonic culture was simply 'disinterested intellectual inquiry'. The ultimate aim of Platonic knowledge was action; the difference between Plato and the Sophists lay in the degree of preparation for action they thought necessary. The Sophists were more immediately pragmatic; they looked to rhetoric as an immediate means of affecting people and hence policy. Plato demanded a long initial philosophical training, leading to the knowledge of the Good; but the final aim was still the practice of statesmanship; the understanding so gained was to purify the life of

Even the goal of 'disinterested scientific curiosity' Whitehead considers is the 'marriage of action to thought . . . No man of science wants merely to know.' (p. 74) This, actually, is untrue in fact; thus an American sociologist recently observed, in a critique of British research: 'Many scholars intentionally select subjects which in their judgment, have no foreseeable application.' It suggests that what Whitehead is doing is perpetrating a disguised value judgment—that is, he prefers 'practical' science to 'pure' science and suggests that 'disinterested' intellectual appreciation is in some unexplained way a mark of 'decadence'.

Such a view, does, however, lead him to an important conclusion about the relation between 'technical' ('practical') and liberal education: the traditional antithesis between them he describes as 'fallacious'. Now, this desire to assimilate the 'liberal' and the 'practical' has affected modern notions about the nature of 'knowledge' and hence about the curriculum a good deal. If one equates earlier ideas of what constituted 'liberal knowledge' with knowledge for its own sake, without immediate practical application[1] and regards the traditional view of 'technical' knowledge as that which enabled people to *act* efficiently within a certain range of situations calling for the application of learned skills, one can see that, in our thinking about the curriculum in recent years, we have tended to extend the range of educational situations within which 'activity' rather than an assimilation of 'disinterested' knowledge would be advocated. In *this* sense the 'technical' has invaded the liberal.

For instance, what were formerly regarded as bodies of knowledge have come to be regarded as modes of apprehension,

---

action. Cf. 'On the Origin and Cycle of the Philosophic Ideal of Life', reprinted in Werner Jaeger, *Aristotle*. It is doubtless true, however, that the ideal of the theoretic life does derive from certain aspects of Plato, certain emphases of his later works.

[1] This, as Paulsen shows, was implicit in the development of the German universities in the nineteenth century, when 'as a rule the university teacher has gradually forsaken active practice for the pursuit of pure science' and the philosophical faculty in particular became 'purely theoretical' (p. 64). Hence the tendency, in academic circles influenced by German developments in that period, to look down on technical knowledge as inferior—a tendency which has persisted in this country, but which in Germany in 1907, Paulsen considered, was quickly disappearing (p. 113).

'tools' for thinking with, or describable in other terms which suggest an active and instrumental orientation. To put it another way, 'knowing how' has come to seem more important than 'knowing that'.[1] I will illustrate something of what I mean from Professor Nowell-Smith's inaugural lecture on 'Education and the University'; for his view of the university curriculum has its relevance to the school situation. After asserting that a University is 'an institution for the advancement and dissemination of knowledge', Nowell-Smith considers what is meant by 'knowledge': 'For the word "knowledge" is ambiguous. It may mean "information" and this is what it does mean to many undergraduates and, I am sorry to say, to many dons. But it may also mean skill, know-how, the ability to find out. And this, I suggest, is what it should mean when we speak of a University as an institution for the advancement and dissemination of knowledge. It is an institution in which the dons apply to the advancement of knowledge the skills they have learnt and in which they transmit these skills to their students. To avoid this ambiguity I shall drop the word "knowledge" and speak of information and skills. Our aim should not be to pump into the students as much information as they can absorb in three years; it is to teach them skills, to equip them with the ability to find out.' (p. 4.) Now, Professor Nowell-Smith weights the scales, in some degree, by equating 'knowing that' with 'information', which is a word often carrying a pejorative implication ('The merely well-informed man is the most useless bore on God's earth.') The use of the words 'skill' and 'know-how' indicate the extent to which knowledge is coming to be looked upon as a tool, as a device either for the further amplification of knowledge (which surely, here, must mean 'knowing that'?) within a particular field or for use in the elucidation of 'problems' in

[1] Recently there have been attempts to point out that science itself progresses because it has given up the idea that the job of the scientist is in any way the contemplation of truth: 'The whole reason why modern science is inherently progressive, where classical natural philosophy was not, is that the scientific revolution abandoned treating theory as "truth" and regarded it merely as a tentative formula for *doing* things—with the implication (utterly alien from classical culture) that it is by handling the world that we live and know.' (J. Ward-Lewis, *Time and Tide*, 24 August 1961.)

everyday life, when it becomes assimilated to Dewey's instrumental view of knowledge. (Nowell-Smith appears to hold both views, for his aim in the education of scientists would be to enable people to think scientifically, and in that of the Humanities, to 'teach those skills that are required for living'.) I will begin by dealing with the first of these.

This shift in our attitude to knowledge has been assisted in our time, by a view of man which tends to equate what he *is* with what he *does*, so that what constitutes intelligent 'thought' is equated with the overt manifestations of rational behaviour—'thinking', as it were. The emphasis in Ryle's philosophically influential *Concept of Mind* is on 'knowing how' rather than 'knowing that', in that 'Efficient practice precedes the theory of it': 'In ordinary life . . . as well as in the special business of teaching, we are much more concerned with people's competences than with their cognitive repertoires, with the operations than with the truths that they learn. Indeed even when we are concerned with their intellectual excellences and deficiencies, we are interested less in the stocks of truths that they acquire and retain than in their capacities to find out truths for themselves and their ability to organize and exploit them, when discovered.' (p. 28.) And again: 'To find that most people have minds (though idiots and infants in arms do not) is simply to find that they are able and prone to do certain sorts of things, and this we do by witnessing the sorts of things they do.' Ryle does not deny the possibility of the assimilation of a body of truths—'knowing that'; but he assigns to it a very subordinate place.

The effect, then, is to equate the valuable in learning with what it enables people to do rather than with what it permits them to know; and this is in line with an educational programme which stresses, in the notorious words of the Primary School Report, 'activity and experience rather than . . . knowledge to be acquired and facts to be stored'. Hence, when the Spens Committee agreed with those witnesses that 'the studies of the ordinary secondary school should be brought into closer contact with the practical affairs of life' (p. 162), its view was tempered by the belief that such practical affairs, involving the encouragement of the 'utility phase' in children's development, could itself be made an agency of 'liberal education'; for it would lead to activity being permeated by insight so that the resulting operations could be described as 'intelligent' in Ryle's connotation of the conceptual working of the term.

But, of course, the advocates of 'pure', 'theoretical' or 'disinterested' learning continue to press their case—the three adjectives have different connotations, but they are often used as though they were roughly synonymous. I think that the quarrel between those who advocate this type of learning—roughly, 'knowing that'—as the proper job of the bright child at school and even more particularly at University, and those who stress the desirability of acquiring skills, know-how, etc.—'knowing how'—could be illumined if it were realized that 'subjects' differ in the extent to which they offer scope for the two types of knowing; and, secondly, that, as I have hinted above, what is at stake is usually a value judgment as to the relative merit of the different sorts of knowledge. What, then, is needed is once again a conceptual analysis of what it *can* mean to 'know' history, a science, a modern language, English literature, and the like. This would reveal, for instance, that we can be said to 'know' a subject—let us say, history—in a number of different ways. Thus, one way of 'knowing' history would be to know a great number of facts about a particular period etc.; and to know history in this way is, to some people, intellectually satisfying. Another way in which we may be said to 'know' history, however, would involve being able to think historically, that is, being able to comprehend the events as a pattern of occurrences having some sort of significance beyond the mere sequence of events. (This, of course, would be only *one* way of thinking historically, and a philosophical investigation into the nature of history would produce a number of theories as to what thinking historically implied, including, perhaps, the view that it is simply comprehending a sequence of events.)

Now, when we maintain a preference for the latter way of looking at history, as a mode of thinking about the past, rather than as a reservoir of information, we perpetrate a value judgment. We choose to study history in this way rather than that, that is, not because what is meant by 'studying history' could not legitimately be comprised under either heading, but because we think that the consequences of studying it the one way are likely to be more valuable than if we study it the other. There are many ways of studying most 'subjects'; and it may as I have suggested be partly fashion which determines which is most acceptable at any one time. Often it is possible to undertake the same piece of study from two quite different points of view—one 'academic' and 'disinterested', the other 'practical'. Thus Rousseau's *Emile* can be read as an eighteenth-century piece of writing formulating certain problems and their answers which have an interest in the theoretical understanding of how the eighteenth century conceived education. And this would be a perfectly legitimate way of reading the book. But it is also possible to regard it as a practical handbook, as an attempt to provide answers to problems which recur in education and from which we can acquire some understanding as to how to respond to what can be termed 'practical' problems: the handling of children in a learning situation. Some of the ethical advice belongs very much to the category of 'practical' knowledge.

If, then, the 'liberal' and the 'practical' or dispositional (the 'technical' in some sense) are to a certain extent in process of assimilation it is partly because our age values doing over contemplation. Both the 'liberal' and the 'practical' come to be regarded as manifestations of 'knowing how'; and it is through the *activities* of the 'knower' that his superior intelligence can be judged. There is not intelligence and conduct; there is only intelligent conduct. There is not knowledge *and* activity; there is only activity guided by knowledgeable insight. Thus 'subject-mindedness' can be defended on the grounds that 'subjects' are no longer to be conceived as 'inert' bodies of knowledge but are the vehicles to intelligent behaviour in certain branches of human activity. This, in effect, lies behind the Crowther approval of specialization, in that 'the job of the Sixth Form is above all to teach a boy to think and not to memorize facts'.

In appreciating, however, this assimilation of the 'technical' and the 'liberal' in the terms in which they have so far been discussed, it is nevertheless important to recognize that to contrast 'knowing how' with 'knowing that' (in certain contexts particularly) perpetrates a false distinction. For instance, to take the sentence from the Crowther report just quoted, there is no such process as simply teaching children how to think; they must always think about something, and the exact nature of their 'thinking' will be controlled by the nature of the subject-matter. Yet it is not possible for them to begin to 'think' within the subject without some acquaintance with relevant fact; it is through the correlation and manipulation of relevant facts that the thought-process exists at all, for such processes, as we have noted, cannot exist in a vacuum. It may sometimes be untrue that there are *two* processes, that of acquiring the facts and then the thinking about them; there may instead be different ways of learning the facts, of arranging them, or having them arranged, in the mind—simpler or more complex, sophisticated ways. But, conversely, in the very act of 'knowing how' it is also necessary to 'know that'; the facts are part of the total pattern of learning.

I come, now, to the second use of the word 'practical', noted above. Some knowledge is said to be 'practical' in that it enables us to pursue knowledge within its own field—which is what we have been discussing. But some knowledge is also called 'practical' because it involves the use of knowledge acquired within these fields for social ends extraneous to the disciplines themselves. Thus historical knowledge can be used for understanding the present as a precursor to social action; and indeed this is how Dewey would want us to understand history. The danger here lies in the subtle falsification of the past that such an orientation of interest makes likely. The past existed in its own right and not simply as a stage of development in its progress to the present. To seek only for that historical understanding which will illumine the present is to run the danger of projecting the problems of the present into the past in order to seek their origins and thus to falsify the emphases which were characteristic of that past, emphases which initially may have paid little attention to what later came to predominate. Here, to study history for its own sake is to study history as it was, not as the concerns of the present would have us think it was.

Finally, there is knowledge which is called 'practical' because it is *by nature* knowledge which springs out of the actual activities carried out by men, and thus inevitably has specific social repercussions. Undoubtedly most of the fear of the practical (in university circles, for instance) stems from the last usage. For one thing, it is feared that the acceptance of the need to pursue the 'practical' in this last sense may well lead to the pursuit of trivial disciplines because they seem to serve strident social demands; the American University, as analysed by Flexner, proliferates 'university faculties of cookery and clothing', schools of journalism, business and the like and has obviously not escaped this danger; and it is right and proper that we should fight such trivialization of the curriculum here. But it does not follow from this that all manifestations of the 'practical' leading to social utility should be condemned. I would indeed suggest two criteria in terms of which the 'practical' in this sense should be admitted. In the first case, the pursuit of the 'practical' is not to be of such a kind that it distorts the nature of disciplines as a result of introducing extraneous criteria of arrangement and classification and thus does violence to the subject; secondly we need to judge the acceptability of any 'practical' skills by assessing the degree of mental complexity involved—the extent to which the activity in question depends on intelligence and the assimilation of principles which require, for their understanding, high mental capacity.

I would conclude, that we must be very careful before we try to replace the notion of knowledge for its own sake by the notion of knowledge as a tool. That it is correct, in certain contexts, to regard both as legitimate ways of learning carries with it, in an era dominated by Deweyan pragmatism, the need to reassert the importance of seeking disinterested understanding, both as a means to personal satisfaction and as a mode of comprehension demanded by the nature of certain disciplines in certain of their guises. Each discipline differs, of course, in the range of opportunities it affords; our aim should be to exploit this range of possibilities to the full.

The emphasis on 'practicality' is very much in line with recent emphasis on technical education as such as a means to the further implementation of the affluent society. Whatever the virtues of technical progress—and it would be stupid to deny that they are considerable—a too exclusive emphasis on the technical contains dangers for our psychic health which apologists for 'progress' too easily brush aside. I can best illustrate what I mean by considering the difference in kind between the scientific-technological and literary modes of apprehension, a difference which has recently been popularized under the heading of the 'Two Cultures'. I will consider, in this respect, Sir Charles Snow's Rede lecture; and I will use the opportunity to explore Sir Charles' indictment of the literary writer and to comment in particular on his preference for the current technological trend of events. For his views ('educational imperatives' he called them in his broadcast version) have important implications for our sixth-form curriculum.

III

Ever since the seventeenth century, the widening gap between literature and the sciences has evoked controversy and mutual recrimination. Newton dismissed poetry as 'a kind of ingenious nonsense'; Thomas Sprat, the historian of the Royal Society, referred to the wits and writers as 'this pleasant but unprofitable sort of men'. In due course, the writers came to reply in kind. Swift makes us laugh at the Academy of Lagado. Blake prayed:

> *May God us keep*
> *From Single vision and Newton's sleep!*

Though in Blake's day and for some time after, writer and scientist were still capable of understanding what each was up to.

In his recent Rede lecture, Sir Charles Snow is concerned about the fact that today scientist and writer comprehend each other so little that it is almost as if they were living in two separate 'cultures' or societies. The intellectual life of the Western world, he asserts, is being split into 'two polar groups'; at the one pole we find the literary intellectuals, at the other the scientists, particularly the physical scientists. Between the two there is a gulf of 'mutual incomprehension' of such magnitude that they can no longer find much common ground even on the emotional level. The non-scientists regard the scientists as 'shallowly optimistic', he thinks; the scientists look upon the literary intellectuals as lacking in social foresight, unconcerned about their fellow men, 'in a deep sense anti-intellectual'. Members of both groups can perhaps equally appreciate man's personal tragedy of isolation and aloneness; but they have very different views from one another about man's political and social condition. 'Most of our fellow human beings,' Sir Charles asserts, 'are underfed and die before their time. In the crudest terms, that is the social condition.' The scientist, he thinks, wishes to serve his fellow-men by helping to banish hunger. But he describes as 'broadly true' a statement by a scientist to the effect that nine out of ten of the writers who have dominated literary sensibility from 1914 to 1950 have been 'politically wicked' and that their influence, for example, brought 'Auschwitz that much nearer'; he mentions specifically Yeats, Pound and Wyndham Lewis.

Now this is a surprising indictment. For it is possible to argue that what has characterized the twentieth-century writer has been the extent to which he has felt drawn towards the social problems of the day. During the thirties it was the writers who warned about the growing menace of Nazism; as they saw many of their fellow-men take the road to Wigan Pier, they committed themselves to palliatory political programmes at home by moving 'forward from liberalism'; a number sacrificed their lives in Spain:

> *We were the prophets of a changeable morning*
> *Who hoped for much but saw the clouds forewarning*
>
> *　　　*　　　*
>
> *Spain was a death to us, Munich a warning*

as Day Lewis put it. Indeed, it might be urged that it was the all-too-direct commitment of writers like Koestler, Orwell, Spender, Auden—to mention only a few who were influential during the thirties—which detracted from the quality of their work by associating them with attitudes too over-simplified to produce great writing. Certainly to suggest that they and their like are responsible for Auschwitz is inaccurate. To press the political wrong-headedness of an untypical figure like Pound would be the equivalent of indicting post-war scientists because of the defection of men like Fuchs and Pontecorvo. And it is perhaps relevant to add that gas chambers were not invented by literary men.

The main point of Sir Charles' argument, however, is that this division between literary intellectuals and scientists, 'this polarization is sheer loss to us all'. If we ask him why, we find in effect that he has two answers. One is an intellectual one. He hints at stimulating intellectual results which would come about as a consequence of a closer rapport. He thinks that there are creative possibilities when two subjects or disciplines cross-fertilize or in some way stimulate or rub up against each other: 'In the history of mental activity that has been where some of the breakthroughs came,' he considers.

Now, I have some sympathy with this view of loss sustained. Certainly writers too easily sneer at 'illiterate' scientists without appreciating their own ignorance of what precisely it is to pursue the intellectual adventure of science. They have not been ready, as Wordsworth thought they should, to carry 'sensation into the midst of the objects of . . . science itself'. If the writer's theme, following Henry James, is 'felt life', then the 'felt life' of scientific discovery, for instance the effect on human personality and human relationships of pursuing knowledge under certain conditions, is as relevant a subject as any. Whether any such attempt to treat of pure science would induce the sort of 'breakthrough' Sir Charles has in mind, however, is more questionable. Had he been speaking of the social sciences, where human behaviour is in question, the prospects for cross-fertilization would have been a good deal rosier. There, the nature or even statement of a problem can often be illumined by a literary insight. But without deprecating Sir Charles' belief that the scientific edifice of the physical world 'is the most beautiful and wonderful *collective* work of the mind of man' (the emphasis is mine), it is difficult to see how literary insight and scientific theorizing can cross-fertilize except in the most general and abstract way. Twentieth-century science is admittedly a very

147

L

different matter from nineteenth-century science; so that we need to admit a degree of personal involvement and a certain arbitrariness in conceptualization which has destroyed the earlier scientists' claim to depict 'reality'. Here, then, perhaps, we can note an 'artistic', because personal and subjective element, in scientific work. Furthermore, since the eighteenth century and the decay of Christian and classical mythologies, the writer may be said to have been 'scientific' to the extent that he has sought the visible universe unencumbered by allegorical convention. Yet when we look at the concrete particulars of the way the two disciplines develop, we see that the *degree* of personal involvement is very different in the two cases. As an important part of its function, science is concerned with making descriptive statements about the regularities in our experience and is to that extent in the grip of the facts. The greatest writers, on the other hand, express a unique vision which is only imperfectly communicable. They generalize to the extent that they deal with our common world; but through their highly personal use of language, they explore their view of our common experience in a way which demands of us a high degree of empathy leading at best to a relatively imperfect assimilation. The coherence they seek is an emotional one; one of quite a different nature from that of the scientist. Moreover, the 'pure' scientist reports on what he finds, irrespective of its implications or of his feelings about it; his question is 'How do things behave?' The great novelists and dramatists select in accordance with a scale of personal values, revealed through the choices of behaviour made by their characters; the writer's problem is the ontological mystery. What perhaps the literary artist can give the scientist is a degree of personal flexibility. What the scientist can give the artist is a measure of impersonality which tempers the idiosyncratic by the need to assimilate common features of a common world. Furthermore, the fact of antagonism is very real on the part of many of the greatest writers; and it suggests that in some way the writer feels the scientific approach to be inimical to his outlook and attitude.

However, the other reason why Sir Charles regrets the lack of understanding between the two cultures is, from his point of view, much the more important one. For he most regrets the indifference or hostility of the literary intellectual to the applications of science. By such application, he asserts, people can be fed and kept alive: 'Industrialization is the only hope of the poor.' He lumps together a number of literary objectors to industrialization—Ruskin, William Morris, Thoreau, Emerson and Lawrence—and dismisses their protests as 'kinds of fancies which were not in effect more than screams of horror'.

Now, of course, here Sir Charles is being a moralist. Although he *talks* of a mutual impoverishment brought about by the cleavage between the two cultures, his sympathies seem to be with the scientists; it is they who have most to offer. Their arguments, we read, are 'usually much more rigorous, and almost always at a higher conceptual level than literary persons' arguments'. Above all, where the moral life is concerned, the scientists, he says: 'are by and large the soundest group of intellectuals we have; there is a moral component right in the grain of science itself'. He looks at the purpose inherent in the practice of applied science and technology and finds that it is good. So that in fact the main aim of his paper is to persuade us to accept the 'scientific revolution', leading to the 'industrial society of electronics, atomic energy, automation'; he wants us to get on with the job of preparing our youth more fully for it. In this way we will catch up with the Americans and Russians, who are praised for being 'more sensitive to the world they are living in'.

Now here, in this matter of the *application* of science, what is at stake between the two cultures is not so much a gap of incomprehension as a clash of moralities. For many writers have been aware of the moral component at the heart of applied science, which can be summed up in the Baconian precept 'Knowledge is Power.' The notion 'Knowledge is Power' implies as much a moral imperative as a statement of fact: such knowledge, such power, it is suggested, are good in that they are 'for the benefit and use of life'. The utilitarian ethos is implicit in the Baconian undertaking as it has been in that of the engineer ever since: the criterion of usefulness has implied a moral contract that it shall be a use for good.

The literary intellectuals have protested because they have grasped the implications of the Baconian position and disliked them. And they have for a very long time protested in a way which makes Sir Charles' dismissal of them as uttering mere 'screams of horror' irresponsible. At the heart of their discontent, repeated time and time again and especially during the nineteenth and twentieth centuries, lies a distaste for that stimulation of the assertive will which appears always to accompany the development of technical control over the forces of nature. During the period of the renaissance, artistic culture was replaced by the desire for technical mastery. The difference this made can be sensed, as Professor L. C. Knights has pointed out, in the varied use of metaphor as employed by Shakespeare and Bacon. In Shakespeare, the complexity of metaphor is exploratory, a mode of defining the meaning; in Bacon, the function of metaphor is purely illustrative, exemplifying a meaning already fully defined. And Bacon looks forward to a sort of writing 'reducing all things as near the mathematical plainness as they can', of which the Royal Society approved. Men, it is argued, have been the worse off for the change, in that they have been denied sensitivities of apprehension and definition relevant to balanced psychic development.

Against this spirit of rationality the romantics protested, as they protested against that alienation of man from nature which has also sprung from his increasing desire to control its processes. Their stress is placed on 'The gravitation and the filial bond / Of nature, that connect him with the world.' And as, in the *Prelude*, Wordsworth defines this relationship, it is seen in essence to be a very different sort of relationship from the one implicit in the engineer's exploitation of the natural world for material ends.

My point is that the objections of the literary intellectuals to the trend of events Sir Charles is concerned to further have a long history; moreover, they are based ultimately on considerations of psychic and spiritual health. The writers whom Sir Charles dismisses as uttering 'various kinds of fancies' in fact commit themselves at the profoundest levels to an examination of the human condition in the sort of society Sir Charles has in

150

mind. D. H. Lawrence is one of the writers he refers to. Now, one of Lawrence's major themes involves a concern for the psychological implications of the sort of rationalistic civilization in which we live, one brought about by technical developments with their ethics of abundance. Far from ignoring the question of starvation, Lawrence faces it quite squarely when, in *Women in Love*, Birkin asks Gerald Crich what he lives for:

' "What do I live for?" he repeated. "I suppose I live to work, to produce something, in so far as I am a purposive being. Apart from that, I live because I am living."

' "And what's your work? [asks Birkin]. Getting so many more tons of coal out of the earth every day. And when we've got all the coal we want, and all the plush furniture, and piano-fortes, and the rabbits are all stewed and eaten, and we're all warm and our bellies are filled and we're listening to the young lady performing on the pianoforte—what then? What then, when you've made a real fair start with your material things?" '

Even then, while we accept the force of Gerald Crich's reply:

' "We haven't got there yet . . . A good many people are still waiting for the rabbit and the fire to cook it." ' even, that is, as Lawrence faces us with the fact of scarcity and want, we are made aware, in the outcome of the book, that means to abundance such as Sir Charles has in mind contain implications for human relationships which need to be questioned. For example, Gerald Crich wishes to rationalize the working of the coal mines; his purposes are bound up with what Lawrence calls the 'plausible ethics of production': 'He had a fight to fight with Matter, with the earth and the coal it enclosed. This was the sole idea, to turn upon the inanimate matter of the underground, and reduce it to his will. And for this fight with matter, one must have perfect instruments in perfect organization, a mechanism so subtle and harmonious in its workings that it represents the single mind of man, and by its relentless repetition of given movement, will accomplish a purpose irresistibly, inhumanly. It was this inhuman principle in the mechanism he wanted to construct that inspired Gerald with an almost religious exaltation.'

Some Problems in the Provision of Academic Education

It would be perfectly proper to ask Lawrence to reveal positively those aspects of our human nature in terms of which he indicts industrialization and mechanization for its 'inhumanity'. In effect it was a major effort of his whole work to make just such a definition. If, therefore, I urge in generalized terms that he wished to reawaken the old spontaneous intuitive faculties, the direct sensuous awareness of the external world in immediate contact before perception was clouded by the abstractness of modern rationalism, and an acceptance of the 'otherness' of other people which denies the right of the assertive will to dominate in personal relationships, it must be realized that such generalities have behind them a great deal of concrete presentation in the body of his books. Without such intuitive contact, he thought, rightly or wrongly, the life of the great majority of people was a dislocation. And with the widespread incidence of neurosis characteristic of our times, who will dare simply to dismiss his diagnosis as a 'scream of horror'?

Yet Sir Charles has forcefully faced us with a fundamental issue of our times. He sees in the further development of industrialization an escape from the horrors of starvation and deprivation; and, of course, he is to that extent right. It is, however, matter for regret that he so peremptorily dismisses profound insights which, accepted and assimilated, might help us to make the further spread of industrialization a more humanly satisfying thing than it has been in the past. We have been warned before that Man does not live by bread alone.

I would conclude, then, that the ways in which the pure scientist approaches experience and the way in which the literary artist does are considerably different, and that where the *applications* of science are concerned, it is two different views of the moral, human personality which are at stake. There are, indeed, certain incompatibilities of outlook as between the 'two cultures'; and it is as well to take this into account when framing syllabuses.[1] For what are in question are two conflicting views of the ends of human existence.

[1] Another way of approaching the problem of the two cultures and of revealing their incompatibilities is that adopted by Professor Stuart Hampshire in a recent review in the *New Statesman* (6 January 1961): 'We now have the habit of writing

152

IV

In view of Sir Charles' open preference for the scientific approach, a preference which carries with it a growing preponderance of intellectual opinion, so that, in fact, Sir Charles exhibits a trend (the very popularity of this lecture which, when all is said and done, contained little that men like Huxley were not stating, rather more carefully, in the later years of the last century, is symptomatic), it is as well to reassert the grounds on which the centrality of literature is based. In general, the syllabus for our able children contains too little emphasis on the arts, for they must be the great vehicles through which the affective life is ordered. Here, however, in speaking of able children, we shall be concerned with the study of literature in its most conscious and sophisticated guise. This will inevitably raise the question as to the extent to which such extension of consciousness can be expected in the community at large.

The great apologist for literature of our times, the man who has made the highest claims for its educative function, has been Dr. Leavis. It is pre-eminently to an education in literature that Dr. Leavis assigns the task of that training in moral awareness and sensitivity which reacts centrally on the problems of living. Not only is it true, from the side of the literary 'specialist', that

about two cultures, the scientific and literary, of deploring their separation and of looking for a cure in education. But there is a deeper and older division concealed beneath these facile terms: the division between reason and imagination. After the standards of reason had been finally set by the physical sciences and mathematics, there remained the philosophical defence that still the human mind itself is substantially outside the reach of any similar rational understanding. This has been the anxious theme of philosophical speculation from the time of Kant and Hegel until the present day. If an imaginative and not a rational understanding of human institutions, of art, religion and social life is alone possible, we can set a limit to scientific method; speculative philosophy and creative artists still have a territory of their own. But we cannot be sure of this dividing line, as earlier philosophers could not be sure of the possibility of an adequate physical science. The lists are drawn up on either side, and it is not an accident that almost all the great writers of this time have been suspicious of scientific method, and of the claims of reason in human affairs, while modern philosophers have been divided by the issue into two opposing schools. It is not easy to decide upon the relative place of the arts and sciences in education until this philosophic doubt is resolved.'

153

a 'real literary interest is an interest in man, society and civilization' (*The Common Pursuit*, p. 200); the obverse that a 'living
critical inwardness with literature, and a mind trained in dealing
analytically with it, would have improved much work undertaken in fields for which these qualifications are not commonly
thought of as among the essential ones, if they are thought of as
relevant at all' (ibid., p. 200) is also made. It is urged explicitly that 'thinking about political and social matters ought to
be done by minds of some real literary education, and done in
an intellectual climate informed by a vital literary culture.'
though the caveat 'I don't mean the ordinary academic kind'
is uttered.

Accepting the pervasive Leavisian invitation—'this is so,
isn't it?'—a closer scrutiny of the precise nature of the claims
being made and of the grounds and evidence on which they are
made, is necessary. The claims are large; no less, in fact, than
an asserted connection between a way of managing language and
spiritual health. Regarded diagnostically, the stages involved in
the argument are revealed in a comment on Shelley: 'in the
examination of his poetry the literary critic finds himself passing,
by inevitable transitions, from describing characteristics to
making adverse judgments about emotional quality; and from
these to judgments that are pretty directly moral; and so to a
kind of discussion in which, by its proper methods and in pursuit
of its proper ends, literary criticism becomes the diagnosis of
what, looking for an inclusive term, we can only call spiritual
malady.' (' "Thought" and Emotional Quality', *Scrutiny*,
Spring 1945.) Though Leavis would want to assert, I think, that
ideally the whole process is too subtle a one for wholly convincing demonstration and elucidation, he has, in fact, made a
number of references to the act of reading which provide further
insight into what he has in mind.

The claim that literature has a peculiarly powerful educative
role to play is, of course, no new one. Homeric poetry provided
one of the fundamentals of Greek education; that this was no
conventional influence (such as could be attributed to the study
of the Bible today) is attested by Plato's anxiety concerning the
moral influence exerted by some of the incidents and the censor-

ship he proposed. The basis of the influence, however, was mimetic, as of so much of Greek education, the imitation of models proposing themselves in characteristically heroic moulds, the *paradeigma*. This formed an important element even in later, more intellectualized education: '. . . if we remember that Plato's whole philosophy is built on the conception of pattern, and that he describes the Ideas as "patterns established in the realm of Being", we can easily see the origin of the category. The Idea of the "Good", . . . that universally applicable pattern, is directly descended from the models of heroic arete which were part of the old aristocratic code.' (Jaeger, *Paideia*, I, 34.) In earlier times, then, imitation provided the main influence; and it continued to form the basis of Plato's educational scheme for the less able in the *Laws*. Literature, rightly conceived, continued to provide the correct affective influence: 'That the child's soul . . . may not learn the habit of feeling pleasure and pain in ways contrary to the law and those who have listened to its bidding, but keep them company, taking pleasure and pain in the very same things as the aged—that, I hold, proves to be the real purpose of what we call our "songs". They are really spells for the soul, directed in all earnest to the production of the concord of which we have spoken.' (*Laws*, 659.) The influence was obviously conceived in good part to work at the unconscious level; the impact of poetry was a matter of assimilation rather than one of bringing to consciousness—the offspring, as it were, of a conversation in the Leavisian mode.

Leavis's approach to literature differs widely in that it involves a much greater emphasis on consciousness. We are, he and Denys Thompson assert in the introduction to *Culture and Environment*, committed to more consciousness; and the whole process of Leavisian criticism out of which his recommendations for the teaching of English are implied, stems from a conscious process of bringing to awareness this, that or the other facet of the complete *œuvre* before one—bringing to awareness for the very practice of discussion and 'verification' I have previously drawn attention to.

Yet to over-intellectualize the process is also to misrepresent it: 'Words in poetry invite us, not to "think about" and judge

155

but to "feel into" or "become"—to realize a complex experience that is given in words.' (*Common Pursuit*, p. 212.) In a sense, the final appeal is to the 'feel' of the situation: the 'tests of realization' depend on a complex interplay of feeling and awareness; the emphasis is on 'What the living thing feels like': 'the difference between that which has been willed and put there, or represents no profound integration, and that which grows from a deep centre of life' (p. 225). The difficulty of defining the precise boundaries between the more conscious intellectual part in creation and response, and that which 'affects', as it were (a defining which exists only for the sake of analysis and an intellectual 'thinking about', for, of course, in the perfected work the two aspects are perfectly fused),[1] is admirably illustrated in Leavis's analysis of Johnson and Shelley in *The Common Pursuit*. For Johnson, Leavis asserts, 'a moral judgment that isn't *stated* isn't there'; Johnson 'cannot understand that works of art *enact* their moral valuations' (p. 110). According to Johnson's implicit view, 'The dramatic must start with a conscious and abstractly formulated moral and proceed to manipulate his puppets so as to demonstrate and enforce it'. On the other hand, Shelley's faults lie at the other extreme to those of Johnson: 'His handling of emotion may not be "statement"; but in order to describe it, we need a parallel term. It is a matter of *telling* us; telling us "I feel like this", and telling us how we, the audience, are to feel . . . While Johnson starts with an intellectual and moral purpose, Shelley starts with an emotional purpose, a dead set at an emotional effect, and pursues it in an explicit mode that might very reasonably be called "statement" in contrast with the Shakespearean mode, which is one of presenting something from which the emotional effect (or whatever else) derives.'

While, therefore, Leavis's criticism may seem very much to be a matter of pointing, a proffering of evidence, a bringing to consciousness of this, that and the other 'effect', the criticism itsel is subsumed—if that is the word—by a sensitivity in depth which

---

[1] Note the Leavisian caveat: 'It is as pointers for use—*in* use—in the direct discussion of pieces of poetry that our terms and definitions have to be judged.' ('Imagery and Movement', *Scrutiny*, September 1945, p. 124.)

responds to movement and presentation as an essential, an integral part of what is itself abstracted for consideration and discussion; and the same is true of the imagery: 'What we are concerned with in analysis are always matters of complex verbal organization; it will not do to treat metaphors, images and other local effects as if their relation to the poem were at all like that of plums to cake. They are worth examining—they are there to examine—because they are foci of a complex life, and sometimes the context from which they cannot be even provisionally separated, if the examination is to be worth anything, is a wide one.' (*'Imagery and Movement'*, p. 119.) It is impossible to realize his intention in his essay, 'Imagery and Movement' without appreciating his extreme sensitivity to shifts and blends that characterize themselves in movement, in (to quote) 'a given kind of effort': 'In reading a successful poem it is as if, with the kind of qualification intimated, one were living that particular action, situation or piece of life; the qualification representing the condition of the peculiar completeness and fineness of art.' (*'Imagery and Movement'*, p. 123.) At the very moment, then, that one asserts the essential bringing to consciousness which is implicit in the Leavisian criticism, the force of 'living', 'enact', 'feel into' need their due stress—as matters of empathic projection as much as of consciousness.

The first stage in the process of Leavisian analysis, then, involves a completeness of reading, a nervous response to complex organizations of words that manifest some inevitable loss in abstraction as at the critic's behest, one's eye lights on 'this, that, and the other detail'. The passage in *Education and the University* is, of course, the classic expression of the activity involved: 'Analysis, one would go on, is the process by which we seek to attain a complete reading of the poem—a reading that approaches as nearly as possible to the perfect reading. There is about it nothing in the nature of "murdering to dissect", and suggestions that it can be anything in the nature of laboratory-method misrepresent it entirely. We can have the poem only by an inner kind of possession; it is "there" for analysis only in so far as we are responding appropriately to the words on the page. In pointing to them (and there is nothing else to point to) what we are doing is to bring into sharp focus, in turn, this, that and the other detail, juncture or relation in our total response; or (since "sharp focus" may be a misleading account of the kind of attention sometimes required), what we are doing is to dwell with a deliberate, considering responsiveness on this, that or the other node or focal point in the complete organization that the poem is, in so far as we have it. Analysis is not a dissection of something that is already and passively there. What we call analysis is, of course, a constructive or creative process. It is a more deliberate following-through of that process of creation in response to the poet's words which reading is. It is a re-creation in which, by a considering attentiveness, we ensure a more than ordinary faithfulness and completeness.' (*Education and the University*, p. 70.) And, it must be insisted, the process is one of collaboration: 'the poem builds up in this way, doesn't it?', 'this bears such-and-such a relation to that, don't you agree?' (*Education and the University*, p. 70.) Furthermore, it is one contained within the work in hand: 'The analysis and judgment of works of literary art belong to the literary critic, who *is* one in so far as he observes a disciplined relevance in response, comment and determination of significance. He is concerned with the work in front of him as something that should contain within itself the reason why it is so and not otherwise. The more experience—experience of life and literature together—he brings to bear on it the better, of course; and it is true that extraneous information may make him more percipient. But the business of critical intelligence will remain what it was: to ensure relevance of response and to determine what is actually *there* in the work of art. The critic will be especially wary how he uses extraneous knowledge about the writer's intentions. Intentions are nothing in art except as realized, and the tests of realization will remain what they were. They are applied in the operation of the critic's sensibility; they are a matter of his sense, derived from his literary experience, of what the living thing feels like—of the difference between that which has been willed and put there, or represents no profound integration, and that which grows from a deep centre of life. These tests may very well reveal that the deep animating intention (if that is the right word) is something

very different from the intention the author would declare.'
(*The Common Pursuit*, pp. 224–5.) It is necessary to lay stress on
the 'disinterested' nature of the process—the word is Leavis's
and, of course, Arnold's. And yet, paradoxically, as this, that
and the other detail become realized in the mind of the critic,
inevitably there takes place a process of assimilation, an assimilation to past experience, a delicate process of testing that issues
in judgment.

But this further stage—though to call it this is again to assert
distinctions where no distinctions appear in the total nature of
response—is most certainly not a matter of measuring against
an abstractly formulated standard. The word 'standard', peculiarly Leavisian though it is, offers notions of criteria indepen-
dently arrived at and applied which is foreign to Leavis's own
estimate of his practice: 'The critic—the reader of poetry—is
indeed concerned with evaluation, but to figure him as measuring
with a norm which he brings up to the object and applies from
the outside is to misrepresent the process. The critic's aim is,
first, to realize as sensitively and completely as possible this or
that which claims his attention; and a certain valuing is implicit
in the realizing. As he matures in experience of the new thing
he asks explicitly and implicitly: "Where does this come? How
does it stand in relation to . . .? How relatively important does
it seem?" And the organization into which it settles as a con-
stituent in becoming "placed" is an organization of similarly
"placed" things, things that have found their bearings with
regard to one another, and not a theoretical system or a system
determined by abstract considerations.' ('Criticism and Philosophy', *Common Pursuit*, p. 213.) The obvious influence is that
of Matthew Arnold's touchstones: 'Critics give themselves great
labour to draw out what in the abstract constitutes the characters of a high quality of poetry. It is much better simply to have
recourse to concrete examples.' ('The Study of Poetry.')

The process of evaluation, then, is one of throwing the assimilated and 'read' arrangement of words against a previously built
organization of responses. One imagines it to be a matter of ear
('feel') and sense combined. Consciousness is involved, for it is a
question of 'making fully conscious and articulate the immediate

sense of value that "places" the poem'. This process is one 'of relating and organizing, and the immediate sense of value should, as the critic matures with experience, represent a growing stability of organization (the problem is to combine stability with growth). What, on testing and re-testing and wider experience, turn out to be my more constant preferences, what the more relative permanencies in my response, and what structure begins to assert itself in the field of poetry with which I am familiar? What map or chart of English poetry as a whole represents my utmost consistency and most inclusive coherence of response?' Leavis suggests that perhaps a 'theoretical statement' derived from the particular judgments would be 'possible'; but the work he describes is, in his estimation, what needs to be done first. And he suggests that any such theoretical formulation would be 'too clumsy to be of any use': 'My whole effort was to work in terms of concrete judgments and particular analyses: "This—doesn't it?—bears such a relation to that; this kind of thing—don't you find it so?—wears better than that", etc. If I had to generalize, my generalization regarding the relation between poetry and "direct vulgar living" or the "actual" would run rather in the following way than in that suggested by Dr. Wellek: traditions, or prevailing conventions or habits, that tend to cut poetry in general off from direct vulgar living and the actual, or that make it difficult for the poet to bring into poetry his most serious interests as an adult living in his own time, have a devitalizing effect. But I cannot see that I should have added to the clarity, cogency or usefulness of my book by enunciating such a proposition (or by arguing it theoretically).' ('Criticism and Philosophy'; Dr. Leavis is replying to an attempted formulation by Dr. René Wellek.)

I think we can come to see more closely what Leavis is getting at in his view of poetic 'realization' by examining what is implied in a disagreement he has with Dr. Wellek in this same essay. The poems concerned are Wordsworth's *Simplon Pass* and Shelley's *Mont Blanc*. The passages quoted are the first eleven lines of the latter and lines 11 to 17 of the former. Briefly Leavis finds that the two poets 'react characteristically to similar concrete occasions' and praises the Wordsworth in terms of its more coherent grasp on the experience, the more delicate fusion of 'inner' and 'outer', an ability to present the emotion involved through the object contemplated, not in and for itself. What are at stake, in the Leavisian analysis, are contrasted forms of emotional organization, one of which finds its adequate 'objective correlative' and hence *presents* its emotional reaction through the objects of contemplation, the other of which involves the reader in its own confused emotionality, *un*recollected in tranquility, as it were. (To put it another way, what is at stake is a difference in degree of impersonality.) The point is that this type of comment arises out of a particular responsiveness to an organization of language discussible, one suspects (Leavis does not here go this far), in terms of experience and movement, not as statement. Characteristically Wellek extracts from the Shelley 'an epistemological proposition' rather than a response to a particular situation ('. . . to me,' says Leavis, 'the opening paragraph of *Mont Blanc* evokes with great vividness a state of excited bewilderment and wonder'), and finds that the Wordsworth 'has philosophically nothing to do with' the Shelley. (He thus, according to Leavis, 'confirms my conviction that philosophy and literary criticism are very different things'.)

When one examines Leavis's gloss on the affair, one cannot help thinking that he arrives at his view of the *Mont Blanc*, in part at least, by taking the opening lines

> *The everlasting universe of things*
> *Flows through the mind, and rolls its rapid waves,*
> *Now dark—now glittering—now reflecting gloom—*

as a particularized response evoked by the scene before the poet rather than as a generalization concerning the nature of mind, with its idealistic implications. This is the evocation of a mood, a mood summoned up in a particular act of contemplation, not a serious attempt to state a principle. To note this necessitates an awareness which brings into prominence particular aspects of the reading—the weight of the opening line, the precise implication to be assigned to the movement implicit in 'flows' and 'rolls', etc. This, of course, is my comment, not Leavis's; but it seems to be in line with the nature of his reaction to the lines.

Poetry, then, is not philosophy rhymed, rhythmed and with a little padding for metrical reasons. But the next stage is more difficult. How does one pass from response to morality, from comments on the texture of verse to comments concerning moral fitness? (Leavis, of course, is not the only one to make this transition; Coleridge speaks of having 'formed the opinion that true taste was virtue and that bad writing was bad feeling'.) The process can be illustrated from Leavis's analysis of Shelley's 'When the lamp is shattered'. (Behind my brief summary of the progression of the argument lies a good deal of detailed comment, involving a close analysis of the poem.) What, in brief, Leavis shows is Shelley's indulgence in poeticalities—the staled currency of sentimental banality; the emotion has been un-alloyed by processes of intelligence; what is revealed through a close analysis of meaning is the self-regarding, self-pitying im-plication of the final stanza. And this leads out to a general indictment: 'The antipathy of his sensibility to any play of the critical mind, the uncongeniality of intelligence to inspiration, these clearly go in Shelley, not merely with a capacity for momentary self-deceptions and insincerities, but with a radical lack of self-knowledge.' For all his pretended altruism Shelley, in fact, is 'his own hero'; and his self-regarding quality is mani-fested in his being 'peculiarly weak in his hold on objects— peculiarly unable to realize them as existing in their own natures and their own right'.

We pass, then, from comments on a particular way of handling thought and emotion through language—closely analysed and illustrated so that disagreement is possible in specific readings —to the implications of this in moral terms. There are two facets to this moral condemnation, though they represent a common phenomenon—two sides of the same coin. There is the failure in concrete apprehension, an experiential muzziness. Read closely, the poem demonstrates a series of local incoherences and discrepancies; certain clichés invite to vagueness and stock response. There is thus a submission to the test of *reality*; how profound has been the experience, what has the writer made of it? Looking at this from another angle, it is seen that the poet's involvement with himself—so that the poem reveals itself as an indulgence, seeking to evoke sympathy to minister to a pervasive self-pity—falsifies his grasp of the external world and invites a moral condemnation. 'Reality' is seen (by implication) to be a function of disinterestedness or impersonality (the words are used in Leavis's essay on '"Thought" and Emotional Quality'), of an ability to transcend the experience and 'present' it, even 'place' it, not to become emotionally involved with it.[1] Intelligence as well as emotion is necessary: 'feeling is not divorced from thinking.' In other words, emotional integrity and 'reality' are two aspects of the same struggle for expression; a failure in one involves a failure in the other and the breakdown revealed in analysis emerges as a moral weakness, involving questions of 'emotional hygiene and moral value— more generally . . . of spiritual health'. Implicit is a moral ideal of the self seeking truth ('reality') and being disciplined against a variety of possibilities for self indulgence. Only through the control of emotion, it is implied, can emotion have its proper place; and the controlling element is the intelligence which 'places': it is a matter of delicate balance: too much thought emerges as 'will', 'thinking about'—as in *Lady Chatterley*. Paradoxically, it is only through such control that the self can be released for 'life'; for, to speak out for 'life' remains one of the most persistent Leavisian positives. And this cannot be willed but can only spring from the 'free play of mind', richly apprehending the external world of people and objects without palpable design upon them.[2] There must be 'some kind of separation or distinction between experiencer and experience'. The endeavour remains Arnoldian: to see the object as in itself it really is. It also stems from Eliot. Here, we are at the heart of the Leavisian experience.

Not, then, to come to terms with 'reality' in some such way is to become guilty of a moral failure, a moral failure which

[1] One detects the influence of Eliot here: cf. Eliot's comment on Baudelaire whom he admires for his power of bringing 'imagery of the sordid life of a great metropolis' to a pitch of the 'first intensity—presenting it as it is, and yet making it represent something more than itself'. Cf. 'Thought and Emotional Quality', p. 58.

[2] *Scrutiny*, winter 1952–3, 'Reality and Sincerity', pp. 93–4. A close examination of the comments on Emily Brontë and Hardy could reveal a great deal of the force behind the Leavisian demand for the 'concrete', the 'particularity of experience'

M

falsifies the world at the behest of the too urgent desires of the self: 'To analyse your experience you must, while keeping it alive and immediately present as experience, treat it in some sense as an object'—Leavis is speaking of the metaphysicals, but he points to this as 'the strength of all the most satisfying poetry'. In this sense, literature becomes a form of revelation concerning the nature of life.[1] But, of course, implicit in this is the assumption that 'life' implies a selective process. *It is here that 'impersonality' is underpinned by affirmation.* The Leavisian 'life' is also the good life. In Leavis's sense of speaking for life a thing isn't life simply because somebody does it, otherwise the notion of the moral would have no possible relevance. Such 'life', indeed, has a different connotation from that implied in 'nihil humanum a me alienum puto', which is used to excuse concentration on any human phenomenon, however perverted. It suggests, for instance—the word is Leavis's—affirmation as opposed to an indulgence in nostalgia or a looking back; it thus involves a potentiality for new experience.[2] There is a good deal of the Leavisian positive implied in his criticism of Mr. Eliot's remark, made during one of the latter's derogatory comments on Lawrence, 'afin de rendre l'amour supportable'; what Leavis would imply by love would emerge in the positive comments he has to make on Lawrence.[3]

[1] But note, in his comment on Lionel Johnson's *By the Statue of King Charles*, that Leavis explicitly asserts: 'We do not, of course, argue from the poem to Lionel Johnson's personal qualities. It merely shows what an unfortunate tradition can do with a mind of some distinction' (p. 65). This, however, does not seem to me to be typical of Leavis's approach.

[2] I would suggest that Lawrence's comment in his essay 'Morality and the Novel' is relevant here: 'A thing isn't just life because somebody does it. This the artist ought to know perfectly well. The ordinary bank-clerk buying himself a new straw hat isn't "life" at all: it is just existence, quite all right—like everyday dinners: but not "life".

'By "life" we mean something that gleams, that has the fourth dimensional quality. If the bank clerk feels really piquant about his hat, if he establishes a lively relation with it, and goes out of the shop with the new straw on his head, a changed man, be-aureoled, then that is life.' I take it that this is something of what Leavis would imply when he stresses the importance of keeping experience 'alive and immediately present as experience'.

[3] Leavis speaks elsewhere of the 'rejection of life implicit in Mr. Eliot's attitude to sex', and considers Lawrence's preoccupation to be 'much less fairly to be called "obsession" than Mr. Eliot's, and very much preferable'.

But the attempt to define what Dr. Leavis would imply by 'satisfactory living' would too easily fall back on abstractions which it is his very genius to have avoided. His morality is something one absorbs as a set of expectations and movements towards, from the specific judgments he passes on particular poems and novels, not something that emerges as a set of moral principles. (I recommend, as an example, comments made in an analysis of Lawrence's 'The Daughters of the Vicar'.[1]) At most, one could, in general terms only, suggest a preference for 'this' rather than 'that'—and 'this', whatever it may be, as something fully realized, presented, not just talked about. Moral philosophers in our time have avoided, as I have noted, 'abstract high-level principles', preferring arguments of a more definite empirical content. Leavis would take them a stage further; his judgments attain a specificity which is consciously hostile to all attempts at generality; at such a level all he would seem to offer are gestures which would themselves point to the necessity of particularized examination.

Something like this, then, I take to be the nature of the Leavisian experience through literature, of those judgments among the whole range of the English literary tradition which define for him the special range of writers he finds valuable and whose insights contribute, in his estimation, to satisfactory living. The Leavisian morality is the sum total of the judgments he passes. The claim is explicit: '. . . we know that, in such a time of disintegration as the present, formulae, credos, abstractions are extremely evasive of unambiguous and effective meaning, and that, whatever else may be also necessary, no effort at integration can achieve anything real without a centre of real consensus—such a centre as is presupposed in the possibility of literary criticism and is tested in particular judgments. But "tested" does not say enough; criticism, when it performs its function, not merely expresses and defines the "contemporary sensibility"; it helps to form it. And the function of *Scrutiny*, as we conceive it, is (among other things) to help to persuade an

---

[1] Cf. especially pp. 74, 84, 85, 90 and 91 of Leavis's book on Lawrence. 'Life', indeed, is a quality of individual connections, found now in aristocratic, now in proletarian relationships.

effective "contemporary sensibility" into being—for that, rather, is what the critical function looks like when decay has gone so far.' In Leavis's own practice, the teacher and critic have been indistinguishable; the approach, ideally through conversation ('this is so, isn't it?') lends itself with an especial fitness to the teaching situation; the characteristic Leavisian prose, with its frequent asides and interjections, its dependence on the personally insisting 'I', translates itself easily to the seminar or the supervision period. The figure of the demonstrator, pointing, analysing, offering judgment, obtrudes, the often criticized clumsiness of his writing revealing itself as the quick darting insistence of a rapidly moving and complex intelligence (if one's standards are those of the 'incomparable Max', of course, one objects).

Yet, the obtuse and frequent failure to cope with the prose points to a certain restriction of audience. In what circumstances is such teaching even possible? To whom can it appeal? 'We are committed to consciousness,' Leavis asserts. As William Walsh has pointed out, 'To state the purpose is to define the character of those to whom it could be significant. The object could only appeal to, the method be undertaken by, Leavis's "intellectually given minority", Coleridge's "possessors of ideas", and Arnold's "small circle apt for fine distinctions".' To assert this, of course, is not to deprive all others of their literary heritage; what is at stake is a mode of procedure not a principle of exclusion; and, here, the operative stress falls on the possibilities of consciousness and the relative emphasis to be laid on 'affective' response and full conscious awareness.

To be more explicit, no one who, like myself, has taught in a training college, has examined orally, and through their work set forth at leisure, some considerable number of training college students (they represent the upper ten per cent of the population) can remain happy at the continued insistence on a self-consciously elaborated and written response to works of literature such as we exact in our present system of examinable education. Of course, Leavis himself is not responsible for this particular tradition of written criticism; he has merely carried to a high pitch of refinement what has always been implicit in the written practice of criticism as one involving a stated and defined reaction to the work under consideration. But the number who benefit from this sort of task seems to me to be more limited than we commonly admit. Either our techniques of teaching preparation need drastic overhauling (they do), or we ought to seek some more affectively based, some less self-consciously elaborated, methods of inducing literary appreciation for the majority—the stress, perhaps, should be on *participation* through speech, mime, drama and movement. The danger of Leavisian analysis as practised by the merely clever lies in the omission of the emphasis on the 'inner possession' of the work concerned and the substitution of a series of analytic tricks which enable a 'right' judgment to be arrived at. Such a process is not educative. The danger for the less bright is a blank incomprehension at the effort of consciousness involved. Even, then, at what appears to be 'minority' level we need to explore more fruitful ways through which students can come to an 'inner possession' of their heritage—through participation in drama, choral work, indeed, rather than through self-conscious elaboration.

What is clear, however, is the immense benefit conferred on the really able in school and university—we are here concerned with them—by the discipline implicit in the Leavisian practice— a benefit which goes beyond the immediate practice of close analysis into the wider life of our times. The corpus of Leavisian criticism—the authors discriminated and offered in all their diversity and his seriousness—permits an incomparable extension of the moral sensibility. In the criticism of Leavis in our times (the debts to Arnold and Eliot allowed for) literature stands forth as providing the closest educative possibilities of a moral 'way' our humanistic age is likely to provide. That such an offering should remain uncontaminated by any suggestion of a 'holy writ' is implicit in the very Leavisian challenge of 'This is so, isn't it?' It is not Leavis's fault that a habit of domination has been fathered on to him.

Fundamentally, great literature affords us the means of moral and perceptual growth; and, of course, it helps to awaken our intuitive awareness so that we are enabled to see more fully into the life of situations; and it does this, not by telling us, but by enabling us to 'feel into', making possible a measure of what I will call 'empathic' projection; the control is of the emotions—but through the intelligence. To that extent it is life-enhancing. These characteristics, related as they are to the qualitative aspect of our lives, provide, in my estimation, a sufficient answer to an over-emphasized technical slant on our educational 'imperatives'. They counter assertive will by 'impersonality', the Faustian urge by the free play of mind—this is their great contribution.

Yet the problem of balance as between technical advance and moral sophistication is complex; that we must not forget. Few have seen the issues as clearly as Henry James did in *The Princess Casamassima*: 'The monuments and treasures of art, the great palaces and properties, the conquests of learning and taste, the general fabric of civilization as we know it, based if you will upon all the despotisms, the cruelties, the exclusions, the monopolies and the rapacities of the past, but thanks to which, all the same, the world is less of a "bloody sell" and life more of a lark.' We can see today, more clearly even than James when he wrote *The Princess Casamassima*, the price at which our welfare has been bought, the sacrifice, precisely, of that high civilization which in the last resort Hyacinth Robinson refused to betray. Now that quality has become quantitative, we see more of what he and his creator were after. *Our* dilemma is to keep off the 'cruelties, the exclusions and the rapacities' and yet preserve the 'conquests of learning and taste' so that children can achieve that refinement and ordering of feeling which the education of the arts, rightly conceived, can afford. There can be no return to pre-industrialization; the effort is itself one of impersonal assessment: how to give the technical its due in a world whose life ends necessarily transcend the technical.

Hence my belief that the arts have too small a role in the education of able children. Science and technology play a universally important part in the modern world, and it is right that their claims to attention, in so far as they provide a degree of mental stimulation, should be met in the schools; but they do not provide that moral insight, that degree of affective control, that ordering of the emotional life through intelligence, that

168

self-awareness through psychological insight, that sensitizing to the life of situations which great literature can afford: 'The arts are our storehouse of recorded values. They spring from and perpetuate hours in the lives of exceptional people, when their control and command of experience is at its highest, hours when the varying possibilities of existence are most clearly seen and the different activities which may arise are most exquisitely reconciled, hours when habitual narrowness of interests or confused bewilderment are replaced by an intricately wrought composure. Both in the genesis of a work of art, in the creative moment, and in its aspect as a vehicle of communication, reasons can be found for giving to the arts a very important place in the theory of Value. They record the most important judgments we possess as to the values of experience.' (I. A. Richards, *Principles of Literary Criticism*.) It has all been said before, of course. But, in the indifference of our times, it needs to be constantly brought to mind.

V

So far I have been concerned with particular problems in the education of our able children. The fundamental issue for our times in our educative aims with these children—and, indeed, with those not quite so able—is contained in a brief remark made by Mr. Philip Rieff in the course of a review of Durkheim's *Education and Sociology*: 'Perhaps in a mass society, the school cannot be the transmitter of civilized values but only a complex of training programmes for various skill groups.' One must be realistic enough to appreciate that in an age which demands certain highly complex forms of expertise which carry with them both a high rate of remuneration and a great deal of social prestige, the inculcation into 'skills' (by which I intend the great academic disciplines so reduced) must not only absorb a good deal of educational effort but attract much of the attention of children who have taken from their homes the notion that this is precisely the role the school is intended to play. One's appreciation of the force of social group pressures—derived from family and peers—are such that a deep concern about human

169

values and the more intangible rewards of an education which is intended to reflect on the general quality of one's existence are not likely to be transmitted without a struggle.

Partly this is a matter of lack of tradition in educational matters, one which is likely most to affect sections of the present-day grammar school population. At its most poignant, the dilemma is that of Richard Hoggart's 'Scholarship Boy'; and two quotations from Miss Stevens' recent book on the grammar school help us to get the feel of the tensions so easily involved. Two children write: 'But also many difficulties. My friends rather think I am a "snob" and say "Oh she goes to a Grammar School" and I find myself thinking deeper than them and feeling on a different level.' 'When first I came, I thought "teddy-boys" and such were ridiculous; now I even envy them their freedom, because school almost entirely rules my life both at home and anywhere else. My parents think that I should only have a thought for superior things (i.e. classical music etc.) and I spend much of my time trying to be what I am not.'[1] (*The Living Tradition.*)

The great theme of modern literature (perhaps it is a constantly recurring one, but it has taken on a special significance in our era of uncertain values) is the search for identity—I mean, of course; among the giants, Conrad, Eliot, Lawrence, Yeats, and, in a more simple and therefore manifest way, Forster and Myers. For such a theme is implicit in that oscillation between isolation and relationship within a decaying moral order which is overtly the subject-matter of so much modern writing. Against such a background—and it is the background, conscious or unconscious, of us all—the grammar school curriculum affords opportunities which yet are in practice almost always neglected. Rightly conceived, as I have indicated the 'subjects' constitute

[1] I have a particular repugnance for the current habit, in educational discourse, of exploiting the *obiter dicta* of children in an attempt to harrow our feelings. The thing is rapidly coming to take on the appearance of a disease, so that whole systems of education are threatened because (an actual example) 'my friend wouldn't come birds-nesting with me the day I passed the eleven-plus and he didn't'. As a result, some educational writing has the emotional aura of a cheap novelette. But this does not mean that everything that children say should be ignored; what is needed is a little discrimination. I find these two expressions of opinion genuinely touching.

ways in which man has attempted to make some sense out of his puzzling universe, out of himself in relation to his environment through literature and the arts, out of his society through the humanities and the social sciences and out of the material universe through the physical sciences. They constitute, that is to say, stages in the development of his thought about himself and the environment, social and physical, which he inhabits.[1] Yet the particular unity which binds each set of subject 'facts' together can be lost when the tools become the master; the poem which, rightly apprehended and responded to involves a species of self revelation, remains a hunting ground for 'references' or difficult meanings; it is reduced to an external vocabulary test, or a matter for a 'context' examination.

Yet the need for the other, profounder approach is there staring one in the face from the very words of the children themselves, out of their dawning self-awareness. In the one extract is the fact of alienation, the growing appreciation of difference and the tensions with which such a movement apart is inevitably involved; for it is equivocally regarded, both by the child and the home. Her remarks continue: 'My parents are rather inclined to think that I need "pulling down a peg or two" even . . . Also, I often think that maybe I am becoming narrow-minded.' Here, then, starkly, the complexities of the situation stand revealed—what goes on behind the sociologist's abstractions about social mobility, and equality of opportunity. The least that can be expected of the school is that it shall attempt to meet the situation half-way. This is not accomplished by lowering its demands or its standards. If these children have both the 'brains' and the temperament for high learning, they must accept the pains that are the inevitable concomittant of 'spiritual' development; as they achieve the level of consciousness which is in them, as they are helped to realize natures which will make them, to a certain extent, 'different', they must be strengthened in the loneliness which, in some degree, is to become part of their lot; and if they cannot accept the challenge, with all the help we

[1] 'Education I will take to be the process of learning, in circumstances of direction and restraint, how to reorganize and make something of ourselves.' (Michael Oakeshott, *Rationalism in Politics and other Essays*, p. 302.)

can bring them, they must reluctantly be allowed to slide back. This, at least, is an answer to Mr. Eliot's statement: 'To be educated above the level of those whose social habits and taste one has inherited, may cause a division within a man which interferes with happiness . . . Too much education, like too little education, can produce unhappiness.' For I see no reason to assume that happiness consciously aimed at, is often achieved; and the unhappiness which springs from one's sense of an essential un-at-homeness—which is part of the human situation and not a pre-emption of those who have achieved social awkwardness through education—is more worth-while than the pig-like contentment of the sty.

Yet that does not mean that the school has no responsibility in the matter of acceptance; it cannot make things easy because the decision is not an easy one to make. But it can make things clearer. The other *cri de cœur* is just as revealing: 'I am being made out to be what I am not.' In both cases there is a search for identity, for a sort of involvement to which the school pays too little heed. Technically, the grammar school is reasonably efficient; it enables the children to go through the various relevant motions, produce the necessary answers, accumulate the essential data; but, too often, it remains data, with all the implication of externality which the word carries with it. The syllabus is not thought of as a means of revelation, a means to clarification of the self and of the world, physical and social outside self, which, as I have argued, in effect it should be.

This, again, doesn't mean Deweyism—the concentration on the narrow circle of social relevance; it means respecting the nature of disciplines for what they are, but progressively making clear what in effect they are. Its aim is not self-centredness, but self-transcendence—that I have made manifest. But it means, too, the admission of where the self is now, pinched and mean through straitened and unpropitious circumstances. It means thinking of the syllabus much more from the standpoint of those who have, in the self-conscious sense of the word, been culturally deprived, as a set of meanings in relation to a tradition, largely, of blank incomprehension, and considering, therefore, where meaning can begin.

It means thinking, too, about presentation; but not as a matter of 'method', isolated from the meanings that are to be clarified. It is not, that is to say, simply to be a case of adding a few visual aids or a few 'gimmicks' as a means to stimulating 'interest'. It can only spring—I must insist—out of a mature elaboration of the philosophic nature of the field involved and a reference back to the comprehensions possible to even able children at the age to which they belong.

Let me attempt to clarify what I mean by reference to the teaching of 'composition'—one of the most difficult 'subjects' to teach, yet one very obviously and closely related to the search for identity implicit in the children's remarks. The nature of writing is the ordering of experience through words, and the sort of writing relevant alters in accordance with the nature of the experience to be conveyed. There is, in fact, no such exercise as writing—there is only writing a something to a somebody, even if the somebody is only the self. The first requisite, then, is a context—and the contexts chosen must be relevant to the child's understanding and capacity for experience.

An important context will be the world of work. Particular communicative demands will be made by the various disciplines the child is involved in learning, so that a good deal of the work in English will necessitate the writing up of requirements in other disciplines: 'Tell me how you perform this chemical experiment'; 'Describe for me (who know nothing about it) this historical situation'; 'Show me, in words, how to play this game.' It is in this way that children ought to be taught how to handle ideas—in relation to what is known intimately at first hand.

Another context will be the immediacies of social relationship —how to write a letter of explanation or thanks, how to give directions in response to specific requests—in a word, how to move with confidence and delicacy in the world of specific relationships—with superiors, with equals—and how to meet the demands of literacy which it may involve.

But the core of literacy will be the imaginative; and this will involve the exploration of the 'I' in relation to a concrete, sensuous awareness of the world of persons and things, by

which the 'I' is surrounded. At first it will be essentially egotis-
tic—as befits the stage of development involved—*I* like, *I* feel,
I respond to. But gradually, with skilled teaching, it will come
to apprehend the world of persons and things as entities other
than the self and having a 'life' apart from the 'I'. Only in this
way, can the nature of the 'I' be clarified and education become
truly 'child-centred': for to be child-centred is not to be spoilt-
child-centred, as with Dewey. It means allowing the child to
realize himself—and as a very part of that realization fostering
an appreciation of selves other than self; for, paradoxically, only
thus can the self come to maturity. In this sense, and only in this
sense, can the purpose of education be said to be self-realization.
But a realization of self, in *these* terms, would avoid the sadness
of 'I spend much of my time trying to be what I am not'; the
first step along the complex road to the admission of others lies
in the acceptance of self as it is; for the prime motive in the
attempt to be what one is not is precisely the social effect one
hopes to create on others—as L. H. Myers, among others, has
revealed. By insisting on the role of the imaginative in the day-
to-day routine of the classroom, then, the schoolmaster, through
the normal disciplines of learning, can do his bit in the maturing
of attitudes and individuals.

The reply, then, to Mr. Rieff's pessimism lies in an assertion
of the essentially civilizing function of the great disciplines,
which are the 'skills' our able children acquire. If I have insisted, in this chapter, on the superior role of literature and the
arts, this is partly in rectification of a significant trend of events
which may increasingly deny their value; but also because I
think they touch what is more fundamental in the human situation; literature, indeed, is concerned with what is basic to all
human strivings; values and the chaos of the passions. The disputed relative emphasis to be placed on literature and the
sciences neatly indicates the extent to which social needs and
demands are allowed to usurp the place of more permanent
human requirements. Because the material conditions of our
civilization have grown so much out of scientific achievement,
it is urged that science ought to play an ever larger part in an
'education for the twentieth century', as the cliché runs. In

actual fact, the very nature of twentieth-century specialized education can make it unnecessary for more than a fairly small percentage of experts to be produced whose talents lie in the scientific or technical direction; these can keep the machines running or our understanding of the material world advancing. Beyond these, it becomes largely a matter of intellectual taste and interest whether science is studied;[1] certainly, a knowledge of scientific fact is in no way essential for a high state of culture, as the previous, pre-scientific history of mankind goes to show. Science, indeed, is simply a way through which the creative talents of certain people express themselves; and it is perfectly possible for the majority to live qualitatively rich and fine lives without the slightest knowledge of science— for science cannot help to define the nature of such moral fineness as is open to them, though it may provide relevant factual data.

Nevertheless, the scientific approach, as a mode of apprehending the world, remains a great achievement of the human spirit. Whereas, then, knowledge of scientific fact or law (Sir Charles Snow's insistence on the Second Law of Thermodynamics is in evidence here) is, even for highly educated people, largely irrelevant, such people could hardly be called highly educated unless they knew something about the *sort* of activity science is. What an educated man needs is some comprehension of the way a scientist approaches and correlates the phenomena he is investigating; to what sorts of questions he seeks an answer and which matters lie outside his purview; what is the status of law and hypothesis and to what extent are the patternings he arrives at subjectively influenced—in a word, it is philosophical science

[1] The one doubt I have about the general truth of this statement lies in the fact that the categories in terms of which we see the world and judge its behaviour owe so much to scientific modes of explanation. If, then, we seek 'understanding', science has its importance. Furthermore it is arguable that these categories tend to dilute what I will call the 'density' of experience in certain ways which make the task of artistic creation more difficult. 'Fire' we understand today in terms of the principles of combustion. Conceived as the gift of the gods it assumes a whole range of associations, an emotional potency, which the modern phenomenon of 'fire' quite lacks. To appreciate this, it seems to me, is to penetrate at least some way into the nature of the modern malaise and its 'affective' starvation; and this cannot happen without some understanding of science, of the sort noted below.

he needs to know, not the detailed facts of any particular science.[1]

In a world as complex as ours has become, it looks as if we are going to have to reconcile ourselves to the fact that there cannot be one prototypic model of the 'educated man'. It has become necessary to accept a number of different models, men who can lay claim to be educated even though the nature of modern knowledge is such that there is only an imperfect degree of communication possible between them—certainly to the level of their adopted specialism. These men would share only certainly limited characteristics in common. For one thing they would be deeply versed in a specialism—but versed in a manner which implied a mastery of the *nature* of the subject-material involved as well as of the material itself.[2] Furthermore, they should have some insight into the nature of other important disciplines, at least in a general sense, even if they remain unacquainted with the detailed structure of them. But there ought to be one further demand—a close acquaintance with the one discipline which reflects on and sensitizes to general human behaviour at its most concrete level of daily intercourse. Such a discipline I have taken to be literature—which requires no special vocabulary and which, even if not read with the deepest understanding, must yet inevitably extend the range of the non-specialist's awareness of the human situation. The point has been made by Dr. Leavis in *Education and the University*: 'We have

[1] There are, of course, two objections here. One is the complaint of practising scientists that they can never recognize the theoretical account of their behaviour which philosophers of science produce; the other is the related objection that only participation in the actual work of a laboratory can give any convincing picture of what is involved in the work of a scientist: 'Those who ask for more and better interpretations of science can be wholly satisfied only if they join the scientist in his laboratory and learn to share his scientific experience' (B. C. Brookes, 'The Difficulty of Interpreting Science', *The Listener*, 1 October 1959). Where finer points are concerned, this may indeed be true. Nevertheless, reflection on the results of science may afford an approximate picture of the approach to experience that science involves: and this, in the nature of the case, is sufficient. (And cf. Michael Yudkin, 'Sir Charles Snow's Rede Lecture', reprinted in F. R. Leavis, *Two Cultures? The Significance of C. P. Snow*.)

[2] Martin Mayer, in his recent survey of *The Schools*, expresses it with his usual forthrightness: 'Ignorance of most of the universe is an inescapable aspect of the human condition, most gracefully borne by those who are not equally ignorant in all directions.'

176

not to debate whether it is to produce specialists or the "educated man" that the university should exist. Its essential function is to produce both—though to say "*the* educated man" is perhaps misleading. The problem is to produce specialists who are in touch with a humane centre . . .; but this centre is not best conceived as a standard "educated man". There will be "educated men" with various stresses, various tendencies towards specialization.' (p. 28.) I would refer to that book for a further concrete amplification of the notion of literary studies as providing the humane centre—with the proviso that it is here the University that is in question.

To put what I am saying another way. I may be a fuller being by the study of science; but by the mere necessity of making choices in conduct I am involved, willy-nilly, in the stuff of literature.[1] This, ultimately, is the answer to Sir Charles Snow's hierarchy of 'educational imperatives'.

VI

The self-realization through self-transcendence I proclaim as my aim can only be achieved within a culturally rich social order which encourages the refinements of the self the history of civilization shows man to be capable of. To bring about those social circumstances which best serve such an order helps to ensure conditions most favourable to the quality of our lives. With this in mind, I will reflect on some of the possible social implications of 'equality of opportunity'.

Mrs. Floud and her colleagues, no longer satisfied with the equality manifested at eleven, seek a similar one at sixteen; and her analysis of the forces opposing the achievement of her desire

[1] I may seem to contradict here what I have said above (cf. p. 98) concerning the increasing 'specialized' nature of literature itself—in the sense that modern literature of any degree of greatness is highly complex. This is true: but there exists a whole tradition of literature which is comprehensible to the 'common reader' of educated tastes; and modern literature itself presents no insuperable barrier to such a reader who has learned to read with care and attention and with a realization that the comprehension of any work of art requires some degree of effort. It should not be too difficult to get this notion across.

—for she seeks explanation in largely environmental terms, being convinced that 'measured intelligence is widely known to be largely an acquired characteristic'—suggests, firstly, that she accepts as the criterion of the ability to go forward the stripped and denuded conception of human personality which is implicit in the notion of such an intelligence, and, secondly, that the in‑hibiting factors militating against further selection warrant social investigation.

The precise nature of the hindrances placed by their home 'in the way of educating working‑class children in grammar schools urgently needs investigating both for its own sake as an im‑mediate problem of educational organization, and for the light it would throw on the problems and possibilities of the com‑prehensive school.'[1] (p. 148.) The truth is, that too many of these children are leaving at fifteen before they have completed their course. The key words are 'urgent' and 'immediate'; the impression of breathlessness implies a consciousness of wastage, an anomaly that needs clearing up; the ordering and sorting machine is not yet working at full efficiency.

Yet, if we ask her and her colleagues why it should, conscious of the small, nagging irreverence of a persisting 'What for?', what end in view has the great sorting and ordering machine, the only discoverable answer which comes from their book is

[1] A recent attempt to diagnose the working‑class educational malaise has appeared in B. Jackson and D. Marsden's *Education and the Working Class*. This book is methodologically highly suspect; even its impressionistic aim is marred by its emotionally charged repudiation of middle‑class values and its largely uncritical acceptance of working‑class virtues. Beneath a surface appearance of fairmindedness, it reveals its authors' conviction that the Grammar school must be wrong. If the working‑class children fit into its ethos, this is wrong because 'There is something infinitely pathetic in these former working‑class children who lost their roots young, and who now with their rigid middle‑class accent preserve "the stability of all our institutions, temporal and spiritual" by avariciously reading the lives of Top People (*sic*), or covet the public schools and glancing back at the society from which they came can see no more there than "the dim" or the "specimens".' (Note the emotionally tendentious force of 'infinitely', 'avariciously', 'rigid'; this is not untypical of the book as a whole.) If the working‑class child doesn't fit into the ethos of the school, this is wrong because it indicates that the school is geared to a false set of values: 'we have come to that place where we must firmly accept the life of the majority', whatever that may mean. It is quite possible to combine an equivo‑cal appreciation of middle‑class virtues with a regret that in this book an oppor‑tunity for a serious and soberly impersonal assessment has been lost.

178

that of 'the loss of qualified man-power to the national economy'. (p. 118.) Now, the language of such a statement no longer causes the raising of eyebrows; it has become a commonplace—and that in itself is perhaps an indication of the extent to which we have substituted a technical for an educated language in the way in which we discuss our educational difficulties. Dr. McIntosh has recently sought to *channel* the 'pool of ability . . . into the national reservoir' of the highly educated; a newly published survey of Britain's scientific ability speaks of *funnelling* able children into the desired occupations; and *The Times Educational Supplement* recently advocated that we *syphon* 'wasted adult ability into the professions which need it'. I cannot think that the attitude to human beings which is implicit in these quotations is a healthy one; or is my delicacy irrelevant in the face of these demands for educated manpower presented as a dire (though usually unexamined) social need?

The point is, that there is implicit in the demand for more efficient machinery in the selection of the élite, a narrow and illiberal view of the function of the élite—the view, in fact, inherent in these dismal associations of 'educated manpower', with their overtones of a narrowly conceived social functioning and an emotional aura of a pressed and conscripted population, acceptable at best in the face of great and dire external danger of wartime. Such crudities, with their collectivist implications, render all the more palatable, by contrast, the warnings of Mr. T. S. Eliot against the emergence of just such an élite as the notion of educated manpower summons up. Mr. Eliot has been attacked by Lord James on the grounds of illiberality; and, indeed, his views on education do, as Lord James points out, cut right across the assumptions about the desirability of education and its infinite extension which has been part of the almost unquestioned social policy of the last few decades . . . as, indeed, it cuts across most of the more general social assumptions of our time.

Mr. Eliot is concerned with defining the conditions under which a high state of culture is likely to exist; he finds them in a hierarchic condition, when the body politic is divided, not on the grounds of 'brains', but on those of 'classes'. His beliefs about

N

the extension of education which has followed the breakdown of classes, with the consequent expansion of opportunity, can be summarized as follows. He considers that the more education is extended, the less it is likely to be prized. Furthermore, for any high state of culture, continuity of experience is essential; hence the need for 'classes', in contrast to élites. For, through classes based on heredity cultural continuity is possible, whereas an élite, as a constantly changing social group chosen solely on account of 'brains', implies a lack of cohesiveness which is likely to be fatal to a high cultural state, in that it will fail to 'foster the hereditary transmission of culture within a culture'. Basically, Mr. Eliot believes that a culture cannot ever be fully 'known' in any intellectual sense; that there is much of value which comes simply from having been nursed in a certain environment, when what is 'known' is only known in Keats' sense of being known along the pulse. This, obviously, is not something that a school education can provide. It is not something which can be provided through the study of 'subjects', particularly if for examination purposes;[1] it is something which can be achieved, if at all, through the 'atmosphere' of a school, and then, presumably, only through a boarding school, when it would be hard to decide whether it emerged from school or background.

Any notion of hereditary 'classes' as distinctive elements in the state is likely to be unpalatable and unacceptable today, when the whole notion of class is in almost universal disrepute. At the same time, the growing lack of continuity between the generations, the lack of a settled social 'style'—manifested as an accepted system of manners and morals, the one refining the other—which the influx of men drawn from different social traditions prevents from developing, carries with it penalties both for the health of the body politic and for the mental ease of the invaders. The strains are already apparent in the comments of Miss Stevens' school children; and the lack of an educated 'public', with clearly defined standards and a reasonably settled mode of expectation, is part of the literary and artistic history

[1] Cf. what has been said about the nature of modern school learning and its rootless quality, its inability to provide any *comprehensive* way of life: cf. p. 127.

of our generation. The 'cultural' effects, indeed, of a policy of 'equality of opportunity' in the terms in which this policy is being implemented need more consideration than they receive. For one effect, certainly, is the too rapid assimilation of the culturally impoverished who have high I.Q.s into sections of the community which carry a good deal of social and economic prestige; the rise of the merely clever in these terms to positions of social influence is a culturally doubtful manifestation.[1] Our present concern for science and technology affords social prestige to what, given the necessary 'brains', can be acquired with a fair amount of ease. The sort of conduct implicit in scientific education is one which, given laboratory space and teachers, can be easily imitated by the able, for its demands are always open to inspection via the acquiring of a special vocabulary which may take time to learn but is never in doubt when learnt. This is because the conventions of scientific investigation are wholly transferable in a way in which the conventions of sophisticated social and moral behaviour and intercourse are not.[2]

The general situation can be presented in terms of a conflict between Justice and Sanity, as indeed it has been by Dr. F. Musgrove in a recent article.[3] Dr. Musgrove sees the current emphasis on social justice as a factor leading to social disruption and individual distress: 'Social justice, suicide and alcoholism

[1] The point is made by Professor Arnold Toynbee: 'One of the most effective privileges hitherto has been the privilege of being heir to a richer cultural heritage than is accessible to the unprivileged majority, and this richer heritage is transmitted through the family as well as through schools and colleges. This becomes apparent when children with a poorer cultural heritage are admitted to the minority's schools. They find it difficult to obtain as much benefit as their privileged schoolfellows obtain from the same course of formal education, because they bring less with them. To him that hath shall be given. This is not just, but it is one of the facts of life. It takes more than one generation for a family that has made its way out of a less privileged into a more privileged social class to acquire the full cultural heritage of the class to which it has won admission.' (Final chapter in E. D. Myers, *Education in the Perspective of History*, p. 270.)

[2] It may indeed be true, as Dr. B. C. Brookes has argued in a recent broadcast, that 'there can be no short cut to understanding science'; but, even here, all Dr. Brookes is arguing against is the notion that science can be easily popularized in non-technical language. The language has to be learnt—but it is technical simply because it is only in such a language that 'new discriminations can be precisely and publicly made and repeated by others'.

[3] Cf. *The Times Educational Supplement*, Nov. 18, 1960.

maintain their annual increments', strikes the keynote of his indictment. In this process, the Grammar School—and, of course, he could have added, the University—plays an important role: 'The grammar school is the agency for collecting local talent, equipping it not only with the requisite technical skills but also the attitudes and role dispositions needed for "success", and redeploying it on a national scale, distributing it throughout the economy and the anonymous avenues, drives and crescents of outer suburbia.' And he points out, rightly, that this is the system which is being exported to other cultures: ('. . . our concept of social justice has successfully eroded entire African societies'.).

The article is an important one even if, within the short space at his disposal, Dr. Musgrove is forced to dramatize the dangers of the situation in terms of stress disorder, ulcers, thrombosis and the like. Many of the effects on individuals are likely to be subtler—matters of social insecurity, shynesses and aggressivenesses—the minor neuroses. Any form of social organization necessarily exacts a price, of course; a fact which is likely to be apparent to any but the most hardened of environmentalists who dream of social harmony achievable through social engineering. No such possibility as this is likely; and one's evidence for one's belief is human history. What is needed is a calm assessment of the complexities of the situation. There is nothing self-evidently right about our conception of social justice and the way we interpret it today. And, indeed, such a concept of justice could be criticized on the grounds that it generates nearly as much negative jealousy as it brings positive advantage,[1] or that, in any case, justice is a cold virtue.

Again, it must be realized that the particular concern which we manifest over the question of selection and opportunity reflects back on the terms in which we conceive the syllabus which we teach in our grammar schools. It makes of it an instrument, not an end in itself; it strengthens the concern for results in assessable terms, through examinations. It reduces knowledge

---

[1] Henry James saw this in *The Princess Casamassima*, where he speaks of the 'ulcer of envy—the greed of a party hanging together only that it might despoil another to its advantage'.

to the level of 'technical knowledge'.[1] The extent to which Miss Stevens indicates that the grammar school rests content with its chains—the examination syllabus—should have been deducible from the nature of the social policy which examinations are expressly designed to support. Furthermore, along with conventional examinations there has arisen a whole industry of mental and attainment testing, much of it resting on dubious philosophical grounds. Such paraphernalia is an essential concomitant of the need to select people; though it must not be forgotten that such selection is an essential concomitant of a proliferating social and economic system which makes the sort of demands that ours does.

This is not, of course, a plea for a denial of chances to the able; what has been said earlier should make that clear. But in the midst of the great sorting process it is as well to bear certain things in mind. In the aggressive drive for talent—and aggressive is the word to apply to certain expositions of the need—it should be remembered that there are other sources of high satisfaction in life for some who, if in terms of ability they appear fitted for a university education, have not the temperament to respond to the demands made on them or to the opportunities afforded. There is the danger too—recognizable to any university teacher as manifest in certain students—that some will carry with them deep cultural resentments, anxious to

[1] I refer to what Professor Oakeshott, in his famous essay on 'Rationalism in Politics', terms 'technical knowledge'. Professor Oakeshott's diagnosis of the rationalist's view of education and the type of training it implies deserves pondering:
'From the earliest days of his emergence, the Rationalist has taken an ominous interest in education. He has a respect for "brains", a great belief in training them, and is determined that cleverness shall be encouraged and shall receive its reward of power. But what is this education in which the Rationalist believes? It is certainly not an initiation into the moral and intellectual habits and achievements of his society, an entry into the partnership between present and past, a sharing of concrete knowledge; for the Rationalist, all this would be an education in nescience, both valueless and mischievous. It is a training in technique, a training, that is, in the half of knowledge which can be learnt from books when they are used as cribs. And the Rationalist's affected interest in Education escapes the suspicion of being a mere subterfuge for imposing himself more firmly on society, only because it is clear that he is as deluded as his pupils. He sincerely believes that a training in technical knowledge is the only education worth while, because he is moved by the faith that there is no knowledge, in the proper sense, except technical knowledge.' (*Rationalism in Politics and other Essays.*)

exploit what the university can give in terms of status and job prestige, but reacting against the ethos of an institution towards which their life experience has made them hostile because of the inadequacies it reveals in themselves.

For, in the last resort this aggressive drive for talent is itself a manifestation of the assertive will which is the concomitant of the scientific and technological state. Under the guise of a concern for individuals, the bullying will asserts itself in a thousand scholastic institutions at the behest of a pressure for 'educated manpower'. 'I am not,' complained Lawrence once, when his peace of mind had been disturbed by someone who had snatched him away from the scene of peace and sensuous beauty he was contemplating into the 'desert void of politics, principles, right and wrong and so forth'—'I am not allowed to sit like a dandelion on my own stem.' No one 'cared' more than Lawrence but he knew, intuitively, the dangers of 'caring': 'They care! They simply are eaten up with caring. They are so busy caring about Fascism or Leagues of Nations or whether France is right or whether Marriage is threatened, that they never know where they are. They certainly never live on the spot where they are.' There is a wisdom, in a true education, which would see the relevance of this, too, in our present educational dilemmas.

What, then, am I arguing for? Certainly, it must be re-emphasized, no drastic curtailment of opportunity.[1] But, any principle, however good in itself, contains, when pushed to extremes, dangers of offence in the infinitely complex human situation in which we find ourselves; as Conrad observes in *Nostromo*, 'a man haunted by a fixed idea is insane'. The possibility at least exists that the pursuit of the policy of equality of opportunity can become as rigid, as destructive of human well-being and achievement as over-attention to the opposite policy of rigid stratification. For it expresses an impracticable ideal in that, born into an historical situation as we all inevitably are, the conditions under which we develop can never be called

[1] What I am saying here, indeed, must be read in conjunction with what I have previously said about the need for able children to accept the aloneness which is often their lot in the achievement of their potentialities (cf. p. 171). It comes down, once more, to individual decisions in individual cases.

equal. 'Social justice', indeed, in the dogmatic way in which its application is sought in the modern world can be destructive of other felicities and harmonies which may be discordant with its peculiar monotonal demands. It is as well to remember that other principles of social organization have produced their high cultures, their enrichments of our human condition. My point, then, is not to deny what of enrichment the principle itself can bring—and it *can* so fructify. Rather, it is to bring to mind, as part of the essential limitation of our kind, that no discoverable principle of human organization can pre-empt, to the exclusion of all others, in the business of earthly satisfactions and achievements; and that, while not accepting Mr. Eliot's diagnosis in its entirety, it is as well to ask whether some explanation of that sort of cultural impoverishment from which we suffer and which inevitably reacts on the range of choices available for self-realization, is not aggravated in the situation he analyses.

We should bear this in mind when we come to expand our system of higher education—*which we must*. We hear a good deal of what universities can do for their students; we think a good deal less about what a large influx of purely status-minded students will do to the university, or of those who, in the recent words of Mr. R. M. Ogilvie, are 'able but lacking in any interest or drive, both in scholastic work and in the conduct of life'. Such students need a sort of teaching and pastoral care which the universities, with their concern for fundamental research, with exploiting, that is, the *nature* of their disciplines, are not altogether well equipped to offer. But, more to the point, is the degradation of effort implied in the necessity of wooing the hostile or indifferent; not because such an effort is not worthwhile, but because it belongs to a milieu other than that of the highest academic body in the kingdom.

Ideally, the solution is to develop other forms of higher education which could be more specifically directed to the educative and pastoral problems posed by the new influx of status seekers; or that would recognize that the sort of purely cognitive education provided in universities is not the only or necessarily the best type of education even for those of good intelligence. In general, the Training College performs an admirable educative as well as professional function because it conceives its work in primarily tutorial terms, undisturbed by the demands of research; and in the emotionally under-educated environment implied by the nature of our popular culture—a culture which in certain of its manifestations often attracts the better intellects as well as the poorer ones—the need for 'affective' training through participation in the arts was never more patent.[1] And, of course, such training is never something simply of the emotions—it needs the intelligence as well.

An objection to such proposals comes from those like Professor Richard Hoggart who fear a hierarchical structure and the creation of a second best with the opportunities for snobbery it fosters. The answer surely lies in the need to accept the realities of things—a teaching institution at least can only become what its pupils will allow it to become; and to call an institution a university which, from the character of its intake, has no chance of providing what is essential to the nature of such an institution is merely a distressing form of *bovarysme*. We can't perpetually live in an *Alice in Wonderland* world where all the creatures are to have a prize. And, paradoxically, our society will be the richer for the honesty and clear-sightedness involved. It is by being itself that our university can best serve the community.

[1] This raises an extremely important point concerning the education of those who are capable in some degree of participation in 'minority' culture but who lack the ability to make it in any sense a part of themselves and whose lives then function at much less than their actual potential because they succumb to the blandishments of the mass media (I have in mind particularly the lower ranges of the grammar schools and perhaps some of those in the higher reaches of the secondary modern schools). I shall have more to say about them in my next book on affective education.

CHAPTER SIX

Prolegomena to a Consideration of Technical[1] Education

❖

The fundamental case for technical progress has been stated by Aristotle: '. . . those are clearly right who . . . maintain the necessity to a happy life of an addition in the form of material goods. It is difficult, if not impossible, to engage in noble enterprises without money to spend on them . . .' (*Nichomachean Ethics*, I, chapter 8). The greater diffusion of wealth throughout the community as a result of technical advance has brought benefits which hardly seem to need stressing at this stage in our social development. But the pursuit of material interests to the exclusion of other concerns, as Charles Gould discovered in Conrad's *Nostromo*, brings with it its own hubris, a concentration of purpose which contains within itself a deep possibility of corruption. No one in his senses could advocate the silencing of the machines which maintain our complex and pullulating civilization; to do so would invite the plain murder of millions of our citizens.

Yet, a major pressure of our times in education, as I have pointed out, is the temptation to use education too exclusively as an instrument for feeding the great Economic and Industrial

---

[1] I shall here use the word 'technical' with particular reference to machinery.

Machine—social need, indeed, in these terms. A British sociologist, recently analysing the changing function of the universities, has pointed out that the universities, from being 'nurseries for élite groups', are beginning to fulfil a new function, as a 'mass higher education service in an emergent technological society'. This indeed is what, it is asserted, has lain behind the vast expansion of university education in America, and it is obviously an important factor in the extension of university education in this country. The pressure is being exercised in 'scare' terms: 'The price of survival is to change our culture.'[1] Technology is being groomed to become 'queen of the sciences': 'Technology is henceforth to crown and bind the arch of the economy.' The tale goes that Britain is reasonably well provided with 'pure' scientists but is lacking in technologists and technicians. Furthermore, the onset of automation is going to need a vastly increased recruitment of trained machine-minders. Though in certain industries—notably Aircraft, Chemical and Electrical Engineering —extensive use is made of technical assistance, in general 'Britain uses proportionately fewer technologists in its industrial operations than the United States, relying more heavily on highly skilled and thoroughly trained craftsmen'. (G. L. Payne, op. cit., p. 56.) Particularly is there a need for a greater emphasis on research, in order that Britain's comparatively meagre resources can be more effectively deployed; and by effective deployment is implied the creation of an expanding economy. Thus the Advisory Council on Scientific Policy wrote in 1952: 'We can either assume that there will be a steady and rapid increase in our productivity or that the economy will remain static and that productivity will increase only slowly . . . If the second assumption is correct there is little hope of our remaining a great power, or even of our paying for the imports needed to sustain our economic life. If planning is to have any purpose it must, therefore, be designed both to meet the needs and create the situation of the first hypothesis.'

Not all who are concerned with the economic life of our country, however, seem to take the view that expansion conceived in this way is a vital necessity. Thus Barclay's Bank

[1] G. L. Payne, *Britain's Scientific and Technological Manpower*, p. 15.

Review urges that '. . . the economy of a country should be regarded as a living organism whose natural strengths must be nurtured and whose robust health is diminished by forced growth. The instabilities and social tensions caused by excessive expansion are not the inevitable alternatives to deflation, nor should stability be stigmatized as stagnation.' (Quoted, op. cit., p. 336.) And of course, J. K. Galbraith's strictures on the Affluent Society have their relevance in the English setting. The need to stimulate home consumption through the type of high-pressure advertising we see all about us has its relevance to our present-day cultural plight. (And the question 'To what end?' constantly arises—as I have frequently made clear.) The educational consequences, indeed, can be even more direct; reviewing a book on the education of scientists, Sir Alan Wilson, the former vice-chairman of Courtaulds, points out that 'The primary cause of the narrow outlook of so many scientists is that we are committed to an expanding economy with its consequential strains upon society in general and upon our educational system in particular. No one wants to go back to a static and far less to a declining economy, and we must therefore reconcile ourselves, not only to balance of payments crises and to creeping inflation, but also to narrowness in scientists as part of the price to be paid for increasing their supply at abnormal rates.' (*New Scientist*, 26 January 1961, p. 226.) Sir Alan's point is that all is not lost at graduation day, and that many scientists do develop cultural interests later in life. Nevertheless, his revelation of the current dilemma convinces; specialization of the narrow sort is needed in science because of the ever-expanding body of scientific knowledge and because the particular nature of scientific research demands a concentration on highly restricted areas of understanding; furthermore, the techniques of research are frequently stereotyped so as to permit only a minimum of intellectual resourcefulness.

Economic values, then, predominate; and the call for more technical education needs to be seen in the context within which it occurs, and in relation to the ends which it desires to promote. The upper and middle echelons of our society are to be manned increasingly by those who are capable of a particular level of expertise;[1] such people are likely to exert a considerable degree of social influence. The sort of cultural life implicit in the practise of technical pursuits therefore becomes a matter of vital importance; what sort of future does a technocracy—prophesied these long years—offer to our society? Is the marriage of business and the technical likely to bring about the situation diagnosed by Wright Mills in *The Power Elite*: 'By the middle of the twentieth century, the American élite have become an entirely different breed of men from those who could on any reasonable grounds be considered a cultural élite, or even for that matter cultivated men of sensibility.' (p. 351.)—particularly in view of his previous caveat: 'The training of skills that are of more or less direct use in the vocational life is an important task to perform, but ought not to be mistaken for liberal education: job advancement, no matter on what levels, is not the same as self-development, although the two are now systematically confused. Among "skills", some are more and some are less relevant to the aims of liberal—that is to say liberating— education.' (p. 318.)

The critic of current trends must face the warning given fifty years ago by Thorstein Veblen: 'We must adapt ourselves to the rule of the machine if we would use it and we have to use it not as we would always wish but as it is determined for us. Society has adapted itself to the machine process. Either you learn to think in its terms or not at all unless you want to go back to the farm and a pretty small farm at that.' (Dorfman: *Thorstein Veblen and his America*, p. 244.) In so far as education is concerned not with technical expertise only but with general culture, the cultural effects of the sort of experience inherent in the functioning of the machine are of great importance to our thinking about education. Veblen himself drew attention to some of the implications of machine tending. The workman, he sees, has become a 'factor involved in a mechanical process whose movement controls his motions'. The effect on his thought processes Veblen defines in these terms: 'Mechanically speaking, the machine is not his to do with it as his fancy may

[1] Cf. Sir Charles Snow's recent plea for a greater share on the part of scientists in the affairs of government.

suggest. His place is to take thought of the machine and its work in terms given him by the process that is going forward. His thinking in the premises is reduced to standard units of gauge and grade. If he fails of the precise measure, by more or less, the exigencies of the process check the aberration and drive home the absolute need of conformity.' (Veblen, *The Theory of Business Enterprise*). The intelligence needed 'runs in standard terms of quantitative precision': 'What the discipline of the machine industry inculcates . . . is regularity of sequence and mechanical precision; and the intellectual outcome is an habitual resort to terms of measurable cause and effect, together with a relative disparagement of such exercise of the intellectual faculties as does not run on these lines.' Though he is at pains to point out that of course the effect of hits technology is not yet by any means complete, in that the machine has not yet had time to mould habits so very far to its own image, nevertheless, 'Within the range of this machine-guided work, and within the range of modern life so far as it is guided by the machine process, the course of things is given mechanically, impersonally, and the resultant discipline is a discipline in the handling of impersonal facts for mechanical effect. It inculcates thinking in terms of opaque, impersonal cause and effect, to the neglect of those norms of validity that rest on usage and on the conventional standards handed down by usage. Usage counts for little in shaping the processes of work of this kind or in shaping the modes of thought induced by work of this kind.

'The machine process gives no insight into questions of good and evil, merit and demerit, except in point of material causation, nor into the foundations of the constraining force of law and order, except such mechanically enforced law and order as may be stated in terms of pressure, temperature, velocity, tensile strength, etc.

'The machine technology takes no cognizance of conventionally established rules of precedence; it knows neither manners nor breeding and can make no use of any of the attributes of worth. Its scheme of knowledge and of inference is based on the laws of material causation, not on those of immemorial custom, authenticity, or authoritative enactment. Its metaphysical basis is the law of cause and effect, which in the thinking of its adepts has displaced even the law of sufficient reason.'

Veblen makes the interesting point that the general effect on the mind of the workman (he is referring in the main to the very technically skilled workman) is to change the direction of his intelligence rather than to produce a state of affairs which can with any justice be described as 'numbing' or deterioration: 'The resulting difference in intellectual training is a difference in kind and direction, not necessarily in degree.' The question he does not face is whether there is any distinction in value as between the sort of intelligence involved in pre-industrial work processes and that stimulated by the technical training demanded by the onset of the machine. The sorts of qualities a technical (understood as relating chiefly to machinery) education seems to involve stress a particular range of possible responses to situations, leading, for instance, to an emphasis on a particular type of 'explanation'. D. H. Lawrence's comment on our attitude to children's 'why' questions[1] contains within it the germ of a fundamentally different orientation to that represented by a technically or scientifically biassed interest. The general movement of mind which is symptomatic of the revolution in our approach to phenomena is one which replaces aesthetic contemplation or acceptance by the desire to alter and control. Furthermore, the emphasis on constant change of technique or degree of efficiency may well be partly responsible for that restlessness which is so marked a feature of our civilization: '. . . l'enterprise moderne, aux U.S.A. particulièrement, est sujette à de fréquentes modifications dans les techniques et les méthodes de production, et par suite dans le composition des groupes de travail, dans les fonctions et les secteurs d'autorité des cadres. Ces changements se répercutent sur l'ouvrier. Ses habitudes, ses routines se trouvent alors bousculeés: d'où trouble et nécessité d'une réadaptation.'[2] (*Où Va le Travail Humain*, p. 145.)

---

[1] Cf. pp. 214-15.

[2] It is interesting to note that one of the early arguments for universal education derived from the constant change which technical progress involved. Dr. Hodgson, in his Report on certain Metropolitan Districts, has a fascinating page or two in

Again, technical work, of which machine work is an important facet, is essentially work which is circumscribed in its incidence; it takes place within a narrow context which is cut off from wider issues. Built into the notion of the technical is a concern for means in relation to a previously accepted end. Thus, when we speak of something's being a technical problem, we imply that there is a hiatus between some preconceived aim that we have in view and the present state of affairs which needs to be filled by a careful examination of available resources conceived in terms of their manipulation and subordination to an end other than themselves. This may well necessitate an abstraction—and a high degree of abstraction at that—from the totality of being implicit in what has thus become a focal point of technical attention; in this, technicism is deeply imbued with rationalism. I will illustrate my point from a situation in which man himself has become a technical aid. Taylorism, the notion of Scientific Management which did a great deal to 'rationalize' industry in the early years of the century, deeply imbued as it was with the notion of method ('the one best way') reduced, through its time-and-motion studies, man to the level of an addendum to the machine which he was supposed to be working; bio-psychological and sociological factors, which would admit the human being as something different in kind from the machine he was supposed to tend, were forgotten or suppressed. The steps of the Taylorian

which he urges the need for education among workmen as a mode of self-protection against technical change: 'Progress implies change, and to him who cannot change, progress threatens danger'. Furthermore, 'The savage who makes his own moccasins, wigwam, war robe, bow and arrow, who kills his own game and cooks it, has, so far as his employment goes, a better discipline of mind, a greater training of inventive faculty than the civilized operative, "hand", as he is aptly styled, who spends ten hours a day, for six days a week, for twelve months a year, and for twenty or thirty years in watching the revolution of a wheel, or in polishing a needle's point. Such a man is by a slackness of work reduced at once to starvation's edge; he can turn to nothing else that is not already over-stocked with many such as he. In such times as these of ever swifter progress in mechanism and manufacture, affecting as that must do the lot of innumerable individuals and families; surely it is desirable that men should, while young, be so taught as to have their wits about them (to use a common phrase), to be able to foresee coming changes, to anticipate them, and either turn them to good account, or by steady economy and power of adapting themselves to new circumstances escape from their personally unfavourable results.' (*Reports of the Newcastle Commission* (1858–61), vol. 3, pp. 560–1.)

Method, as revealed by Le Chatelier, indicate admirably what is involved in attention to the purely technical aspects of a problem:

(1) before any action set yourself a definite single and limited aim.

(2) before starting work, study scientifically the best methods to be employed to attain the end in view;

(3) before beginning work, bring together all necessary tools;

(4) act in exact conformity with the arranged programme.

It was only when the rationalistic psychology implicit in Taylorism was replaced by ideas drawn from a different tradition, those involved in the notion of 'gestalt', that the wholeness of the human factor and its many-sided complexity came under consideration.

In the elucidation of the technical, then, there is involved a number of basic stages. There is a philosophical determinism which indicates that a correctly analysed and conceived series of processes will inevitably bring about the desired end. There is a process of Cartesian simplification which involves the breaking down of a problem into its basic factors and their reconstitution as an interlocking series of events bound together in terms of cause and effect; and there is the fact that in most technologies these 'events' constitute variables of a monolithic type which offer independent opportunities for regularization in terms of their effects in the chain of occurrences which may be said to constitute the completed 'technology'. The failure of Taylorism as a human technique of industry provides a clue as to a basic incompatibility between the human and the mechanical; so that the 'human factor'—a significant term—needs to be seen as a factor different *in kind* from the other factors in a technical process.

Now, all this has its implication for technical education. For a concentration on the sorts of processes which are normally implicit in the development of technical 'know-how' contains as part of its make-up a condition of thought which may prove essentially dehumanizing—the sort of mistake made by Taylor and his associates in application to industry reveals something of the confusion and degradation which the proliferation of the technical mind may bring about. Prolonged concentration on a particular mode of procedure easily leads to the transference of its typical thought patterns into areas where they do not apply; and the sorts of situation where the notion of the technical is applicable and those in which it is not need careful delimitation. The broadly anti-traditional element involved in all technical discovery, too, reinforces those elements in our culture which tend to think of social problems as essentially technical ones, to be cured by what is significantly called 'social engineering'. Furthermore, so many of the problems in industry which the technicians face are short-term; this is a fact which may give such technicians an advantage over the operatives, whose work is not even of this nature; it is nevertheless one which in the end may well lead to psychic dissatisfaction: 'Les techniciens eux-mêmes, directeurs de fabrication, ingénieurs du *planning* ou des études, souffrent de ce manque de motivation à long terme. Ils ont sur les manœuvres l'avantage d'être occupés, sinon satisfaits, par la multiplicité des tâches à court terme que leurs responsibilités impliquent.' (*Où Va le Travail Humain*, p. 252.)

The dangers implicit in this sort of training have been summed up by Georges Friedmann in these terms: 'A tous les échelons, et, ajouterons-nous, dans tous les pays, le progrès technique, certaines formes pseudo-scientifiques d'organisation du travail, les conditions générales d'une impérieuse civilisation industrielle exercent une constante pression qui tend à multiplier un type humain (ou plutôt inhumain): celui qui nous avons appelé le "techniste", l'homme qui envisage tous les problèmes de l'industrie, et en général tous les problèmes de l'existence, de l'économie, de la culture, sous l'angle exclusif de la technique . . .'[1]

In such a situation, ends tend increasingly to be lost sight of. The major question of technical education, I take it, is how a discipline which offers such dangerous possibilities can achieve at once a measure of intellectual 'respectability' in its own right and at the same time lead on to that 'humanization' without

---

[1] Symptomatic of such an age is a view of sex education which reduces it to a matter of physiological detail.

which the technical remains a desiccation. In the workshops, the former problem can be seen as: 'Faire de leurs ateliers un milieu éducatif aussi favorable au travail de l'intelligence qu'à celui des mains.' (p. 289.) The need, it is suggested, is to bring out the abstract intellectual principles on which the *techne* is based: to treat it, in fact, as an intellectual discipline as well as a practical problem, as a technology rather than as a technique: 'Par contre, la technologie générale, partant du concret, par l'observation et l'expérimentation, s'élève vers l'abstrait . . . "La technologie générale expliquera les changements, le fonctionnement, cherchera le facteur constitutif des causes, étudiera leurs variations et les variations correspondantes des éffets techniques. Elle montrera ce qu'il y a de commun sous une multiplicité de phénomènes différents, elle abstraira une qualité ou une propriété d'un produit, d'un outil, et l'étudiera dans d'autres produits, d'autres outils, elle montrera l'évolution et la filiation sous des apparences de stabilité et de discontinuité. Partant de l'observation, de l'expérimentation et de la mesure, tout comme les sciences expérimentales, elle s'élèvera jusqu'à la relation numérique et abstraite." ' The general emphasis, indeed, needs, according to Friedmann, to be more evenly balanced between theoretical and practical work—to the advantage, indeed, of the practical work itself, as well as to the educational profit of the apprentices. Again, it is possible to employ the technical as a centre from which radiate a number of educative possibilities. Thus, from the sort of work undertaken by young students, not yet professionally oriented, it is possible to include: '. . . l'éducation du goût (colloboration de l'atelier avec le professeur de dessin d'art), celle du soin et de la précision (à laquelle veille, en liaison avec son collègue de l'atelier, le professeur de mathématiques), l'esprit d'observation, en liaison avec le professeur de sciences naturelles, l'esprit d'analyse et de synthèse, le gout de l'activité méthodique et aussi (en indispensable coopération avec le professeur de français), l'étude du milieu humain.' (pp. 294–5.)

The problem, as Friedmann sees it—and as many begin to see it in this country—proceeds from the growing realization: 'Notre monde est technique.' To put it in other words: '*Comment faire bénéficier les valeurs nouvelles de la science et de la technique du legs précieux des civilisations du passé?'* (p. 304). The question is indeed 'how?' It is a question which exercised Friedmann just as it exercised the Committee which produced the report on *Liberal Education in a Technical Age*. Solutions suggested are of two kinds: one is to 'liberalize' the technical by considering the 'social, historical and human implications of the subject' (p. 122), the other is to include non-technical liberal studies as part of the course. The former depends on an ability to see the 'liberal' implications of what may seem an unpromising technical field, as the teacher of building crafts, quoted in the report, saw them when he took his students to Hampton Court to study the various work there, so as to stimulate their awareness of the possibilities of their craft. The latter is often likely to be resisted by the students who are too examination ridden to be willing to devote much time and attention to what is not, obviously, of any immediate examinable value.

To realize that the technical in the final resort subserves human ends seems to provide the best way of extending its range and scope. Indeed, in his recent inaugural lecture, 'The Education of an Engineer', Professor Parkes, Professor of Engineering at Leicester University, has insisted that such an education is insufficient if it remains exclusively technological. Not only does he urge the need for a non-specialist engineering course (so that the purely technical aspect of the education itself ranges over the field of engineering by correlating themes relevant to the various specialist branches); he also insists that questions of management and design are of fundamental importance in the training of the engineer. Thus both the human and the aesthetic fields receive their share of attention: sociology and social psychology become important disciplines for what in the past has been too exclusively regarded from the technical angle.

Others, too, have urged the possibility of linking technical work with design as a means of refining the creative element implicit in aspects of technical work: 'La pensée technique . . . est une forme particulièrement précise de la pensée concrète. L'à-peu-près en est exclus par l'exigence des réalités auxquelles elle se confronte. Serait-elle pour cela une forme inférieure de la

197

pensée? Elle se cultive et s'exprime par le dessin industriel qui est par cela même un moyen particulièrement efficace d'excercer et de contrôler l'imagination créatrice, forme supérieure de l'intelligence.' (*Où Va le Travail Humain*, p. 283.) This, Friedmann quotes approvingly from M. Montagnan. Such views are not, indeed, foreign to our own best handbooks in metal craft: thus, the Shirleys write that 'Design is fundamental in all craftwork' and that 'the interest in good design must be deliberately cultivated'.[1] Such notions have some application even to modern mass production, for modern machine tools permit a fineness which has aesthetic possibilities.

Whatever I may think as a student of literature of a world which in so many ways denies the values of the literature I admire, as an educationist I can see that a 'scream of horror' would not be an adequate response. The benefit of the machine lies in the abundance it can produce, the cold and starvation it can obviate; allied to good design, it can make more widely available pleasing and beautiful objects. The dangers lie in certain temptations to the human spirit; these, at an obvious level, might be described as Faustian; in a more subtle way they may prove corroding to human capacities and skills, inducing a particular sort of responsiveness to human problems which denies what Martin Buber would call the 'Thou' quality in others—or, alternatively, the pervasive apathy of unstimulated potentiality.

But—'notre monde est technique'—at least to the extent that many do exercise technical skills, and their number is likely to increase. The time has come for a much more thorough exploration of the nature of technical education and of the possibilities it affords or can be induced to afford for a revised humanism as well as for the intellectual satisfaction it can provide *per se*. Our exploration of the technical field in education is deplorably backward, for the tendency has been to dismiss such an education as humanistically irrelevant or barbaric. With the world turning more and more to what the machine can offer, this is no longer an adequate response. Indeed, the humanization of the technical is one of our most pressing educational problems. For the

[1] A. J. and A. F. Shirley: *Handcraft in Metal.*

demand for machine-minders means that an ever-increasing proportion of our children are going to receive a technical education in the non-technological sense. They will form, indeed the great middle echelon between those whose abilities enable them to study the fundamental disciplines and the unskilled whose education must be thought out in radically different terms. What must be insisted on in all three is the fundamental place of the 'humanizing' process. Where the technically trained are concerned, this means that beyond their technical specialism they will need particular attention to be paid to their affective life in much the way suggested in the next chapter. In this respect, their education will be nearer that of the less able than that of the academically gifted.

CHAPTER SEVEN

The Education of the Less Able Child

———————————◆———————————

I

Today we seem further than ever from the solution to the problems which Matthew Arnold in *Culture and Anarchy* so resolutely faced: 'If England were swallowed up by the sea tomorrow, which of the two, a hundred years hence, would most excite the love, interest, and admiration of mankind,—would most, therefore, show the evidences of having possessed greatness,—the England of the last twenty years, or the England of Elizabeth, of a time of splendid spiritual effort, but when our coal, and our industrial operations depending on coal, were very little developed? Well, then, what an unsound habit of mind it must be which makes us talk of things like coal or iron as constituting the greatness of England, and how salutary a friend is culture, bent on seeing things as they are, and thus dissipating delusions of this kind and fixing standards of perfection that are real!' Yet perhaps the problem itself is not quite so simple as Arnold thought. He inherited an essentially aristocratic view of 'culture'—'the best that had been thought and said'—and hoped that, because the apostles of culture were, as he saw them, the true apostles of equality, the spread of culture, *his* sort of culture, was feasible and would in the end promote that particular type of egalitarianism implicit in his view of the role of culture. There is indeed an unresolved tension between his realization of the need for 'superiorities' and his concern for equality. To some extent he, too, was the victim of the utilitarian faith in the spread of education as an instrument of rationality, so that men had only to receive the tools of enlightenment for enlightenment duly to follow. Today, at least, we can see that this is not so; just as we can see that the culture of the minority can never be that of the majority as well; so that, as Mr. Eliot has stated: 'It is an essential condition of the preservation of the quality of the culture of the minority, that it should continue to be a minority culture.' The notion of the 'minority', of course, is not a simple one, as I suggested in Chapter Four. The area of human understanding has so increased that we ought perhaps to think in terms of minorities, groups who preserve high standards within particular areas of concern, implementing the 'best that has been thought and said' within their sphere. Inevitably the individuals who go to make up such groups will participate, in certain of their interests, in any revivified mass culture. Furthermore, in certain roles—as teachers, TV and film producers, musicians, etc.—they will have an opportunity to play their part in fashioning the culture of the folk, and the folk will make their own contributions as participants and, in a variety of interests and skills, as initiators. What we need to encourage is a wide range of excellencies at a number of levels. I have, in Chapter Four, tried to indicate that a common culture is a mirage which, if pursued, will not benefit the majority and runs a considerable danger of ruining the minority as well. If I suggest, by contrast, that the whole problem must be seen in terms of at least two cultures, this is only a way of mapping out broad levels of sophistication of interest, of stressing the need for differentiation and range; my aim is not to imply an isolated minority remote from the concerns of the folk majority. As a matter of social reality there will be an enormous variety of levels of achievement; and a new folk culture will inevitably encompass a substantial number of levels. What need to be kept in mind as guiding principles are that as against Dewey's stress on the priority of majority interests some human activities are of greater importance than others ('of greater importance' because they represent a more deliberate, refined and sophisticated exploitation of human potentiality—as poetry is superior to pushpin) and that most human activities offer opportunities of excellence within themselves so that the area of possibilities is extensive.

My reason for urging at least two cultures stems from the need to admit, quite honestly, that minority culture, to whatever extent (on the analogy of past models) it can seek enrichment by majority contacts, will inevitably represent the highest point of aspiration simply because its area of competence will encompass all the more important disciplines in the sense in which I have defined important. The onus of responsibility, indeed, lies with the minorities; it is largely (though not exclusively) from them that the impetus towards a purified cultural order must come. It is the virtue of the Pilkington Report, with its very varied membership, that, in a social climate where 'responsibility' has come to be regarded as a dirty word, it has dared to make a stand against deleterious and meretricious influences. Indeed, the whole of my book stems from the faith that, though the broad trend of events seems to be towards the further implementation of the values implicit in what I have termed the industrial-bureaucratic state, there is sufficient evidence of expostulation against the vulgarized cultural order which this state has spawned to make a contrary affirmation something more than merely quixotic. The point about Henry James' moral fable *The Lesson of the Master*, for instance, lies in the fact that the counter-vailing protest against the prostitution of talent is made.

To many people, of course, any talk of culture at all in the present world situation is simply a form of the higher time-wasting, expressing an irresponsible type of irrelevance. 'The imperatives of educational strategy', which was Sir Charles Snow's translation of his Rede lecture for broadcast purposes, contained no reference to 'pop' song or Bartok, comics or classics. His concern was hunger and poverty and behind them, the exigencies of *weltpolitik*: who, in fact, is going to get the technicians there first? ' *Erst Kommt das Fressen, dann kommt die Moral,*' he quotes from Brecht. His criteria are quantitative rather than qualitative, so many mouths to feed rather than so many souls to save: we seem to hear an echo of Frederic Harrison's words that drove Matthew Arnold into print: 'Culture is a desirable quality in a critic of new books, and sits well on a professor of *belles lettres*; but as applied to politics, it means simply a turn for small-fault-finding, love of selfish ease, and indecision in action.' The words may be Frederic Harrison's, but they would find many an echo today among our practical educators, to whom, even if poverty isn't an issue, the need for greater affluence is. 'We need to make the best we can of marginal talent. This means compulsion'—compulsion, that is, in the raising of the school leaving age. Is it not significant that *this* would seem to be the crucial consideration in the minds of the Crowther committee?

II

It is with these considerations in mind that I want to take up here more specifically some of the points I have already raised in relation to the education of what I shall term, in order to avoid emotional overtones, our less able children.[1] All along, in my criticism of the current ethos and of the degree of social commitment implied both by 'uniformity' and 'diversity' I have been hinting at an alternative tradition. It is not one that ignores the social aspect; it is merely one that sees the 'social' problem in radically different terms. It appreciates that social life springs out of individual lives, that apart from the individual our society does not exist. In this connection it is well to bear in mind the view of L. H. Myers, expressed through the agency of the Guru in the *Pool of Vishnu*: the view that 'Every action is personal at its roots' and that the right ordering of the social life depends on the right ordering of the personal life; a view which admittedly fails perhaps to appreciate the degree to which the two are bound up, but which, in my view, puts the emphasis in the right place. What I have in mind is what is expressed by D. H. Lawrence: 'So let our ideal be living, spontaneous individuality in every man and woman. Which living spontaneous individuality, being the hardest thing of all to come at, will need the most careful rearing.'

[1] I intend by these roughly the least able 40 per cent of the community—apart from those who are diagnosed as educationally sub-normal.

If I am right to take up this general position, that it is ultimately out of the satisfaction of individual lives that such social harmony as is attainable in this world can come and not out of some attempt to bring about cohesion where no such cohesion can exist, the first step towards building up a satisfactory syllabus lies in the recognition of radical difference between natures in our society, a radical difference which talk about a 'common culture' only serves to obfuscate. I have already indicated, in my comment on the passage from George Bourne quoted above (cf. p. 102), that narrowness is not necessarily a weakness. Of course, the situation as described by Bourne is no longer recapturable, even if it were considered desirable in itself, about which one inevitably has many reservations. Yet that does not mean that we should not be willing to listen and learn from the strength which Bourne and others have found in the old preindustrial way of life, and build into any view we may form of the education desirable for the less able members of the community what of value we can discover of former satisfactions. For such 'narrowness' is by no means incompatible with a morally stern individuality which represents something finer than, for instance, Dewey's pressure for like-mindedness in action.

One element in the situation which has certainly changed is the satisfaction to be derived from the work that the less able are likely to undertake. It is surprising that the Crowther Report has not implemented its members' encouragement of an increasingly technical trend of events by some consideration of the sorts of problems which factory work poses. They would have found a good deal to make them think in Georges Friedmann's admirably balanced *Industrial Society*, with its highly relevant account of the decline in subtlety and skill engendered by the technological rationalization of the earlier years of the century, implicit in the movement towards 'scientific management' referred to as Taylorism. Much production work at the assembly line, for example, Friedmann reveals there, in his *Où Va le Travail Humain*, and in his *Travail en Miettes*[1] is only really suitable for those who can achieve total abstraction from their work:

[1] Recently translated as *The Anatomy of Work* (1961).

'Seuls les individus capables de cette rigoureuse séparation
[entre le *série physique* des gestes plus ou moins automatisés et
par conséquent n'exigeant qu'une activité médullaire, et la *série
mentale* des idées et des images qui alimentent la distraction, la
rêverie, ce que les Anglais appellent le "day-dreaming"] et
dont l'esprit, durant les longues heures de travaux "mono-
tones", effectués aux lisières de la conscience, peut errer à sa
guise, sont aptes à travailler longuement et avec succès à la
chaîne.'[1] (*Où Va le Travail Humain*, p. 232.) Furthermore, such
work, after a time, takes away initiative, the ability to make
decisions: 'La chaîne, me disait un contremaître américain,
enlève aux gens "la volonté de prendre un risque", en cherchant
ailleurs un autre métier, en s'instruisant en dehors des heures de
travail. Tout se passe comme si l'accoutumance progressive aux
travaux "dépersonnalisés", dépourvus d'initiative et de respon-
sabilité, favorisant le traintrain quotidien et la rêverie, provo-
quait peu à peu, malgré l'exutoire de la sociabilité, une sorte
d'usure de l'énergie et d' "assoupissement" de l'individu.'
(pp. 150–1.) Though some amelioration can be sought through
the camaraderie implicit in the social groupings which form in a
factory, so that human intercourse to some extent compensates
for lack of job satisfaction,[2] in effect Friedmann paints a sombre
picture of lost skills and frenzied leisure pursuits in compensation: such leisure pursuits, among the black workers of Detroit,
for instance, involve an extravagance which '. . . exprime, bien

[1] Alan Sillitoe's *Saturday Night and Sunday Morning* is written by someone who
knows the life of the factory from the inside, and it contains interesting evidence
concerning the degradation of work implied in operative 'skills' and the stimulation
to fantasy living it engenders: 'If your machine was working well—the motor
smooth, stops tight, jigs good—and you spring your actions into a favourable
rhythm you became happy. You went off into pipe-dreams for the rest of the day . . .
'Time flew while you wore out the oil-soaked floor and worked furiously without
knowing it: you lived in a compatible world of pictures which passed through your
mind like a magic-lantern, often in vivid and glorious loony-colour, a world where
memory and imagination ran free and did acrobatic tricks with your past and with
what might be your future, an amok that produced all sorts of agreeable visions.'
The mental and moral bankruptcy of such a world is demonstrated in the body of
the book. The obverse to the factory is that 'cosy world of pubs and noisy tarts'
(and married women) through which Arthur Seaton finds his spiritual fulfilment.
The contrast with Dewey's optimism (cf. p. 50) is worth noting.

[2] Recently, too, such phenomena as 'job enlargement' have done something to
mitigate the narrowness of skills employed.

davantage, un besoin de s'affirmer coûte que coûte durant les heures de liberté, hors du travail qui ne permet, lui, aucune affirmation de soi.' (p. 149.) while, where work is concerned: 'La fabrication de série, telle qu'elle se développe aux U.S.A. (et mutatis mutandis en Europe) porte en elle de gros dangers. La spécialisation des professionnels, formés dans le moule standardisé des tâches parcellaires, accentue l'éclatement et le déclin des métiers globaux, fondés sur la culture professionnelle et la fierté dans l'achèvement d'un produit (*pride in work*).' (p. 161.) We are told that automation will demand a rising standard of technical knowledge—and, indeed, the idea is implicit in the Crowther committee's concern. Furthermore, it is said to need a new flexibility of outlook, to allow for increased technical change. But I would like to know a good deal more than seems to be clear at the moment what exactly, in terms of skill and sensibilities engaged, the new race of machine-minders are to be involved in; and there still remains the question, posed with brutal frankness by Sir George Thomson in *The Foreseeable Future*: 'What is the future of the stupid?'

Certainly, the sort of situation revealed so soberly by Friedmann is profoundly disquieting, not least because so much of the culture of the folk in the past grew out of work—some of their music and a great deal of their art. Where work is unsatisfactory, as for a considerable percentage of people it must appear to be today, leisure comes to take on more and more importance; and with technical advance it comes to look as if 'the stupid'— the unskilled—may find it more and more difficult to find work, while at the same time the hours of work will gradually be reduced for the rest.[1] In other words, we may well be forced to

---

[1] Opinions vary as to what is likely to happen, of course. Sir George Thomson considers that 'the stupid' will find it difficult to get suitable jobs; and he is supported by Professor C. F. Carter of Manchester University, who thinks that within twenty-five years there will be considerable difficulty in finding any form of employment for the unskilled, the untrained and those of lower intelligence: '. . . there is little doubt there will be a shortage, a contraction in the amount of unskilled work to be done. I would suggest this is probably one of the reasons why the present total of unemployment in the United States is proving quite intractable, because there has been a displacement of labour by automation, labour of a kind very difficult to absorb into any other use.' On the other hand, officials in industry with whom I have discussed this problem consider that this has been a perennial

face the profound problem of turning over from a work-oriented society to one which will have to find its serious *raison d'être* in its leisure-time activities, a transformation which raises the gravest psychological and moral problems.[1] These are some of the realities which lie behind the cry for increased production.

So it is in leisure—perhaps rather than through attempts to humanize the factory—that man may have to express himself; the human relations movement in industry carries with it the danger of false 'personalization'. Indeed, David Riesman, in *The Lonely Crowd*, urges the importance of leisure as a means to the autonomy of 'other-directed' people in the modern world where work has itself come to take on many characteristics of such false personalization. As the psychological rather than technical pressures of work continue to grow (as in the human relations movement), the way out to some measure of personal responsibility and autonomy is not, he thinks, through personalizing, emotionalizing and moralizing the machine process or attempting to introduce joy and meaning into the industrial process itself: '. . . perhaps it is possible to gain from layout engineering greater results in making work more tolerable and less exhausting than are gained from the manipulative practices of the mood engineers. Pending automatization, assembly work can be rearranged to reduce monotony; plants can be relocated to reduce travel time. This means working with rather than against the grain of impersonality in modern industry.' (pp.

cry since the times of the Luddites and that new industries will arise or other forms of employment, perhaps to cater for the very leisure created, will absorb the displaced labour. Nevertheless, the threat persists.

[1] A fact which is demonstrated by the way in which in a number of industries the shorter working day is sought simply as a means of gaining more overtime work at higher pay. It is suggested that people don't want more leisure—they don't know what to do with it. I was told this by a high official at one of the largest steel works in the country who instanced the clamour for overtime at his works as a pointer to the truth of his remarks. Yet the dilemma persists of the need for more leisure to compensate for the unsatisfactory nature of much work: '. . . it must seem highly probable that for several generations yet there will remain a multitude of jobs in which the worker can find no outlet for his tastes, his deeper wishes or his personality. Even a radical reform of society . . . will not endow such work with the scope and interest necessary to make it the centre of his life and a means of self-fulfilment. Thus everything points to the growing importance of leisure time for the humanization of our technical civilization.' (G. Friedmann, *The Anatomy of Work*, p. 121.)

318–19.) It will come through play rather than work: 'The first step may consist of giving play a far higher priority as a produce both of societies and character than we give it today . . . play, far from having to be the residue sphere left over from work time and work feeling, can increasingly become the sphere for the development of skill and competence in the art of living. Play may prove to be the sphere in which there is still room for the would-be autonomous man to reclaim his individual character from the pervasive demands of his social character.' (pp. 326–8.) Both the 'work-directed' puritan heritage and 'outer-direction' have made play difficult to accept 'seriously', as it were.[1] The changeover may be essential—but it will require a profound psychological reorientation which much talk about education for leisure fails to note.

The upshot of all this is that the vocational appeal in schools must be used with some care; technological advance seems likely to make the 'work' of the less able either less satisfying, or to do away with their need to work at all. The vocational bait, then, is likely to become less legitimate in that at the very best the sorts of jobs the children are likely to be given will demand only the minimum of training—and moreover the sort of training that can best be given in a few hours or days on the spot. In considering the 'needs' of the less able, I think these points are of fundamental importance. Furthermore, other strains are introduced by the fact that the basis of moral conduct is becoming increasingly a matter of rational assessment and less and less a

[1] As Bruno Bettelheim puts it in *The Informed Heart*:
'I do not know whether and to what degree automation will . . . (free) the worker from having to repeat the same task over and over again. It should certainly do away with much drudgery in the productive process. But as less of man's labor will be needed for survival, more of his time and energy will become available for other tasks. Unless he finds ways to expend this time and energy on tasks deeply meaningful to him, his personal agony will increase to the degree that less of his physical and mental energies go to assuring survival for himself and his family. It is relatively easy to find life meaningful if most of one's energy is constructively spent in securing the essentials of living for oneself and one's own. It is quite difficult to find that much meaning in less essential or less obviously meaningful tasks. We can all derive a great deal of self respect and deep satisfaction from the knowledge that we are helping others and ourselves survive; very little meaning can be wrung from the ability to provide ourselves and others with ever less essential conveniences.' (p. 57.)

matter of appeal to authority. This, to certain classes in the community, may constitute a gain; but, to those who find rational analysis difficult, it may constitute a considerable loss.[1]

Such children, then, are probably going to have more and more leisure; and, in that leisure, they are going to be subjected to a number of depersonalizing influences which will blur their apprehensions of the real world of relationships in which they live. Modern mass communications will induct them, in part at least, into an unreal world of powerfully communicated fantasy—the fantasy of the advertising commercial, the 'pop' song, the railway bookstall novel, the rampant infidelity of the cinema to anything approaching real life experience—all stimulating to various forms of *bovarysme*. It is a compensation culture evoked, in part, by an unsatisfactory work situation. Foremost among our requirements, then, will be an education that educates to 'reality', the sort of reality that George Bourne depicts

[1] Karl Mannhiem makes the same point more fully in *Ideology and Utopia*:
'Without, however, a social life-situation compelling and tending toward individualization, a mode of life which is devoid of collective myths is scarcely bearable. The merchant, the entrepreneur, the intellectual, each in his own way occupies a position which requires rational decisions concerning the tasks set by everyday life. In arriving at these decisions, it is always necessary for the individual to free his judgments from those of others and to think through certain issues in a rational way from the point of view of his own interests. This is not true for peasants of the older type nor for the recently emerged mass of subordinate white-collar workers who hold positions requiring little initiative, and no foresight of a speculative kind. Their modes of behaviour are regulated to a certain extent on the basis of myths, traditions or mass-faith in a leader. Men who in their everyday life are not trained by occupations which impel toward individualization always to make their own decisions, to know from their own personal point of view what is wrong and what is right, who from this point on never have occasion to analyse situations into their elements and who, further, fail to develop a self-consciousness in themselves which will stand firm even when the individual is cut off from the mode of judgment peculiar to his group and must think for himself—such individuals will not be in a position, even in the religious sphere, to bear up under such severe inner crises as scepticism. Life in terms of an inner balance which must be ever won anew is the essentially novel element which modern man, at the level of individualization, must elaborate for himself if he is to live on the basis of the rationality of the Enlightenment. A society which in its division of labour and functional differentiation cannot offer to each individual a set of problems and fields of operation in which full initiative and individual judgment can be exercised, also cannot realize a thorough-going individualistic and rationalistic *Weltanschauung* which can aspire to become an effective social reality.' (pp. 31–2.) And, of course, modern industrial conditions can offer it even less than a peasant society in the nature of its work.

his peasants as facing—so that their life had strength as well as narrowness—only translated into twentieth-century terms, where his valley has disappeared for ever. This, of course, will raise the whole question of the level of consciousness at which we can aim. What, in fact, is required is a new folk culture—to replace one whose strength lay precisely in its mature acceptance of the conditions of human existence, which displayed remarkable subtleties and beauties within the various media in which it expressed itself, and which was, therefore, at the opposite pole to that which so often passes for popular culture today;[1] though we must fear lest those who, in effect, 'created' this culture were the more intelligent of the 'folk' (minor 'mute inglorious Miltons') who are now creamed off by the efficiency of our selective system. The dangers and implications of this need more investigation than they have received.

First, then, I would support Mr. A. W. Rowe's contention, in his *Education of the Average Child*, that 'Many of the traditional subjects, taken over *en bloc* from the grammar school curriculum, are of little use in educating the average child'—a sentiment which I would adopt as the foundation of my thinking about the curriculum for less able children. (The common curriculum, indeed, is one of the enormities of the comprehensive school.) We have got to begin by asking what, in the situation as I have diagnosed it all too briefly in the earlier part of this book, are the essential things in the development of the non-academic child; what fields of interest and importance are relevant to his level of consciousness. I have distinguished four: the affective life, the physical life, the domestic life, and the environmental challenge of the machine; these are often interrelated but they are necessarily distinguished for the sake of analysis. There is, first and foremost, the affective life—the life of the emotions. It is roughly in this sphere that the modern world most lets down its young people, for, of course, it is closely connected with the moral life as well; or, to put it another way, it is highly relevant

---

[1] I am not, of course, so foolish as to think that the school by itself can create such a culture. But it can take a stand against deleterious influences; and in the training of the affective life desiderated below, it can re-awaken the folk tradition in music, literature and the arts as well as encourage 'creative' elements.

to the *quality* of our lives, with the realization that in the inti-macies of our day-to-day living it is possible to function at a variety of levels in accordance with the way in which our feelings are directed. When then I refer to the affective life, I refer to the life of the emotions with their moral implications for conduct.[1] Partly this will be a matter of the relationships within the school —of the *manner* of approach both to child and subject-matter; but what is to be taught is what perhaps more concerns us here.

We have, I am sure, to think primarily in terms of affective satisfactions, related to immediacies of feeling and response.[2] In general, the question of the *level* of attention at which we can expect the less able child to function has been thought about too little; the move towards a common culture, with its rationalist basis and its emphasis on helping people to learn how to think has induced the belief that we can expect an extension of con-sciousness *in these terms*, at the level of rational generality, to all members of the community.[3] Yet even with the Grammar-school

---

[1] In view of the enormous influence of Greek culture on our way of life—and this has been true of our thinking about education—it is surprising how little attention has been paid to Greek modes of education, where the less able are concerned. Plato in *The Laws* fully appreciated the importance of the affective life in the ordinary man. There, as Mr. Gould points out in his *Development of Plato's Ethics* it is through the emotions that the legislator is to work. As Plato himself puts it: 'Passionate sensations of pleasure, revulsion and desire are basic characteristics of human nature; they are precisely like pulleys or strings which operate on every mortal creature, inevitably and with fundamental effect' (*Laws*, 732). Thus, songs become 'spells for the soul'; the arts, religion and the festivals they share work for that concord of the soul which leads to virtue. (A good account of the education of *The Laws* is to be found in *Plato's Cretan City*, by Glenn R. Morrow.) These aspects of Greek education seem to me to point ways of engaging the sensibilities that ought to be of fundamental importance for the modern world. I shall hope to explore these possibilities more fully in my next book.

[2] 'I suggest that there is a close connection between the non-involvement of the personality in the fragmentary jobs required by factory and office and the need for self-expression which is equally excluded from the various duties of every-day life.' (G. Friedmann, *The Anatomy of Work*, p. 110.) Some of the most philosophically cogent justifications for treating the life of the emotions 'seriously' are to be found in the work of Ernst Cassirer and Professor Susanne K. Langer.

[3] 'Consciousness comes to them willy-nilly,' as Birkin retorted to Hermione's sentimental primitivism in Lawrence's *Women in Love*. What I am pleading for is not, it must be emphasized, a regression to the primitive; such a regression is an impossibility even if it were considered desirable, which it is not. But we need to grasp the question of level of consciousness, particularly in relation to the ability to arrive at rational decisions based on the capacity to conceptualize, to abstract

211

pupil, one notes the unhappy effect induced by an attempt to think and argue at too high a level of abstraction, so that the concrete reality and particularity of individuals is forgotten: 'we produce the political, the emotional idea, evading sensation and thought,' as Mr. T. S. Eliot puts it, apropos his comment that Henry James had a 'mind so fine that no idea could violate it'.

Such ways are doubly unfortunate with the less able child in whom intellectual control is always precarious, and whose ordering of experience needs to be achieved on a different basis. Traditionally, his world is an oral one and, as George Bourne pointed out, it is among the immediacies of home and local environment that he moves with the greatest ease. The extension of his world through wireless and television has not fundamentally altered this, even if it has offered a number of substitute figures and situations for the immediately known ones of former times. It is still the homely and intimate that catch on, even with their new soft centre—the Archers, the Dales, Wilfred Pickles, Coronation Street. When it is the exotic, it is the marvellous, the thrilling, the horrific, the pathetic that appeals. The logic of such things is bound together by narrative, though it tends to operate imagistically, that is to say as a series of imagined situations with their appropriate emotional reaction. [The folk tale rarely seeks psychological elaboration but exists as a series of 'strong' situations strung together with the minimum of comment; analogous is the modern reader's liking for books 'with plenty of conversation in them', where dramatic clash is evident, rather than description, however atmospheric.] Concern for motivation and explanation is comparatively lacking— these are sophisticated, rationalistic accretions, the offspring of another 'culture' trained in the logical relations of cause and effect.

It is for this reason that, in times past, the sophisticated, when they have needed to address the folk, have addressed them

and to generalize, processes which play a large part in our rationalistic civilization but endowment in which is patently not shared equally among our people. Obviously one would want the area of decision-making to be extended as far as possible; but to consider that all are equally endowed in this respect is as sentimental as to opt for a return to the primitive.

in terms of symbol and image, as the Church addressed them in medieval times through fresco, or, in sermons, through concrete presentation of abstract virtues and vices, and, as the advertiser today knows how to approach them, through the pictured image. Professor Owst's *Literature and Pulpit in Medieval England* reveals the extent to which the preacher introduced what, in his terminology he calls the 'commonplace' and the 'realistic' into his sermons. He quotes with approval Miss Evelyn Underhill's statement that 'It is characteristic of the primitive mind that it finds a difficulty about universals and is most at home with particulars. The Catholic peasant may find it easier to approach God through and in his special saint, or even a special local form of the Madonna. This is the inevitable corollary of the psychic level at which he lives; and to speak contemptuously of his "superstition" is wholly beside the point.'[1] And adds: 'To some extent it is already true to say that the characteristic features of English medieval preaching so far revealed in our studies exhibit this same desire to escape as far as possible from the abstract and universal in religion, and to be "at home in particulars". That special devotion to the person of a romantic Queen of Heaven exhibited it in our first chapter. So also does the impersonation of Vices and Virtures, and the whole emphasis upon familiar concrete *figures* and illustrative scenes . . .' (p. 110).

Another feature of interest in these sermons is the repetitiveness of the *exempla* employed to illustrate or enliven the sermon: 'On the whole there is amazingly little originality in the choice of tales. The old favourites are repeated again and again, as though there was no risk of creating boredom with their perpetual staleness.' Despite a century and a half's emphasis on romantic 'originality' such features of repetition still play some part in our mass culture. The radio show, like ITMA, with its repetition of well-known characters each with his/her appropriate formula, and above all, the phenomenon of the Western, where the variations are usually small, show something of the appeal that repetition can have. The folk mind, of course, has altered; but insights into the *way* in which it works and the ways in which it can be appealed to should not be neglected because of

[1] This is borne out in C. M. Bowra's recent *Primitive Song*, cf. p. 92.

that peculiar twentieth-century arrogance which thinks to have 'progressed' so far beyond more 'primitive' times.

The lesson of all this is that certain long-standing traditions of English teaching need careful re-examination. The sort of writing attempted—an alien mode to these pupils, be it remembered—must rehearse the logic of their own minds rather than the logic of an unpalatable, more rationalistic 'culture'; and an imagistic, symbolic type of poetry writing meets their capabilities much more easily than does prose writing, with its more rigid structure and its greater technical demands of grammar and punctuation. By and large, the logic of a prose paragraph is a logic of sense and connectedness that is yet 'artificially' broken up in accordance with the demands of sentence structure. Moreover, the purpose is statement rather than evocation, each sentence adding its tithe in a linear structure.

By contrast, the sort of free verse poetry I have in mind can be impressionistic, its structure pointilliste rather than that of the completed brush stroke. What provides the structure is an emotional reaction, a series of disparate raids on the inarticulate rather than a coherently interlinked configuration. Indeed, in poetry, logical discontinuity is not necessarily a fault: the ordering principle is emotional, evocative, imagistic rather than logical, connected and rational. What I intend is admirably illustrated by parts of Lawrence's poem *Bat*, where, in the views of the bat, the comments are momentarily impressionistic (a series of camera angles and sound shots, if the terminology serves) followed by the instinctive emotional frisson: 'Not for me.' Lawrence, of course, had a theory about the sort of poetry he wished to write; it was to be essentially that of the moment; and in this he curiously betrays the mind movements of those who belonged to the environment from which he sprang—at least on his father's side—and the sort of coherence to which they can aspire, the 'natural' way in which they can most fully order their experience which is quite different from an intellectual ordering. It was such experience that enabled Lawrence to notice a very different feature of children's 'Why' questions than that assumed by the ordinary, positivistically trained child psychologist: 'He will ask "why" often enough. But he more often asks why the sun shines, or why men have moustaches, or why grass is green, than anything sensible. Most of a child's questions are, and should be, unanswerable. They are not questions at all. They are exclamations of wonder, they are *remarks* half sceptically addressed. When a child says, "Why is grass green?" he half implies, "Is it really green or is it just taking me in?" And we solemnly begin to prate about cholorophyll. Oh, imbeciles, idiots, inexcusable owls!' (*Fantasia of the Unconscious.*) It was why Lawrence also stated categorically that 'For the mass of people, knowledge *must* be symbolical, mythical, dynamic'; and why he urged, in the education of children, 'The voice of dynamic sound, not the words of understanding'.

So then the way is through poetry, paradoxical as this will seem to be to those who find poetry—the wrong sort of poetry, usually—so much of a drug on the market; and anything else in the arts which will touch the affective centres, even if some concessions must be made to the rationalistic State in terms of instruction in letter writing, form filling and chores of a like nature.

But there is another basic need for such children—the moral need to come to terms with the 'real' world, particularly in view of the insincerities of the mass media, the world of relationships. A more general view of the role of the arts will take this in mind, so that, as I have indicated, what I am asking for is not a thin aestheticism but a grappling with the real world through the relevant medium. In this way, at least, we give him a chance to become sensitized to what *is*, capable, in some degree, of ordering, with regard to the logic of his senses, his experience, and, in some small degree, one would hope, armed against other affective challenges which many are shrewd and clever enough to employ. We can hope to influence his conduct, so that what I have in mind will have its effect on behaviour.

Let me begin, then, by distinguishing a number of basic media through which the affective ordering may be helped. [Perhaps the really disturbed child cannot be touched in this way—though achievement in any of these fields would be of great assistance— art and drama, after all, can be used 'therapeutically'.] There is, it is agreed, the use of language—that will need attention.

There is the desire for movement, one branch of which leads to dance with its association with music, the other to mime and drama—role playing, in effect, with its possibilities of empathy. There is the desire to shape and make—partly technical, let it not be forgotten—and partly a matter of imitative, yet trainable delight in shape and contour. In all these matters there is a folk tradition to reawaken. Furthermore, in contemporary terms, all impinge immediately and concretely on everyday life as the modern teenager sees it. He (and she) talks; he will 'twist', or whatever the latest craze may be; he will spend a great deal of his spare time and money on pop music. He will attend the cinema or watch the television; he will read the cheap newspapers, and these things, it is relevant to remind ourselves, will affect his attitudes much more than what passes for formal education. My point about all this, is that we must not shut our eyes to what these various things mean to him in out-of-school terms. We must be prepared actively to combat and demonstrate—for example, in the analysis of newspapers we can try to show the falsity of advertisements (with their links with the domestic life) so that the children become used to asking qualitative questions in relation to the concrete things they all see and use; and through free verse poetry writing show how far short in descriptive power the modern press falls in its handling of words. We must encourage our children to read, by reading to them, by getting them involved in books, not by focusing attention on irrelevant grammar. And we must be prepared to accept as a starting point some of the forms which our modern mass culture has evolved for itself and to work from them, not ignore them; teen-age 'pop' culture points to affective needs unfulfilled by our rationalistic education. For example, we might conceivably explore the skiffle group—I would add the resuscitated calypsos, a form capable of development—as a starting point for music making. Again, I think film making on a group basis should be seriously considered as a school subject. This would, where possible, involve discussion of old masterpieces of the past, after some introduction to the technicalities of film-making, the writing of scripts—preferably documentary films, which can often be very successfully made by amateurs; fictional attempts are usually a failure—the consideration of images and their juxtaposition, the need for cutting. The television should be utilized and discussed.[1] Where drama and movement are concerned I would like to see a development of the work sponsored by Laban and his followers. Here I would draw attention to the recently completed thesis of a higher degree student of mine Miss V. Bruce, *Dance and Dance Drama in Education*, which gives the fullest account of such work yet attempted.

The common factor involved in all this is some return to the concentration on symbol and image rather than on intellectual processes; handwriting, painting, pottery, weaving, as well as the traditional wood and metal crafts, are what I have in mind; and the 'teddy-boy' uniform and the recently popular brightly coloured stockings worn by young people are an indication of the contemporary craving for colour in a drab world. But these things should be treated from the point of view of forming taste in relation to contemporary design, as well as from the technical standpoint. This, too, will link with the sort of domestic training that aids home-building.

IV

My second centre round which the curriculum should be built is the domestic life. This will receive a greater emphasis in the education of girls, of course, but there is no reason why boys should not be involved to some extent. Lawrence suggested: 'The rudiments of domestic labour, such as boot-mending, plumbing, soldering, painting and paper-hanging, gardening—all these minor trades on which domestic life depends, and in which every working man should have some proficiency.' ('Education of the People.') This would give us something of a start, at any rate; and, even if some items on the list have an

---

[1] Indeed, there is a case to be made out for the possibility that any new folk culture which evolves must be primarily *visual*, employing the media in which, in the modern world, the folk find themselves most at home. The old folk tradition, though re-invoked, cannot simply be resuscitated; nevertheless this folk education I have in mind is in an essential part of itself a re-invocation, a re-assertion of a past tradition reinterpreted. It will need to evolve its own symbolism, its own mythologies.

old-fashioned sound, it gives an indication of the sort of approach involved. It is with the girls, however, that the effort must be made—to break down the idea that the home is a sort of prison from which any escape is better than none—or alternatively a dream world of popular song where there are no problems. What is now considered as domestic science could be used as a core, though with a good deal more time devoted to it. Here, if anywhere, are the proper exercises for such rationality and decision-making as these children are capable of—rather than on the abstract notions of citizenship or what Lawrence called the 'desert void of right and wrong'. The purchase of goods for the household can be considered in relation to advertisements on the one hand and the rational advice given by *Which* and *Shopper's Guide* on the other. Learning how to spend money wisely becomes essential in our 'affluent society'; and it involves making decisions in relation to concrete actualities of a sort more easily comprehensible to these children.

Much more concern for cooking should be fostered—if only to try to disgust our populace with the typical English restaurant meal; some biology, too, for the brighter girls, and a little dietetics. Training in mothercraft and some preparation for marriage (which means much more than sex education) for the older girls—to do something to drive out the cheap romantic notions they derive from the films and 'pop' songs. There must be needlework, making clothes, household articles, darning and mending. The school flat (or flats, if possible) should become an important centre of activity—with some real training in the choice of furniture and articles in the flat to be chosen for quality—not cheapness, as I suspect must have been the case in a number of school flats I have seen. Visitors might be entertained in the flats; certainly, some training in how to entertain would be desirable.[1] Of course, it is a tremendous fight against

---

[1] The notion of learning how to entertain perhaps summons up notions of trivialities such as are sometimes found in American schools (together with courses on how to use the telephone). It is interesting then, to consider how the Japanese have traditionally regarded these arts: 'Several social arts were developing . . . cultivated to some extent among the people as a whole. These arts were those of flower arrangement, gardening, the tea ceremony and incense smelling.

'The art of flower arrangement . . . was regarded not merely as a decorative art,

the cheap furniture shop, and one will often lose; but the effort is worth making. Laundering should be taught. For some of this the assistance of part-time outsiders—real cooks, launderers and so on—can be sought, so that the jobs seem important and worthwhile.[1]

For boys, the main emphasis must come on the machine rather than on the domestic life. The internal combustion engine, the mechanics of the radio set, the television and tape recorder (where there is the necessary ability); the electric motor, the steam engine, together with some basic principles involved, provide centres of treatment which fascinate many boys. A course in mechanics could be based on practical work with bicycles and engines of many kinds. In this way the door is left open for later specialization on the technical side.

Finally, of course, there is the physical life: what I am thinking of here are games, physical education linked with the new interest in movement and dance drama mentioned above, and a much fuller exploitation of the Outward Bound ideas, and those stimulated by the Duke of Edinburgh's award—camping, canoeing, hiking, rock-climbing and so on, in accordance with the opportunities of the locality. And what geography is done can be done in relation to local excursions and should include, for instance, map-reading.[2]

What goes out? Certainly formal history and geography and

but as a means of cultivating gentleness of spirit and disinterested attention to things of the spirit by using common objects to produce aesthetic effects . . .

'The tea ceremony—an elaborate, almost ritualistic refinement of the smallest act and gesture in the preparation, serving and drinking of tea—was a grace of culture . . . It was regarded as a soul-calming art . . .' (E. D. Myers, *Education in the Perspective of History*, pp. 148–9). I do not, of course, suggest the resuscitation of such arts for our children! I merely draw attention to possible implications of what can too quickly be dismissed as beneath the dignity of the modern school.

[1] A good deal of this, of course, goes on now. What I am asking for, however, is that these skills shall become one of the main ingredients of the curriculum, rather than peripheral as at present.

[2] I have said nothing about religious instruction which, of course, remains a compulsory 'subject'. Every effort ought to be made to convey the Christian message and its morality. But can one seriously hope that there are enough devoted teachers to make it live in the minds of our blankly incomprehending children to whom it remains at most a fugitive echo irrelevant amidst the pressures that go to make up their world? We can only hope to re-awaken a Christian morality through the expectations of conduct we arouse in the implementation of the syllabus.

a good deal of the arithmetic which is still often taught might well disappear. There should be no second language—by and large unimportant for English children of 'average' ability—and as little in the way of commercial subjects as possible—typing and shorthand do not 'humanize'. At the same time, any history that is taught can come, for instance, through the domestic course—the social history of domestic life. Geography, as I have stated, can come through Physical Education. There will need to be a great deal of breaking down of subject barriers in accordance with the aptitudes of the individual teachers. I do not think there is much point in some of the social studies at present undertaken. I believe that children come to be 'good citizens' rather through the activity of joining together in the sort of enterprises I have noted than through self-conscious attempts to learn about local government or the functioning of parliament. Nor do I think that sophisticated efforts to train for democratic life through school parliaments and committees are very effective. Much more important is the general atmosphere of relationship within the school itself.

I would make two suggestions here: one is that true social adjustment comes from people who are actively engaged in work that satisfies, and, as it were, releases them; the other is that a good deal of well-meaning emphasis on citizenship fails to touch the vital affective sources of conduct in children. Drama with its opportunity for empathy and 'working out' is potentially a better instrument of social vitality and harmony than any amount of information about how aldermen and councillors are elected. This is particularly so at a time when an internationalism is being substituted for local and national loyalties, an internationalism beyond the interest and capacity of many people to understand. Patriotism has its dangers; but the resultant hiatus when the emotional satisfactions of national loyalty are removed deserves attention also.

I would hate to present a system. What I have tried to do is to think out, tentatively, the basis on which a system could be built, and to explain a little why I have made the choices I have. But I have made no allowance, for instance, for opportunity. By that I mean the opportunity which comes to a good Head to seize on capabilities in his staff which aid the promotion of what I have called the humanizing process. What we need in our teachers is a touch of the charismatic, and, if we have a teacher who can interest children, because of his own fascinated absorption in, shall we say, so unlikely a subject as archaeology (and I know of one such teacher) then he should be given his head. I wish more schools would make use of their own teachers' individual enthusiasms and hobbies in the way suggested and adopted by Mr. Rowe.[1] But what I have said must be taken as a feeling towards some new thinking about the syllabus, and the social, economic and industrial facts which lie behind the need to think in these terms; I have not tried to provide a blueprint for all schools.

One final point needs to be made. Intellectually, these children are inferior—let us be blunt and honest about it; but simply to dismiss them in this way—to lump them together in Sir George Thompson's description as 'the stupid'—is to ignore possibilities of growth, sensitivities and awarenesses which our 'rational' education leaves untouched. What I want is a schooling that will enable these children to realize their natures as much as in their own way our able children realize theirs through intellectual accomplishment. This means that there is within the work proposed a discipline and a demand on the self no less exacting at its level than that involved in high academic work; but one more suited to the sorts of sensitivities and level of consciousness traditionally revealed by the folk.[2] Furthermore, these fields provide opportunities for decision-making in relation to concrete choices and actualities of a sort these children can encompass, one which forms an essential element in the growing independence of the psyche at whatever level it can best be exercised. In this way the children can, in part, fulfil themselves

[1] Cf. his book, *The Education of the Average Child.*

[2] The hope, indeed, is that implicit in Professor Hoggart's diagnosis: 'There may be some prophetic truth in discussions about "the vast anonymous masses with their thoroughly dulled responses". But so far working-class people are by no means as badly affected as that sentence suggests, because with a large part of themselves they are just not there, are living elsewhere, living intuitively, habitually, verbally, drawing on myth, aphorism and ritual.' (*The Uses of Literacy*, pp. 31–2.) Cf. too, the analysis of the role of myth and ritual in Susanne K. Langer, *Philosophy in a New Key.*

and, at the same time, make their contribution to that cultural richness we seem latterly to have lost to the more trivial manifestations of the mass media. For, adequately treated, what I have in mind has profound moral implications—could form, for these children, indeed, some introduction to a 'Way' of life based on what is most fundamental in their existence. I do not offer it as a soft option.

I also feel that this sort of education can best take place in an institution specially devoted to it, with a staff trained for the purpose—the sort of training provided, for instance, at the newer 'art' training colleges, like Bretton Hall; indeed, the centrality of this work in such schools might well give these colleges a sense of functional importance which would destroy the feeling that in our society their work is only peripheral. Certainly, these less able children would benefit from the more intimate atmosphere procurable in the smaller institution—for reasons which Mr. David Holbrook, whose magnificent work with them forms one of the most hopeful growing points in our present educational system, so movingly displays, directly and by implication:

'A good deal of educational comment nowadays—about the social implications of "streaming", of the "eleven plus", and about the comprehensive school—seems to assume that differences between children are artificially induced by the needs of our society to maintain an "élite" on the one hand and a working mass on the other. Nobody would urge more strongly than I do that in terms of needs of the sensibility children must be regarded as equal. All must be given a sense of significance in life, and a degree of civilization by their school—if education is to mean anything at all. And in such subjects as drama and painting there is little need for "streaming" in the secondary school.

'But there certainly is a very great difference between children's capacities to respond to the varied process we call "education"—and the difference between teaching "A" stream children and "C" or "D" stream children is an utter difference of dimension. So much public discourse on education seems irrelevant, because the people carrying it on simply do not know the "low stream" child.

The Education of the Less Able Child

'To teach children at the "lower" end of a secondary modern school is to enter another dimension, of time and of human capacity. One has to learn to force one's mind to run slowly, to match theirs. One needs to talk more slowly and systematically, and yet to abandon any systematic procedure. And one needs, above all, to work on a plane which would seem almost indecent to the grammar school teacher or the university person—one has to enter a familiarity of manner and an emotional context which are fraught with dangers and stress.'[1]

[1] D. Holbrook, 'Teaching in a low stream dimension', *The Guardian*, 28 October 1961. The reader is also referred to *English for Maturity* by the same author—especially the chapters on folk verse and song.

Conclusion

In this book, I have been concerned with man's fate in an advanced industrial society and the role that education can play in inducing a richer life than that implicit in a rising standard of material comfort. What we have today is both the wrong sort of hierarchy and an impulse towards the wrong sort of equality. The equality we need is that which reverently accepts the essential nature and uniqueness of every human being; the hierarchy, one which recognizes different levels of intelligence, consciousness and sensitivity and recruits itself on this basis. That this latter has been the cry, in an unresponsive world, from Plato's philosopher kings to D. H. Lawrence's 'priests of life' ('the first quality will be the soul-quality, the quality of being, and the power for the directing of life itself') and that our times are almost fantastically opposed to any such differentiation (though implicitly accepting a much more crudely based discrimination) in no way obviates the need to urge the finer morality in what, in education, is essentially and inescapably a moral situation.[1] At the core of the problem lies the question of human freedom—the problem I examined in *Freedom and Authority in Education*. The view that I expressed there—that freedom is something to be realized, not simply something to be accepted as an absence of restraint—stands, of course. What is needed is an education which provides an ample opportunity to achieve the highest level of realization which very diverse natures can encompass. And

---

[1] My evocation of Plato and Lawrence here is not intended to imply concurrence with the social systems of either.

this means an education which accepts the phenomenon of diversity as its primary datum, not one which seeks to hide the truth in a mistaken philanthropy of an excessive 'equality of opportunity'. For, in the context of the modern world in which this phrase is used, it is relevant to ask 'opportunity for what?'. The answer—to further the ends of the contemporary industrial-bureaucratic state—is one which, in the body of this book, I have found wanting. Not, be it emphasized, completely wanting: some can find their fulfilment in technical advance; some will find their lives enriched by it. But many will not; for, at the heart of modern industrial society lies a profound paradox—a paradox of enrichment and deprivation. These will need a different sort of opportunity. In this book, my aim has been partly diagnostic, partly to begin the long task of suggesting alternative provision. (In general, we need much more willingness to analyse what is implicit in current curricula and to debate alternatives. The organizers have held the field long enough.)

We need, I think, a much greater attention to the affective element in human nature which is nearer the springs of life for the majority of people than our present, cognitively based education with its emphasis on consciousness and decision-making recognizes, though the latter emphases remain vital for the really able. Some counterbalance, too, at more self-conscious levels, is needed against the will to power which is characteristic of technological advance. I have touched on this need for affective education at various points in this book; and it will provide the major theme of my next. It is a theme which lends itself to every sort of pretension and woolliness—to sound the note of 'creativity', for instance, in most modern educational discourse is to send a shiver down the spine of any reasonably fastidious person, and to decide what precisely is intended by the 'education of the emotions' is matter for prolonged conceptual analysis.

I have not tried to be precise about numbers.

Those who urge that improving social conditions, more money spent on education, better selection techniques, more concern for talent, growing parental interest in education, etc., will increase the number of those who can benefit in some measure from a more prolonged acquaintanceship with the major disciplines *may* be right.[1] But I cannot see any time in the foreseeable future when the whole population will gain from such an education. Even, then, if the percentages capable of tackling profitably the different levels of syllabus I have proposed should alter, the need to think out curricula suited to varying capacities will still remain. (This is one reason why I have not made much attempt to suggest relevant percentages in the body of the book.)

There is a final point. Traditionally, whatever has been learnt has usually looked beyond itself to its effect on what we call 'character'—though the word has unfortunate associations with public school aspirations. The sacred texts, which have so often in the past absorbed the educational attention of peoples, were not examined for their own sakes but for the illumination they provided in the affairs of life; they have been thought of as providing a Tao, a Way. I have said little about religion in this book; but, in fact, we face a situation in which the Christian story regrettably makes little or no sense to the bulk of our population. We live, indeed, amidst the dying embers of a Christian morality; and we are faced with the necessity of seeking a new source of ethical enlightenment—or such a rekindling of the Christian one as, despite the efforts of a devoted few, has not happened in our time to the extent that the people have become moved.[2]

The school, cannot, of course, provide a new morality. But while we wait, we can explore the moral implications for our youth of what the school has to offer. The demands the school makes in the discipline it exacts over learning will have some repercussions on character. Furthermore, it needs, in varying degrees, to combat certain tendencies of the modern world. The

[1] Mr. J. Adcock, a higher degree student of mine, has, for instance, shown recently that some secondary modern children are capable of a higher level of reading attainment in the study of narrative prose than is commonly thought. Cf. J. Adcock, 'The Study of Narrative Prose in the Secondary Modern School in relation to contemporary popular culture' (unpublished M.Ed. thesis, University of Leicester).

[2] Here, indeed, 'change' has so worked its way that it must, in some measure, be accepted. But I imply by this no derogation to those who can live their lives in Christian terms. Such 'knowledge' transcends what I have here to offer as the 'way' of the secular school.

attack will be indirect: modern learning does not provide maxims for conduct or a 'revealed knowledge'. Some disciplines, however, do offer the opportunity of moral enlightenment; the humanities have their possibilities for moral insight, as I have tried to show in relation to literature. There, if anywhere, is to be found the morality appropriate to a modern, decision-making, sophisticated minority. More; it offers the opportunities implicit in the notion of impersonality to the too insistent urges of the assertive will, to that desire to control which is inherent in an advanced technology. And this can reflect on the nature of education itself; so that we may be helped to recapture the notion of education as a 'process' rather than as a 'product'.[1]

[1] The words are taken from E. D. Myers, op. cit. Education as a 'product' is something that can be 'got', complete; as a 'process' it implies a continuing discipline of learning.

Q

Index

Index

Buber, Martin, 198

Cardwell, Dr. D. S. L.: *The Organisation of Science in England*, 68 n., 71, 72
Carter, Professor C. F., 206 n.
Case for Examinations (The): Brereton, J. L., 70 n.
Cassirer, Ernst, 211 n.
Change in the Village: George Bourne, 78, 102–3
Chatwynd, H. R.: *Comprehensive School —The Story of Woodbury Down*, 88 n.
Child-centred education, 51, 52, 174
Clarke, Sir Fred: *Education and Social Change*, 65–6 and n.
Classics, in education, 67, 69, 74, 136–7
Coleridge, Samuel Taylor, 166
Common Faith (A): John Dewey, 31, 33
Common Pursuit (The): F. R. Leavis, 24, 154, 156, 159
Communication between people, possibility of, 94–5
Comprehensive education, 44, 88 and n., 92–7
Comprehensive School—The Story of Woodbury Down: H. R. Chatwynd, 88 n.
Concept of Mind (The): Professor G. Ryle, 140
Conrad, Joseph, 184, 187
Consciousness, differing levels of, 47, 59, 76, 81–3, 93–4 n., 100–11 *pass.*, 115–19 *pass.*, 121–2, 124–5, 153, 166–7, 185–6, 225–6 (cf. also Chapters V and VII *pass.*)
'Creativity', possibilities of, in industry, 196–8
in school, 80–1
Crowther Report, 80, 113–14, 142–3, 203, 204, 206
Culture, appeals of mass, 119, 185–6, 209–10, 212
as an acquired characteristic, 101
common, 45, 64, 97–112 *pass.*, 204, 211–12
different meanings of the term, 97 n., 107–8

T. S. Eliot on conditions necessary for, 180
folk, 201–2, 210–17 *pass.*
Greek ideal of, 127–9, 137 n.
Matthew Arnold on, 200
Culture and Anarchy: Matthew Arnold, 200
Culture and Environment: F. R. Leavis and Denys Thompson, 155
Culture and Society: Raymond Williams, 106–11 *pass.*
Curriculum, for able children, cf. Chapter V *pass.*
common, 93, 119, 210
as a crucial problem of our times, 115–17
development of, 136–40
different ways of handling, 121–2, 210 (cf. also 'Subjects')
for the less able child, cf. Chapter VII *pass.*
place of literature in, 153–69 *pass.*
in the nineteenth century, 66, 69, 79
place of science and technology in, 116, 145–52, 174–7
sixth form, 134–6, 142, 145
unsuitability of, in many cases, 83, 166–7, and cf. Chapter VII
value judgments in, 93–4 n.

Davie, G. E.: *Democratic Intellect*, 61 n., 66 n.
Day Lewis, Cecil, 146
Democratic Intellect (The): G. E. Davie, 61 n., 66 n.
Democracy, Arnold on, 84–5
and bureaucracy, 63
conflicting ideals in, 61
dangers of totalitarianism in, 43–4
Dewey on, 38–40, 45
Harvard Educational Report on, 104
de Tocqueville on, 43–4
Raymond Williams on, 106–11 *pass.*
Democracy and Education: John Dewey, 31–5, 36, 39, 40, 42, 50, 53, 55 n.
Democracy in America: Alexis de Tocqueville, 43–4
Democritus, 127

230

Index

Index

Index

Musgrove, Dr. Frank, 181–2
Myers, E. D.: *Education in the Per-spective of Hisotry*, 126 n., 181 n., 219 n., 227
Myers, L. H., 174, 203

Nature, man's relation to, 150–1, 192
Dewey on, 30, 37
Froebel on, 30
Neighbourhood, 'practice of', 109–10, 110 n., 111
Newton, Sir Isaac, 36
Notes Towards the Definition of Culture: T. S. Eliot, 61 n., 112–13
Nowell-Smith, Professor P. H., 139–40
Nunn, Sir Percy: *Education, its Data and First Principles*, 59

Oakeshott, Professor Michael: *Ration-alism in Politics*, 49, 88–9, 171 n., 183 n.
Ogilvie, R. M., 185
Organisation of Science in England: Dr. D. S. L. Cardwell, 68 n., 71
Organization, excessive faith in, 115–119 *pass.*
schemes for secondary schools, 115–119, 178
Où Va le Travail Humain: Georges Friedmann, 192, 195–8 *pass.*, 204–5
Owst, Professor G. R.: *Literature and Pulpit in Medieval England*, 213

Parkes, Professor E. W., 197
Pattison, Mark, 73
Paulsen, F., 65–6 n., 138 n.
Payne, G. L.: *Britain's Scientific and Technological Manpower*, 188–9
Pedley, Dr. R., 92, 93
Peters, Professor R. S., 129
Peterson, A. D. C., 134
Philosophy in a new Key: Susanne K. Langer, 221 n.
Phoenix: D. H. Lawrence, 78
Physical activities in education, 219
Pilkington Report, 202
Plato, 84–5, 94, 127–9, 137, 137–8 n., 154–5, 211 n., 224

Plato's Cretan City: Glen R. Morrow, 211 n.
Power Elite (The): Wright Mills, 190
Pragmatism, of Dewey, 29–33 *pass.*, 35
limitations of, 47
in nineteenth-century education, 66, 69
Primary School Report, 140
Primitive Song: Sir Maurice Bowra, 213 n.
Principles of Literary Criticism: I. A. Richards, 169
Problems, Dewey's conception of, 33, 37
rationalist's conception of, 89
Process of Education: J. S. Bruner, 76 n.
Public Schools and British Opinion: E. C. Mack, 67

Quest for Certainty: John Dewey, 32, 35, 137 n.

Rationalism, in industrial-bureaucratic society, 64–5
in industry, 193–4 (cf. also Taylor-ism)
limits of, 105–6, 150
in moral value judgments, 208–9, 209 n.
nature of, 89
in nineteenth-century education, 57–59, 60, 79
Rationalism in Politics: Professor M. Oakeshott, 49, 88–9, 171 n., 183 n.
Rational man, as educational aim, 15–17, 79–81, 98–105, 211
James Mill on, 15
Rayner, S. A.: *The Special Vocabulary of Civics*, 53
Rees, J. C., 131
Religion in education, 219 n., 226
Richards, I. A.: *Principles of Literary Criticism*, 169
Rieff, Philip, 120, 169, 174
Riesman, David: *The Lonely Crowd*, 207
Rousseau, Jean-Jacques, 51, 120
Emile, 142
Rowe, A. P., 76

235